# RISING TROUT

# RISING TROUT

## by Charles K. Fox

AUTHOR OF *This Wonderful World of Trout*

FOREWORD BY L. JAMES BASHLINE

SECOND EDITION

HAWTHORN BOOKS, INC.
*Publishers*/NEW YORK
*A Howard & Wyndham Company*

*To all*

*who love to be on a trout stream*

*with a fly rod for company*

second edition

RISING TROUT

Copyright © 1967, 1978 by Charles K. Fox. Copyright under International and Pan-American Copyright Conventions. All rights reserved, including the right to reproduce this book or portions thereof in any form, except for the inclusion of brief quotations in a review. All inquiries should be addressed to Hawthorn Books, Inc., 260 Madison Avenue, New York, New York 10016. This book was manufactured in the United States of America and published simultaneously in Canada by Prentice- Hall of Canada, Limited, 1870 Birch-mount Road, Scarborough, Ontario.

Library of Congress Catalog Card Number: 77-92364

ISBN: 0-8015-6394-1

1 2 3 4 5 6 7 8 9 10

# Contents

# PART THREE

# PART FOUR

# Foreword

It has become apparent to me that fly fishermen eventually fall into one of three main categories. The first is the pedestrian angler, who makes a few half-hearted attempts at the game and then settles into an occasional angling sortie when all planets are properly positioned. Next, there is the fly-fishing moth who, in the vernacular of today, is the sport's "groupie." He has all of the books, knows the terminology, and has at least one vintage bamboo rod. Finally there is the addict. He's the star-crossed person who simply can't help himself. He has risen to the charm of moving water, been captured by the trout, and finds himself at the center of the ever-widening rings of the fly-fishing experience. Charles K. Fox is in this last category. He has long been in the center of the angling ring; his rod has cast a long line across the modern history of our chosen sport.

Unknown to many of Charlie's admirers, his expertise does not end with those species wearing adipose fins. While it's true that his first angling love is the stewardship of his beloved LeTort and that his extra affairs with the salmon of New Brunswick are significant, Charlie Fox knows the smallmouth bass of Cumberland County, Pennsylvania, equally well. His creativity in fashioning surface plugs is a historic fact. His ability to coax cautious muskellunge into making a fatal decision is equally impressive. Charlie Fox is not merely an angler. He is a master tactician.

He has written books and a hundred or more articles about bass, muskellunge, and Atlantic salmon, but it is the surface-feeding trout that fascinates him most. In his backyard workshop, the productive little LeTort, Charlie has proven to the satisfaction of most observers that he has come far closer than most of us to being the trout's undoing. (Charlie would be the first to admit that no angler will ever successfully master the rising trout.)

*Rising Trout*—I can't think of a better title. His first delightful fishing trip, *This Wonderful World Of Trout*, is now securely lodged in the top two dozen of American trout fishing tomes. Charlie's own description of *Rising Trout* is that it is a continuation of the first book. But this edition is richer. It has been updated and fattened with an ample supply of new information.

The Fox approach to fly fishing and the data included in this book are applicable to almost any trout stream in the world. The fact that he is a loyal Pennsylvanian does not detract from the copy. In fact, it may be what makes the book stand above the pack. I'll admit that it sounds terribly provincial, but for any author-angler to rise above the cadre of angling notables who have made and still make the Keystone State their headquarters is a significant achievement. It is the rare angler who hasn't heard of at least two of the following: Vince Marinaro, John Alden Knight, James Leisinring, Alvin Grove, Sam Slaymaker, George Harvey, and Ed Koch—Pennsylvanians all. And that's only a few of them. Another covey of nearby states regularly sends their best flyrod practitioners to the streams of Pennsylvania for a refresher course. Among this list of angling celebrities, Charles K. Fox not only holds his own, he shines. His fellow fishermen recognize this clearly. They are all his friends, and so are countless others who have never met the man but know his worth through his writing.

It's impossible for everyone who buys this book to have the chance to sit and trade fishing tales with Charlie Fox. I wish you could. He'd certainly have the time for you. Fox is no prima donna who pontificates with a haughty know-it-all attitude. He enjoys listening to you fully as much as he enjoys sharing his vast mental collection of fly-fishing knowledge. But if your paths cross, I'd advise you to do most of the listening. You'll be a much better angler for it.

The next best thing to spending a few hours on a LeTort bench with the keeper of that little river is to read *Rising Trout*. It is historical at times, nostalgic on occasion, but brimful of practical fishing information that can be applied on your stream. Charlie

Fox instructs and suggests. He never demands or thrusts dogmatic foolishness at the reader. He is too much of a gentleman for that.

I have purposely not told you much about what you're going to find in *Rising Trout*. The fun is in the discovery. But if this is your first trip along the printed stream with Charles K. Fox, a better fishing session you'll never enjoy. Fifty years of trout fishing know-how is about to be shared. Take advantage of it.

L. James Bashline
Honey Brook, Pennsylvania
Spring 1978

# Acknowledgments

A minor portion of this book is quoted material. The author wishes to thank the following editors and magazines for reprint permissions: Arnold Gingrich, *Esquire*; George Forrest, *Pennsylvania Angler*; James Bashline, *Pennsylvania Game News*; Pete Kaplan, *Rod and Gun World*; Frank Moss, *Sportfishing*; Ted Kesting, *Sports Afield*; Donald Zahner, *Fly Fisherman*.

The author expresses gratitude to Ziggy Platter for editorial assistance.

Thanks to Ned Smith for the drawings that appear on the frontispiece and part title pages.

And the author wishes to place another star in the crown of a girl named Gladferd, a fishing widow.

# Introduction

Progress in fly fishing for trout continues without abatement, thus it is a progressive pursuit. Each age has added its development and each age has had its say. Much is owed to anglers of past generations but there is always up-to-the-minute information about fish, fishing, and fishermen. It is because of the latter that more writings on the subject are justified and each should have a value of its own.

Trout fishing is no casual pastime, not fly fishing. As Professor John Crowe of the University of Pittsburgh and author of *Modern ABCs of Angling* advises: "The angler should be a student of cause and effect because the desired effect is produced when the underlying cause is understood." This may be the reason why angling has special attraction for the leisure of the intellectual. In addition, for many, outdoor activity is inborn and instinctive.

Among pertinent decisions of the angler are: choice of equipment, method and style of fishing, and pattern and size of fly. It pays to be analytical, inquisitive, observant, and ingenious. To quote again John Crowe: "Stream craft is the application of stream lore." Problems are the real challenge, the heart of angling. There develops steady and persistent optimism. The spring of split bamboo, graphite, or fiber glass is simply the climax.

A comparison between a recreation and an athletic team sport is fair and in order, so let us consider two of the greatest: football and fly fishing—player and caster, one who tackles, one who uses tackle.

He who participates in the spectator sport has his great day in the morning. Chief satisfaction and reward, and they are great, stem from individual effort and coordinated action, particularly if such activity wins the game or lifts the underdog above the favorite. Then it ends even before youth steals into middle age only to emerge in the world of make-believe to temporarily revert to the glory days. The old player just sits and watches and dreams. The opposite is true of the angler, for he enjoys a lifetime of participation that continues through noon, then on into the sunset, and even into the eventide of life.

In writing about the one hundredth college football game, the first such event, between old rivals (Lafayette and Lehigh, 1964) veteran writer, Al Laney, of the *New York Herald Tribune*, with the following words, may have reached the zenith in sports reporting:

> Returning to the scene of their youth with the mournful scent of burning leaves in the nostrils, they succumb to a melancholy brooding while making contact with a vanished day, envisioning themselves and others as they once were.
>
> Here for a few brief hours they touch a land of ghosts whence comes the breath of autumn days that are past, the rustle of silk long faded, the scent of flowers that are dust. . . . For those coming from far away and long ago it is a game of an earlier vintage. The banners, the bands and the crowds are the same. Only the date and the names are different.

This is not the way with the angler. He too returns to the scene of an earlier day and an earlier contest. But unlike the athletic has-been, the angler is better prepared trip after trip to contend with a worthy adversary. He is ever becoming a better observer, a keener analyst, and a finer practitioner. By comparison his schedule is long, flexible, and of his own making. He enjoys a great day in the morning, a greater one in the afternoon, and the greatest in the evening of his life.

The fly-fishing hobbyist combines a love of nature with the delights of angling. Beauty strews his path. There remains the difficulty of expressing the pleasure of it all, but some good men have done this well.

The Rev. William Cowper Prime in *I Go A-Fishing*, 1873, contributed the following:

The contentment which fills the mind of the angler at the close of his day's sport is one of the chiefest charms in his life. He is just sufficiently wearied in body to be thoughtful, and the weariness is without nervousness, so that thoughts succeed each other with deliberation and calm, not in haste and confusion. The evening talk after a day of fishing is apt to be memorable. The quiet thinking on the way home is apt to be pleasant, delicious, sometimes even sacred.

There comes a time when physique is failing but mentality continues to climb. A master angler, Will H. Dilg, one of the founders of the Izaak Walton League of America, wrote:

Those of us who have reached the half-century mark or more, and whose trail gently leads towards the setting sun, more and more value the yesterdays, especially the angling yesterdays. For doubtless we fishermen dream far more often of our favorite sport than other men of theirs.

Angling is the way to round out a happy life. There is romance in the knowledge that the naturals and the imitations are the same today as they were yesterday; even some of the pools, the hiding places, and feeding stations we know our forefathers knew before us.

A man is the substance of the things he loves. The love of nature was passed on to me and I in turn am passing it along. Maybe in their overcrowded world my boy and my girl will discover escape from the concentrations and complications of people and revel in their own outdoors. Maybe they will be thankful for the wild strain in their blood and that I was their father. They deserve to inherit a stretch of trout water that may remain sufficiently clean, along with a thicket and a swamp. And maybe, too, they will delight to be along a stream with a fly rod for company.

The fly-fishing-for-trout fraternity is a great one, great from the standpoint of participation and great from the standpoint of memory.

# PART ONE

# 1
# Flowing Trout Waters

It is true that the regular angler forgets most of the fish he catches but does not forget the streams in which they were caught. Brooklets, little rivers, big waters—all are rich in memory, rich in hope. Identical waters do not exist; similar ones are rare. The pools, too, vary as much as the streams of which they are a part, being different in size, setting, character, potential, and different in the fascinating problems they present. Trout streams merit the attention of the angler and artist alike, for, all or in part, each possesses an attraction, a beauty, and a nobleness of its own. Man cannot manufacture a stream; that is the work of the Creator. However, man can make a body of water or a pool of almost any size above the appropriate dam. To many fly fishermen, though, ponds and lakes lack the appeal of flowing water. The reason must be that every square yard of the surface of the stream is different, while the acres of a lake—except the shoreline—are similar.

Upon the mountainside in a picturesque setting where only a few sunbeams filter through the boughs, the brooklet sings its melodious song. This is usually a primitive area amid silent solitudes, out of sight and sound of neon and TV. These are hungry little streams wherein the ravenous natives take a fly boldly. By comparison with the more heavily fished little rivers of the valleys, they possess a trout population which is amazing, that is in numbers of fish, not in their size. The rate of natural reproduction of the brooklet is high because there is little silt to rot eggs, but acid water from leaf mold seepage and a lack of penetrating sunshine combine to limit the food supply. In many brooklets a 9-incher is a veritable giant. For those who must eat fish, the flesh of the stream-bred brook trout is most delectable.

One of the best-known trout stream biologists of the day is Dr. Albert S. Hazzard, at one time a member of the faculty of the University of Michigan, later with the Pennsylvania Fish Commission, now retired and residing in his native state, New York. He propounded a new concept in trout management encompassing no killing, no closed season, and fly fishing only. The name given it, which has become controversial, is "Fish for Fun." As editor of the *Pennsylvania Angler*, the publication of the Pennsylvania Fish Commission, I arranged a reprint of his trial balloon article, written originally for the Institute for Fisheries Research, Michigan Conservation Department, in June 1944. Today this zoning is practiced on its largest scale in the streams of the National Parks under the wing of Othello Wallace. In due time some conservation departments converted the idea into trophy fishing by permitting the keeping of the largest fish only.

But what does this digression have to do with mountain brooklets where rate of natural reproduction outstrips carrying capacity? The favorite fishing site of the man who set the stage for consistent fly fishing for good-sized trout is the mountain brooklet, a small one over which one can jump and from which one can keep tiny trout with no damaging effect to the stream. Al Hazzard has even assembled compact fish-fry equipment for streamside utilization.

My introduction to "hemlock trout fishing" was in the thirties by one who had assembled special equipment for this game. Lew Kunkel had a famous rod builder make him a 6-foot fly rod in the days before the "midge rod" and the "flea rod." Upon this was mounted a tiny single-action reel, the spool of which was filled with part of a coil of level-E line. To this was added a home-tied, 4-foot tapered leader. The flies he employed on the brooklets were all Lead Wing Coachman in #16, some tied dry to be fished upstream, the others tied wet for downstream work. Lew would fish his way up or down, as the case might be, by one method then turn around and come back to the car by the other. While I poked and dabbled and untangled tangles with my clumsy equipment for such confined quarters, he merrily and effectively cast away in his

Tom Thumb enterprise. There are two significant things about this type of trouting: there exist many, many miles of mountain brooklets where it can be practiced and there are adherents who love it beyond all other angling. These specialists revel in the personal satisfaction that they are dealing with the real thing, stream-bred trout of the native species in an unspoiled environment. The fish truck is the least of their concerns nor do they worry about the danger of being led by a scientist, as Professor John Crowe formerly of the University of Pittsburgh puts it, "whose preconceptions are fortified by ill-digested and sometimes imagined fact."

The tiny brooklet, populated by the tiny trout, flows through glorious scenes, spilling from one rippling pool into another. As she flashes her smiles she sweeps merrily along her turbulent way. Here and there she melts into grassy landscape and sometimes she disappears under the rocks. Then the negligible streamlet is joined by another of its kind, and still another. Other than the ones that flow under dense rhododendron, stubborn laurel, and scrub willow, all are fishable with a fly. Down the mountainsides they tumble, a network of such brooklets formed by the little freestone springs and swamps.

At some juncture pool, a combination of brooklets reaches the dignity of riverhood. Now there are highlights and deep shadows, multicolored rocks, quiet depths, and the sparkling water makes a rushing sound. Every bend is fringed by a sylvan canopy; every straight stretch is guarded by wooded hills. There are alternate moods of broken shallows and quiet depths. As F. W. Pickard put it in *Sixteen British Trout Rivers*, "The scenery for the angler whose eyes sometimes leave the fly is picturesque, colorful and sometimes on the grand scale." The pools are clearly defined, the flowage varied, and the wading complicated. A trout finds a reason to be satisfied with a place or a pool.

There develops a casting situation that takes nerve along with skill, for many an inviting spot is well guarded. Frequent casting targets are slicks and glides where the stream drops away; other targets are the dimples made by surface-feeding trout of the placid places. The stream presents every aspect of the art and mystery of fly fishing for trout.

It is perfectly obvious in the brooklet of the mountainside, high up in the watershed, where the trout must be located, but in the lap of the mountain it sometimes seems that what is needed is a sixth sense about the location of willing takers. The brooklet is bank fishing but the little river is fished primarily by wading. The smooth areas of the river, the flats, harbor fine fish, but with every hurried step one makes, out goes a wave of information. Little water or big water, there is no use fishing for frightened trout.

Down in the watershed there has been a conquest by the brown trout over the native brook trout species; the fish are portly and they are sophisticated. Here in the valley, unlike the mountainside, there are times when the trout concentrate brain power on one insect. This the fly fisherman calls "selectivity," and he loves it because a challenge is presented that when solved provides action and personal satisfaction, the real reasons behind fishing. The necessary little details are delightful. It is not the rod so much as the hand that wields it that takes the trout, or, better, as George A. B. Dewar in *The Book of the Dry Fly* puts it: "It is the fisherman who makes the tackle, not the tackle the fisherman."

More hours are expended by more anglers fly fishing for trout in the little rivers than are spent in the combined settings of brooklet, big river, and pond. In fact, to some, trout fishing means fishing the little rivers. It must have been about such waters that Charles Hallock, the founder and editor of *Forest and Stream*, prophesied in the December 11, 1879, issue of his magazine:

> . . . in those days, not long hence to come, some venerable piscator, in whose memory still lingers the joy of fishing, the brawling stream which tumbled over the rocks in the tangled wildwood, and moistened the arbutus and the bunchberries which garnish its banks, will totter forth to the velvety edge of some peacefully flowing stream, and having seated himself on a convenient point in a revolving easy chair, placed there by his careful attendant, cast right and left for the semblance of sport long dead. Hosts of liverfed fish will rush to the signal for their early morning meal and, from the center of the boil which follows the fall of the handsful thrown in, my piscator of the ancient days will hook a two-pound trout, and play him hither and yon, from surface to bottom, without disturbing the pampered gourmands which are gorging themselves upon the disgusting viands; and when he has leisurely brought him to

hand at last and the gillie has scooped him with his landing net, he will feel in his capacious pocket for his last trade dollar, and giving his friend the tip, shuffle back to his house, and lay aside his rod forever.

Do you regard this prophecy as a fairly accurate description of fish-truck chasing of today, so dearly loved by the hatcheryman?

There is another type of little river, the limestone meadow stream which meanders through the pastures of an agricultural area, often seen through nature's pageantry of willows and often flashing a silver sheen like molten pewter in the failing light. For those who understand them they are precious; for those who don't they are confounding. The dissolving lime salts increase the food supply and the cover in the form of weeds, in short, increasing the carrying capacity of the stream. There are such streams in the United States. However, the most famous are the Test and the Itchen of southern Britain.

Another English author, who followed Dewar, penned a book entitled *Dry Fly Fishing*, and he too is worth quoting. No doubt R. C. Bridgett had placid water in mind when he wrote the following under the subtitle Trout-Stalking:

> The trout is a wary animal, extremely suspicious of the human form, and when, as in the height of summer, he is well fed and therefore under no compelling necessity to accept anything which arouses within him the slightest doubt, there is no creature of the wild more difficult of approach or more ready to take alarm.
>
> In certain streams, smooth and placid, whose banks are much frequented, trout may, it is said, become so accustomed to the sight of man that they remain totally unperturbed by his presence, and will enjoy, with the utmost indifference to a crowd of spectators, a banquet of flies or nymphae. The merest glimpse of a waving rod, the slightest flicker of light from gossamer gut, the least deviation of a fly from the true path will, any one of them, suffice to tell these trout that danger in the form of an angler has arrived, for, despite their seeming nonchalance, they are fully alive to the perils that surround them. They are even more difficult to lure than their brethren of the wild moorland solitudes, who, though they recognize an enemy in every man, and are therefore to be approached with the

greatest caution, are not quite so well versed in the angler's wiles or so able to distinguish the signs of his dangerous presence.

You may prefer to angle in water where the push of the current has authority, or where there is an emerald torrent, or even where water lashes itself into a fury of foam. Big-trout water features challenging pools, mysterious depths, great undercut rocks, and heavy trout. When fish are not surface feeding, and on most big waters this is much of the time, the trick is to fish far and wide in an effort to locate takers.

Flowing water is deceptive. Buck Raunhorst, the Minnesota trout authority, puts it thus, "The fastest water is in the middle; the surface flow is slower than the middle; the sides are slower than the top; and the bottom water is hardly moving."

Many big trout waters are in distant places—Argentina, Labrador, New Zealand, Lapland, etc.—but not all. Some are cropping up below the deep taps, low-flow augmentation, of large river impoundments near population centers. Those who are good at distance casting, such as the late Joe Brooks, the late Buddy Torrentino, Ted Williams, Al McClane, the late Charles Ritz, Gene Anderegg, and Joe Bates, are in their element here.

Considerable water searching is done with large streamer flies; but a greased-to-float muddler minnow works its charm; and, for midday, high-ceiling, bluebird weather, the Neversink Skater fly reigns supreme. The hair version made from groundhog tail as designed and tied by Charles DeFeo, the artist-angler, is extra fine.

Brooklet, little river, or big river, flowing water in any of its three forms possesses an appeal of its own, each so different from the other two that the fishing therein seems unrelated. Then, too, it is interesting and entertaining to fish beautiful water for the first time, but it is fascinating to fish a stream that is known well.

In writing about the glories of a stream, Cal Queal, the avid Rocky Mountain fly-fishing expert, offers the following:

> A stream is dynamic. It is a living thing with a character and personality the angler must understand, analyze and interpret. It is sophisticated and demands sophistication of the fisherman who would tap its piscatorial riches . . . I further believe the stream offers its greatest pleasure to a man with a fly rod who has learned

through experience that he is dealing with a complex piece of fishing water worthy of infinite respect, hours of walking, casting, and study.

Robert Louis Stevenson commented about flowing water: "There is no music like a little river's"; and Henry Van Dyke in another day added: "Human intercourse is purified and sweetened by the flowing, murmuring water."

Dr. James J. Waring of Denver, Colorado, a fly fisherman and student of angling literature, touched his fellow doctor-anglers when he described in a speech to them, which he chose to call "The Anatomy of Angling," the following relating to the passing of an angler:

> Over thirty years ago a friend and neighbor my own age, a passionate fisherman, lay dying of tuberculosis. During the last week of his life, continuously day and night, his devoted mother ran the water in the adjoining bathroom at his request. As his spirit hung between heaven and earth, his fevered imagination prompted by the sound of running water transported him to scenes and streams where he had fished, and he was comforted.

The stream, whatever the type and size, was murmuring, or singing or roaring in its wilderness even before the wilderness was given a name. They may be becoming less clear as the air becomes less fragrant, but fortunate we are to be able to follow the trails of our fathers along a stream traveling toward the ocean and not too heavily charged with poison.

Generation after generation, fly fishing has appealed to the highest type of mind. This is no casual pastime, it is inborn and instructive, a pursuit reduced to a science. One learns to love the dainty art for its own sake and the little details become delightful. Anglers come and anglers go and the brooklet, the little river, and the big waters flow on. In man's brief passage through time he has wrought destruction and damage. The pertinent question is, will he take care of what is left so that trout thrive therein with the result that the sport of fly fishing flourishes? The answer is in the affirmative, for there must be clean water to sustain human life and that is where the trout will be.

# 2

# The American Beginning

Prior to the time that paintings depicting fly-fishing scenes were lithographed by Currier and Ives, prior to the time that Theodore Gordon cast the first dry fly on a trout stream on this side of the Atlantic Ocean, and prior to the time of the split bamboo fly rod, wet-fly fishing flourished in accessible pockets of valleys in New York State, Pennsylvania, New Jersey, Maryland, and the New England states. It was the time when every stream in our land was nestled in a gemlike setting of great beauty and it was before pollution marked the end of American innocence. There was no necessity for nature's reactions to man's action. Like the early Victorians on English streams, the habitués on our streams cast their wet flies down and across where the expected comes so unexpectedly. There were no hatchery trout or exotic species in those years in the East, only native brook trout, the most beautiful fish that swims.

To resident anglers open-air treatment was customary, and it was the practice of city-dwelling anglers to escape to the country at every provocation. Headquarters and even trout towns became established where there existed the combination of a stream, a railroad station, and an overnight accommodation. Some places were reached by horse and buggy. Sometimes transportation for the fisherman was the combination, iron horse and hay burner. Eastern streams were spawning more than trout; they were spawning great anglers, too.

In their devotion to fly fishing these men pioneered tackle and methods for which the present-day angler owes them a debt of gratitude. But as one by one they laid aside their rods forever, there passed with them into eternal rest much of the acquired knowledge and the experienced glory. Thus a large part of the story of early fly fishing in America became lost in the haze of time. However, scraps have been handed down. Here and there a choice item is on file in a library; there remain, too, a scattered few fishing logs; a limited number of books; and, of course, there are mementos in museums and collections. We know there were shooting stars in those early years in whose afterglow we now cast. This can be called the presplit bamboo epoch or the predry-fly period for the American fly fisherman.

Some anglers of today might look askance at the equipment of their forebears should they have to employ its like, but now the old-time solid-wood rods and horsehair lines command as antiques more than mere passing interest. So do old fishing prints of gentlemen anglers in high hats.

Even by present-day standards the fishing pressure in those precious times of our ancestors was not light in the accessible choice spots. In his valuable historical record, *Angling in America*, privately printed in 1939, in an edition limited to 750 copies, Charles E. Goodspeed reported:

> Contemporary records of this sport indicate that a century ago all of the fishing territory convenient to the larger northern cities, Philadelphia, New York, and Boston, was thronged by anglers in numbers proportionately compared with those found along our streams today. In Pennsylvania, which, in the opinion of one who wrote in *Forest and Stream* in 1879, "is perhaps the best natural trout region in America," trout fishing was followed in all parts of the state.

It was in the year 1814 that Dr. Samuel L. Mitchell was given credit for giving our native trout its scientific name, *Salvelinus fontinalis*, in his book, *Fishes of New York*.

Many have assumed that the cradle of fly fishing in America was the Beaverkill Valley in the Catskill Mountains of New York, the nerve center being the mouth of the Willowemoc, around Roscoe. Later the valley produced two of anglerdom's immortals— Hiram L. Leonard, the split bamboo rod builder, and Theodore Gordon, the sire of dry-fly fishing in America.

There is documentary evidence that early fly fishermen were attracted by the short, deep, slow-flowing streams of Long Island, rendezvous for fishermen including Islip, Southampton, Fireplace, and Brookhaven.

The following is a newspaper quotation: "Mr. Robbins of the Philadelphia theatre visited Long Island in the summer of 1814. During his stay in the place he caught 190 fresh-water trout." Apparently this resident of the city of Brotherly Love one and one-half centuries ago had a trout-catching background.

True or false, we cannot be sure, ardent angler Daniel Webster caught a 14½-pound trout in Carmans River, South Haven, Long Island, about the year 1834. The carcass was taken to Delmonico's famous eating emporium in the big city, where it was consumed by its captor and his cronies. So it was written, but also, so it was challenged in writing.

Some years later it was a "lazy, idle, little brook" of Long Island that provided material for a chapter in the Rev. Henry van Dyke's *Fisherman's Luck*.

But flies were being cast on the waters of another state, too. On the Paradise Branch of the Brodheads at Henryville, Pennsylvania, was built a frame hotel not far from a railroad station. For three generations the operator was a Henry. It was then purchased by angler Al Zeigler, who was married to a Henry. (Unfortunately he passed away in 1968.) Over the years it has been a combination flycaster's mecca, a retreat for escapees from the concrete jungle, and a meeting place for vacationing pedagogues.

Across Route 447 and almost at the streamside was a restaurant called the Lighthouse, which served anglers many early breakfasts and many more late dinners. Fishermen funneled into it, not only to satisfy the inner man but to reinforce the contents of the fly book, later the fly box, and to associate with kindred spirits. Over the years the fishing guests made entries in a fishing log. There were times when the book was located at the Lighthouse, and there were times when it was across the way at the Henry House. Fortunately for posterity it was at the latter that day in the spring of 1957 when the Lighthouse disintegrated and disappeared in the flood that ravaged Analomink and Stroudsburg.

Ernest G. Schweibert, Jr., author of *Matching the Hatch*, while a member of the Princeton University faculty, became a Henry

House patron. He was presented the opportunity to examine the famous log. In his masterful manner he researched and reported on early Brodheads fishing. The great true story and its early historical significance is a chapter in the book of the Theodore Gordon Fly Fishers Club of New York, the title of which is *The Gordon Garland*.

I, too, am proud of the traditions and rewards of my fishing country, an area of great limestone springs. If less beautiful than the mountains, the countryside of the Cumberland Valley in Pennsylvania is more picturesque.

Cumberland County in the early days of fly fishing in America was different in scope from that of the present. This was the sixth county formed in Penn's Woods and it encompassed about one-quarter of the entire state, including what is now Pittsburgh in the western part and State College in the central sector. At that time Carlisle was the jump-off place, anything to the west of it harboring red-skinned savages.

As the early settlers carved out their precarious hold, it became the plan to have everyone within 50 miles of a courthouse, which meant in turn another county seat and a new courthouse. Ultimately the state total became sixty-seven counties, Cumberland being divided and subdivided into dozens, hence the name, "Mother Cumberland." The county was large in the year 1829 when the following appeared in the September issue of the *American Turf Register and Sporting Magazine:*

Sir,

You ask me for a paper on trout and trout fishing in Pennsylvania. This you shall have with pleasure, but as I am no more than a practical man in such matters, you cannot expect much.

Although I commenced wetting flies in times long gone by, my experience extends only to Cumberland County; but trout were formerly found in all the limestone springs in the state. Owing, however, to the villainous practice of netting them, they are extinct in some streams and scarce in others.

In Cumberland there are three good trout streams. Big Spring, west of Carlisle, runs a distance of five miles and turns six flouring mills and affords fine sport almost the whole distance. A law of the state makes it penal to net in this stream and forbids the taking of trout between the months of July and April. It is the only spring branch in the state protected by law; the good effect of which is so apparent that it is hoped other streams will receive the like protection.

The LeTort, which flows past Carlisle, is another good stream. It runs about four miles through meadow grounds and turns three flouring mills. It formerly afforded excellent sport, but owing to the infamous practice of netting and setting night lines, the fish have been much lessened in numbers and size.

Silver Spring, east and north of Carlisle, runs half a mile and turns two flouring mills. This stream breeds the best and largest trout of any in the state—they are from one to three pounds, and it requires nice tackle and an experienced hand to land them.

The rod used is fifteen or sixteen feet long, very delicate, and throws from twenty to thirty feet of line—and in all three streams the fisherman is most successful with the artificial fly. The color used in April is black or dark brown; in May, dun or red hackle; in June and July imitations of the millers or candle flies are found best.

The habits of this fish are soon told. In winter they seek the deep calm pool, and seldom or ever change their position or go abroad. In spring and summer, they delight in rapids. They feed on flies, worms, water snails and prey on small fish. They spawn in September; and for that purpose select ripples and shoal water, with gravel and sandy bottom. When the spawn or young trout is brought, it approaches close to the shore or gets into very shallow water to protect it from the larger fish, for it is a fact that the large trout will kill and eat the small ones. As he gains strength and size he returns to deep water and, in time, becomes the monarch of his pool.

In conclusion I will give you my first evening at Silver Spring. It was long since with a party of five, all bait fishers except myself. The proprietor of the ground advised me to use bait. He had never been successful with the fly. I would not be advised. The evening was fine, a cloud obscured the sun, a gentle breeze rippled the water, and such was my success that in less than one hour I landed twenty trout from one to two pounds each. The proprietor cried "enough." I asked for the privilege of another cast. I made one, and hooked a large trout with my bobbing fly, and in playing him, another one of equal size ran out and was hooked by my tail fly, and both were landed in handsome style. The last throw was fatal to my sports in that pool—for I never afterwards was a welcome visitor, but many is the day I have met with nearly as good success in the other millpool.

The editor of *The American Turf Register and Sporting Magazine* not only chose to publish the trout-fishing notes from Cumberland County, Pennsylvania, from the pen of G., but apparently he requested that more be submitted. The following is a quotation by the same reporter in a later issue of the magazine:

June 28, 1830
Mr. Editor,
    I have returned from my annual visit to Carlisle. In the rich and delightful neighbourhood of that place I indulged in my favorite amusement of trout fishing. Owing, however, to the heavy and frequent rains, the season was a bad one and the great numbers of insects which washed into the streams made the trout capricious in their feeding. At my first visit to Big Spring a dun wing over a red hackle was the killing fly; but in a few days after, at the same place, not a trout would rise at it; and at Silver Spring a miller sucked in the upper pool, while in that below a peacock body and brown wing was the only fly to be relied on. In LeTort a small grey fly was at all times in season. The trout this year were fat, plump and of high flavor, but the number taken by a brother sportsman and myself bears no comparison with that of former years. In our various excursions we took between seven and eight dozen and from all sizes from eight to sixteen inches. I have been particular in noting the color of my flies and the frequent changes necessary for the benefit of young sportsmen, but they too often stick to the same fly and the same spot of ground when they ought to change both.
    At Big Spring I met one of the best fly fishers of the age. "Laughing Joe" adds to his character of a scientific and practical fisherman, that of a modest, sober and hard working man. Joe makes his own lines and flies, holds a rod eighteen feet long and throws thirty-six or forty feet of line with one hand, and no amateur can avoid a bush, flank an eddy, or drop into a ripple, with more certainty or with more ease. And there is one trait in his character decidedly sportsman—he never sold a trout in his life, the product of his rod is made a grateful offering for favors received.

Unfortunate it is that the identity of "Laughing Joe" is lost in the midst of time, for today one of his scions, such as a Trimmer, an Ahl, a Stuart, a Shenk, a Pittinger, or a Reed may cast his "honey wing over red hackle" beside the undercut watercress. Possibly Joe's final resting place is the stone-studded hillside in Newville that overlooks the stream of Big Spring, or the church-yard at the source.

The hamlet of Springfield, overlooking the amphitheater featuring the great spring and until recent years the first of the series of mills and millponds of the stream, produced two founders of business in our miraculous free-enterprise system, one being Rea of the Rea and Derrick Drug Store chain; the other, Laughlin of the Jones and Laughlin Steel Company. On one occasion a proud miller saw to it that Queen Victoria was the recipient of a bag of flour ground in his beautiful limestone mill with power furnished by the flow of this premier trout water.

At an earlier time there was a boundary dispute between the Penns and Lord Baltimore that placed Big Spring in two different states. In resolution of the matter, what was Maryland's loss was Pennsylvania's gain.

Stories have been handed down about the visiting anglers, how they put up at private homes, how in the morning they were taken upstream by horse and buggy to the great head spring to fish their way back, and how private enterprise kept up the road and set up a tollgate.

Historic lore of yesteryear tells us how big a big trout was. Under the date of June 16, 1831, the *Carlisle Republican* proclaimed:

> Comes the report of a large brook trout taken in the Big Spring near Newville last Saturday. The trout measured 19 inches in length, 5½ inches in breadth and 12½ inches around. It weighed more than four pounds on steel yards. The fish was taken by John Lee of Springfield within fifty yards of the door of James Elliott.

Unless our groundwater channels and springs become contaminated, the stream of Big Spring should be safe for posterity, for the upper miles have been purchased by the commonwealth.

In his superb job of research, Goodspeed discovered that the sector enjoyed a trout-fishing reputation (*Angling in America*, page 234):

But it was the fine fish in the limestone springs of Cumberland County which especially attracted the early Pennsylvania trout fishermen. Big Spring, Silver Spring, and Letard [the LeTort]— streams all in close vicinity to Carlisle—offered the anglers of 1830 ten miles of fine trout water.

The LeTort, misspelled in the above, flows from south to north into Carlisle, where it is polluted. It was named after a trader and trapper by the name of Jac LeTort. Today there are large commercial watercress beds at the spring sources where Jac once breathed, bartered, and bred.

Joe Jefferson, who won acclaim as an actor for his portrayal of Rip Van Winkle, cherished Silver Spring, midway between Harrisburg and Carlisle. He loved to play the old opera house in the capital city during the trout season so that spare time could be spent on this stream. Although unsuccessful, he tried to get his frequent fishing companion, President Grover Cleveland, to fish with him there.

Scratch a fly fisherman and there will be found underneath a conservationist. Possibly the legal action described in the following is a first. It was written by a Washington, D.C., angler and published in 1839 in the *American Turf Register and Sporting Magazine.*

For the sake of everything dear to the lovers of angling, do all you can to put a stop to the taking of trout out of season. In Pennsylvania some streams are protected by law: Big Spring near Carlisle is one of them; fishing is confined to the months of May, June, July, and August, and netting trout forbid at all times. Ask your legislature to follow the lead given by Pennsylvania: but should that body doubt the propriety of passing a law of the kind, ask them to appoint a committee to visit Big Spring on May Day. The committee will there see farmers, mechanics, doctors, and persons of every calling all engaged in trout fishing; and should it prove a day of clouds and sunshine, with just enough breeze to make a ripple, your committee will be gratified with the sight of at least three hundred brace of fine, fat, rosy trout.

The three-quarter point of the nineteenth century marked the end of the beginning of fly fishing in America. There followed two

A view of the LeTort just outside of Carlisle, Pennsylvania. *Photo by Lefty Kreh.*

events that ushered in a new era: one was a vastly improved casting instrument made of split, glued, and wrapped bamboo and the other was the introduction of dry-fly fishing.

The indication is that two gunsmiths, who were also violinmakers, living in two different states, independently conceived and built a complete rod of split bamboo, the greatest American contribution to angling. Easton, Pennsylvania, claims the honor for native son Samuel Phillippe, whereas Liberty, New York, believes that her son Hiram L. Leonard deserves the credit. The year was approximately 1874, and it is possible that at that time there was only one dry-fly fisherman in America, Theodore Gordon, even though this phase of angling had already captivated the angling fancy of those who fished the chalk streams (limestone waters) of southern Britain.

Even though nature resists interference, under people pressure many things were destined to change. Those early fishermen would have appreciated the angling achievements that followed their time, but they would have been shocked by the physical changes—pollution, siltation, and litter—of streams. We, in turn, are witnessing stream changes of still a different nature. In the name of progress, of course, the developers are straightening, broadening, shallowing, silting, blasting, and walling. A dam is built, sometimes not because a dam is needed but because it is a good place to build one. In the fullness of time they must redesign. But it cannot happen every place on every stream, and nature will continue to resist and rectify.

Some things won't change. It will be as Lord Grey discovered it to be before the turn of the century. "For to the angler as he looks back, his angling days seem to belong to a world different from and fairer than the world in which he has worked." To this we might add: we are still faced with the same problems astream, we still meet with the same disasters, and we still rejoice in the same triumphs. It was the same then as it is now: creeds and theories, rules and hypotheses; these the trout upset and destroy. This transpires even after the end of the beginning.

# 3

# *The Unpublished Bible*

Legendary Theodore Gordon was more than the father of dry-fly fishing in America; he was a masterful angler and also a craftsman par excellence at the fly-tying table. Born in Pittsburgh, Pennsylvania, in 1854, he moved to the banks of New York's Neversink River to devote his life to outdoor pursuits, mainly fly fishing for trout.

When the frail little man died, a victim of tuberculosis at the age of sixty, the fly-fishing fraternity lost one of its all-time greats. Ironically, with his passing passed the treasure of treasures, his trout manuscript, which was not only unpublished but disappeared. His friend George LaBranche unsuccessfully attempted to secure the typewritten pages for publication. Unfortunately, too, there seems to be but one lone picture of Gordon. Apparently the housecleaning following his death was complete.

In the wake of the diminutive man of great dexterity are "Little Talks on Fly Fishing," published with regularity for over twenty years in the now defunct *Forest and Stream* magazine and "Occasional Notes" written for the *Fishing Gazette* of England in his capacity of American correspondent. John McDonald of *Fortune* magazine assembled for posterity these writings, along with a collection of the cherished letters from Gordon to three fishing friends, G. E. M. Skues, Roy Steenrod, and Guy Jenkins, under the title of *The Complete Fly Fisherman*. The pages of this book demonstrate that Gordon, in addition to being the master angler, was a pleasing and sincere writer. The loss of the manuscript prepared by this respected reporter, voluminous letter writer, and consultant who gave his life to fly fishing for trout is tragedy personified. From this point to the concluding paragraphs of this chapter, the words are those of the greatly admired Gordon.

"I have fished the dry fly for more than twenty years, at first only to trout that I saw rising at natural flies. If one can fish for large trout in sight, sport becomes most exciting, and the next best is a rise which one knows must be a big fish. The greatest good for the largest number is conserved by fly-fishing only, as one can follow many fly-fishers and still have sport. The angler's chances are reduced to a minimum when he is compelled to follow a minnow fisher, who scares the trout and puts them down. Worms are not so injurious and grasshoppers do not interfere much if they are fished by a decent man who has some regard for those who follow him. In a large body of flowing water the trout are less easily alarmed and come on the feed again sooner than in small streams."

"Where artificial fly only has been used, one may fish after many anglers and lose little or nothing by it, or if desirable one may fish over the same water several times. When living on the stream and able to fish at will, one should rest satisfied with a small kill. It is only the larger trout, after all, that are exciting and make history, and we must remember the enormous numbers of anglers whose opportunities are limited."

"I am no purist or ultra purist, and fish wet when I feel inclined that way, but the more one fishes the greater his enjoyment when problems of this kind present themselves. The *perlidae*, caddis flies, etc., flutter and buzz, but the *ephemerida* usually sail down serenely after coming out of the nymphal stage. Nowadays they are not so plentiful as they were ten years ago [dateline June 21, 1913—*Forest and Stream*], but we had good rises nearly every day during that nasty weather in May.

"I have been ill and am even more stupid in expressing myself than usual. I am willing to admit that conditions vary greatly in different waters, but given the flies in the water and trout feeding upon them, I feel confident that the persevering dry-fly man will succeed not only in taking fish, but some of the very largest, provided that they are rising steadily. No doubt there is a very great deal in the manner in which the artificial fly is presented. The best of our artificials are far from perfect, but if one can get the effect of the natural fly in the water, he usually has sport. One gets a pretty good pattern occasionally at first attempt, but more frequently improvements are required. I have fussed with a bug for two seasons before I felt satisfied that I could do no better."

"There is one fly which puzzles me when it is used as a floater. This is the Royal Coachman, which I have always considered one of the 'lures.' There is no use talking about it—trout do not see things just as we do. To see a Royal Coachman floating on quiet water is quite remarkable. It is so frightfully conspicuous that it should scare the fish, yet one frequently hears of success with it."

"Have seen so many Whirling Duns that I have made a little collection from a number of dressers. All were presumed to be the same. We all know the old dressing in Ronald's, but now we have a fine assortment of Whirling Duns to choose from, and I think I have seen four different dressings from the same shop. The Wickham is always with us, yet even this varies a bit, and I fancy that one dressing of this fly, when I can get just the feathers for it, is more killing than any other. The fact is that a man who dresses his own flies will always have more faith in them than they perhaps deserve."

"Nature is a great colorist and the tones in insects are fine and harmonious, but for the most part subdued. I never tried a dun-colored (grey) fly that pleased me that did not prove useful, and I like to have several shades in the box, from very pale to a dark iron or purplish blue. It is easy to use flies too large, yet a big trout will sometimes rise at a large fly when he would ignore a little one. One could easily fill a book with talk about insects, natural and artificial, so it may be well to call a halt."

"In fancy patterns, lures and salmon flies, one must follow the best formulas procurable, but in imitations of insects we should have the natural fly before us. Illustrations and formulas are not of much value in rendering of colors, and an imitation of an imitation will not satisfy the man who collects flies on many waters.

"We wish to reproduce as nearly as possible the effect of the insect as it floats upon the stream, to deceive trout that have had enough experience of flies and of fishermen to make them a bit shy and crafty. When the fish take freely, without discriminating, the amateur flydresser is not satisfied. Something has been lost, and he will be happier with half a dozen good trout which yielded only to the attractions of a special fly, dressed after some study of naturals that are or have been upon the water."

"In dyeing feathers and other materials a little information from an artist on the mixing of colors may not come amiss. For instance, I am informed that to dye bluish grey one should mix yellow and blue until green is produced, then add red carefully, until one gets the dun tint required. Alum or soda is used in removing grease, and vinegar or acid to set the color.

"The hackles on a favorite fly of mine were imitated in this way. Some very successful patterns are not exact in detail, but in combination the materials give the effect desired when the fly is on the water. The numerous legs used on a floating fly have an effect upon the color of the body.

"Fly fishing is more interesting when insects are plentiful than when they are scarce, particularly when the attention of the trout seems to be centered upon a particular fly. One cannot make positive assertions or dogmatise in regard to these matters, but I have known sport to fail at the time of the take, when the trout were rising everywhere, for want of a good imitation. Upon supplying this, one would succeed in at least moving the majority of the feeding fish."

"When trout are feeding freely and have their attention concentrated on *one* species of insect, all of the same color and size, they may fail to recognize an imperfect imitation as a fly. Again, they will accept any one of a number of patterns, and possibly quite unlike the natural fly that is on the water. There is no rule, and this makes the game of fishing all the more interesting."

"Many of our insects differ greatly from those found in Great Britain, yet others are closely akin in color and size to English flies. All manufacturers have their own patterns, and considerable differences will often be noted in imitations which are named the same. We prefer to tie our own and like to think that we follow nature, but the longer one studies the insects, the less easily one is pleased with his counterfeits. We have been as much as two years at work before a pattern was really satisfactory, even though it killed trout. There is so much in the presentation of the fly and in keeping out of sight of the keen vision of the fish. Their eyes are practically their only protection, and they quickly detect movement, yet they cannot distinguish form as we do. They feel pretty safe in a large body of water, but during droughts and in the smaller class of streams, one must use great circumspection if he desires the larger fish. Again, the fishing of broken water, where the surface is disturbed by current, wind, or eddies, is usually much easier than taking trout from smooth calm water, which flows slowly, and has no great depth. We scare lots of trout in such places and seldom know it. It is most interesting to fish for the larger trout that have seen many baits and flies and have probably been hooked several times. One difficulty is to find them in position to feed and in the humor to do so, and the next is to place the fly softly, without splash, and so accurately that it will float over them naturally an inch or two to the right or left of the trout's nose. Of course when lying near the top of a pool they may come some distance and take quite a large fly. They are often ready for any food in such places, and the disturbed water covers any deficiencies in the fly, and to some extent its presentation."

"Anticipation plays a large part in the pleasures of fly-fishing and there is really quite a lot of things to do. Rod and tackle must not be neglected until the last moment, and we must make good all deficiencies. There is much pleasure in inspecting the old stock of artificial flies and in buying or dressing new ones. Time flies fast always, and as the years pass, it seems to get away more and more rapidly. We have not days enough in the week to do all that we wish or intend to do."

"Mr. Halford's refined patterns of sedges, brown ants, etc., are dressed with an enormous number of legs, and even the mayflies are heavily hackled to assist floatation, so we may hope that trout cannot count beyond tthe number six, the usual quantity of legs possessed by an insect. I have never found that the trout objected to surplus tails. I suspect that many of our floating flies would prove inefficient if many insects did not buzz when on the water, as some of the shop flies rejoice in an inordinate supply of hackles, resembling somewhat a miniature toothbrush."

"What a pity it is that G. S. Marryat did not keep a diary, and that his letters do not seem to have been preserved. The loss to the lovers of the floating fly is very great, as he was not only a wonderful fisher but a man of remarkably attractive personality, judged by the few records we have of him."

"This gentleman manufactures nothing but these special leaders and claims to use only the very best gut that can be bought. He is very strong in faith in his theories, which are roughly something like the following: It is most important that the leader should harmonize and agree with the surroundings. If the sky is intensely blue and sun bright and warm, then the sky-blue leader is indicated. If there is much green grass and moss along the stream, a pale green one. The favorite color, however, which meets the needs of the angler is orange, none dark but shading from medium to light orange. This is on many days almost invisible to the fish. There is a whole lot to the business but the above covers the ground sufficiently for practical purposes. I mussed with the leaders but I was so accustomed to something very different that I could not bring myself to use them for the finest dry-fly works. It is almost impossible not to cherish small prejudices when one has been fishing with the fly all of his life (nearly). I wish the colored-leader man well."

"I hear now of great sport with big rainbow and brown trout in several states, and the distance is no great matter nowadays, when a thousand miles may be done in twenty-four hours by one of the fast express.

"The Au Sable, in Michigan, is fishing very well, as it now enjoys a special law which limits anglers to the use of the artificial fly. Consequently there are lots of trout for everyone, and some large fish are killed.

"Such a law as this would be of great benefit to all trout streams . . ."

"It seems to me that they [large sulphurs] are gone, as no angler has mentioned them recently. It seems to me that the appearance of all sorts of flies is becoming more irregular and uncertain in this part of our country. I feel inclined to go on a still hunt for a region where big streams are not so changeable."

(In reference to the limestone streams of Pennsylvania and the Castalia near Sandusky, Ohio, Theodore Gordon wrote:)
"There is much insect life in such spring waters, and they carry an enormous head of fish with anything like fair treatment.

"The rings made by rising fish seemed to dimple the water as far as one could see in the spring months, and during the evening rise every foot of water seemed to have its rising trout.

"Just think of it! Chalk stream fishing in America! Even long ago special flies of smaller size were made for one or two of these streams, and the color of the natural in the water was of the first importance. There was just about enough current in the dams, and not many places in the shallows where there was too much."

"We are fond of all sorts of fishing, but fly-fishing for trout has been beloved. It is a passion that grows with the years, and we can never become indifferent to it, as we are always learning something that is interesting. As a sport it is possessed of infinite variety, but to get the best of it I fancy that we must confine ourselves to the use of the artificial fly. If the fish are not rising freely and we resort to bait of any kind, we lose faith and may never discover the uttermost possibilities in the artificial insect. There is always something to puzzle over and think about, and one solitary trout may defy us throughout a whole season."

"*Fontinalis* is a beauty, but I love *fario* quite as well."

A rising trout.

"A few ultra dry-fly men may assume airs of superiority, but they are mostly good fellows. I have known none of them to kill too many trout. To be able to meet difficulties successfully, yet stick to the artificial fly in all trout waters, we feel that the American angler should thoroughly understand the dry, the wet, and the sunk fly."

"I sympathize particularly with the man who is devoted to the sport, yet has but a week or two to give to it, often during the worst portion of the season."

It was by design that excerpts chosen from the magazine writings of Theodore Gordon encompassed only the last several years of his life. The reasons are twofold: first, it would be his most mature work and most advanced thought; and, second, it might give a better idea of the nature of the unpublished book. Probably in his weakened and feverish condition he realized that he was entering the valley of the shadow of death. It is reported that he spat blood for the last three years of his life.

Gordon is responsible for so much of what we now have and so much of what we now do. He gave his all to angling. Were he here today he would reiterate: "Cast your fly with confidence." His belief was unbounded in direct imitation of the natural and the matching of the hatch. He brought thinking to its present-day status, this man ahead of his time.

The best-known Gordian contribution was the policy to fish the water with a dry fly when there is no rise over which to fish. Possibly the most famous innovation should be the American concept to fish for sport and not for meat, which means return unharmed many of the caught fish.

The New Yorkers who cast in his afterglow have honored the memory of their patron saint by calling themselves The Theodore Gordon Fly Fishers Club. Their creed is, "Limit your kill instead of kill your limit." This has been printed in two colors in conjunction with an appropriate illustration on waterproof material for outdoor distribution by the members. Were Gordon here today he would be most appreciative of this. These posters adorn the thick trunks of streamside trees under which he loitered and under which he cast, and they adorn the trunks of trees he never saw even as saplings. Distribution is good.

With the exception of his fatal illness and the unpublished book, both so disheartening, the Theodore Gordon story is a glory story, and another chapter in the unmatchable literary history of fly fishing for trout.

As for the unpublished Bible, the work was done by the best man at the proper time and no doubt in a superb manner. Its loss to the fraternity is catastrophic, but to offset this, Theodore Gordon fathered and championed the concept of fishing for sport as opposed to fishing for meat. He sold to many the idea of putting them back alive, something the English were not doing.

# 4
# *Vision*

The object of fly fishing is to place the fly within the vision of the fish without revealing, previously or at the same time, that anything is connected to or associated with the offering. That means that body and equipment should be hidden as well as possible. In the case of angling, detection deals with the sense of sight of the quarry to a greater degree than with the senses of hearing or smelling.

The margin between sport and pleasure is not great. The same thing can be said of angling and fishing. Angling, so rich in memory and rich in hope, is to many the tremendous sport. Leisurely fishing is a pleasure to others. Much of the greatness of angling is due to what is seen by both man and fish. Yet, because two different elements are involved, air and water, and because two creatures of nature which cannot communicate with each other or readily observe each other are involved, the situation is complex. Anglers agree that eyes to the trout are the most important of the sense organs, just as they are for humans. Therefore the disciple of Izaak Walton, today's complete angler, desires to have an understanding of what the fish sees and what the human sees.

The scientist will never be able to answer all the questions about the sense of sight of fish because it is impossible to know fully what the sensation of the fish might be. The angler, however, can absorb what the scientist reports, then equate this with personal observation and theory and thus to his own satisfaction be a knowledgeable hobbyist about the important subject to him: vision when angling.

An observant angler knows a great deal about the sight of fish because he has trained himself to watch and appraise action and reaction. It is basic that he comes to understand scientific fact. Though incomplete, the information the scientist provides is extensive.

Light travels underwater in a straight line, although it does not travel as far and as fast as in air. The intensity of the light diminishes as the angle of the light entering the water decreases. Light intensity is also diminished by particles in suspension, and the distance of vision is reduced and darkness increases with depth. When light rays pass from air into water or from water into air, they bend, the bend being an angle between two straight lines, actually a shifting of direction or paths. It is only when the light rays are at right angles to the surface that they do not bend. The greater the angle the greater the bend. The refraction of light is probably better understood by the bow fisherman than any other, for to hit anything he must know where the fish is in relation to where it appears to be.

We know that fish see beyond their element, water, therefore they too contend with refraction of light as we do when we look at them, for the principle of refraction is reversible.

It is light passing from the fish to our eyes by which we see the fish, and the fish sees the angler by the light passing from the

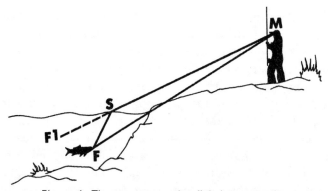

Figure 1. The man sees the fish because the light rays are traveling from the fish to the angler. But because of the refraction of the light, the fish's location appears to be at point F¹, rather than at the actual point F around the corner. *Drawing by Kenneth Kugler.*

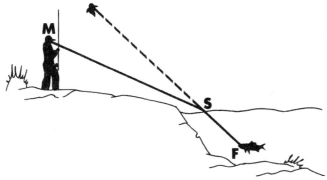

*Figure 2.* Because of refraction of light, the fish sees the angler around the corner, although the angler will appear to be at point M¹. *Drawing by Kenneth Kugler.*

angler to the fish's eye. Were this not proved by the scientist, the reverse passage of light rays might appear to be the determining factor.

The oddity is the fact that the bending of the rays makes it possible for both man and fish to see around a corner, Fig. 1 and Fig. 2. In reality neither is located where he appears to be to the other. However, the point at the surface of the water where the rays bend, S in Figs. 1 and 2, is the exact spot where it appears to be to both fish and man.

As fishermen we talk and read about the fish's window. This is not conjecture or myth; it is a fact with a scientific explanation. Involved is the principle of refraction of light. The sharper the angle at which the light rays approach the surface, the greater the angle at which they are bent. Once the point is reached where rays are bent so they do not go above the surface, the fish can no longer see into the outer element. That area where the bent rays go above the surface forms a conical window (see Fig. 3). The diameter of

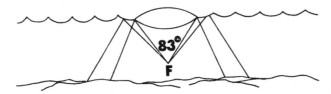

*Figure 3.* Where rays are bent so they do not go through the surface, the fish can no longer see into the air. That area where the rays go above the surface is the fish's "window." *Drawing by Kenneth Kugler.*

the window increases with the depth of water above the fish, but to the fish it does not appear to change, for the apparent size is governed by the angle it subtends.

The angle from the fish to the extremities of the window is slightly less than 90°, actually 41½° to the vertical, or 83°, the result being that the diameter of the window is slightly more than twice the distance from the fish to the surface.

Framing this window is a dark circular band. The bases and bottoms of visible objects around the outer part of the window melt into this ring and disappear. Beyond and around the ring is a mirrored ceiling that reflects the bottom. This is the area of total refraction. In effect there is a great mirror with a small round hole in it.

The picture seen by the fish beyond calm clear water might be a patch of sky and around that: limbs, bushes, banks, grass, or reeds, etc., all dwarfed in height and flattened in shape.

Great distortion takes place in water that is broken by currents and waves. Images are in constant motion due to continuously changing surface angles. The fish cannot see nearly so well through such a window as is the case in placid water. No longer is there a single picture that is steady in motion; rather it is a series of distortions that come and go with a quick glimpse now and then at what would be seen if the water were calm.

When a lure or a line strikes the mirrored section, it would seem that it makes a mark not unlike the cracking of a mirror.

Images come into the window from surface action above and from fish movement below. The first thing seen by the fish is the uppermost part, such as a rod, the head of an angler, the tip of the wing of an upright-wing fly, the gunwale of a canoe, etc. (see Fig. 2). It would appear to be coming downhill toward the fish.

The biologist gives us a good comparison between a fish eye and the human eye, but no one knows just exactly what a fish sees through its eyes. There are differences in the structure of the respective visual equipment.

The fish eye has no lid, yet its owner can sleep without closing its eyes as we sleep without blocking our ears.

A fish eye has an iris, but this iris does not expand or contract to regulate the amount of light that enters the pupil, as is the case with the human iris.

The lens of the fish, the outer eye, is spherical; whereas man's lens is slightly flat and regulatory. It is a case of comparing a globe with a variable disk.

The fluid in the fish's eye handles light coming through water, not light coming through air, as is the case with man.

At all times the fish goes the limit in the degree of curvature of the lens, whereas we humans are able to change the curvature of ours in order to focus objects at any distance on the retina and thereby place an image on a sensitive screen. For short range we make ours more curved, but the fish's lens is permanently at maximum curvature. The large pupil of the fish eye has great light-gathering power, therefore vision is good when there is but a small amount of light. Thus the fish is geared for short-range work; he is nearsighted; his field of vision by our standards is small. Because light travels a long way through air it is natural that man gazes into the distance. But light does not travel far through water, thus it can be expected that fish normally stare at things close by.

Man's eyes, being placed in the front of the head, look forward, both focusing at the same time on the same object; but the eyes of a fish are on the sides of the head and face in almost diametrically opposite directions. Each one of man's eyes is connected to each side of the brain. In the case of the fish, however, each eye is connected to one side of the brain only, right to left and left to right. In spite of fish eyes being located on the sides of the head, there is a common field of vision for the eyes, but it is more limited than the fields of the members of the animal kingdom. These differences tend toward theory and speculation, for it is difficult for man to understand the mysteries of a fish's eye and mind.

Whether fish can distinguish one color from another because of shade or because of brightness is academic to the angler, but distinguish color they do. Many well-conducted experiments with various species have proved this, the general approach being to make food associated with one color safe and palatable and food associated with another dangerous or not edible. Of course these same tests divulge something about memory too. Before the tests were made, the only evidence was circumstantial and arguments were heated. Generations of anglers have speculated that deceiver flies and lures should imitate in color, size, and form their natural counterpart, which generally speaking is somber, and that attrac-

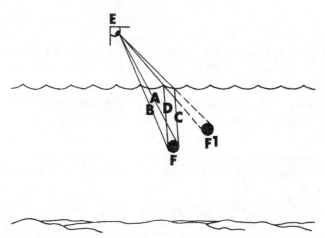

*Figure 4.* When the eye at E sees the fish sideways, the fish seems thinner, higher, and farther away than is the case. *Drawing by Kenneth Kugler.*

tor flies and lures should be bright and flashing, unlike anything in nature. Whatever arguments there were about color have, in recent years, been pretty well settled by the scientist.

Now let us turn our attention to the angler and his application of knowledge and observation to his sport. How do the fish look to him? What is his approach? How does he hide? What does his artificial look like to the fish?

The refraction of light in water changes the appearance of the shape of the fish. A fish viewed sideways appears to be thin underwater, to be more distant than is the case, and to be nearer to the surface than is the case, although the length is not distorted (see Fig. 4). The fish F is in the angle A B E, but the refraction of light makes it appear to be a F1, but this has changed the angle to C D E. The deeper the fish in the water, the greater the distortion. Because of bent rays, more fish back is seen and less fish belly, hence the slender appearance. It can be seen from the sketch that the bow fisherman could hit a large carp in the stomach, below his middle, so the arrow would pass through an area of the fish out of sight of the shooter.

Change your position so this fish underwater is viewed head end-on. Now its breadth corresponds to what was its length and its length corresponds to what was its breadth. In the new position the breadth remains the same but the length is altered, the result being that the fish appears to be much shorter than is actually the case. Thus a submerged fish viewed sideways appears to be abnormally thin and one viewed lengthwise appears to be abnormally short.

There is a certain sunshine condition when the shadow in shallow water is more pronounced than the creature that makes it. Hence there are times when one looks for shadows on the bottom, then casts to shadows.

Naturally fish spotted in the water are of special interest, and the behavior of the individual is fascinating. Some, we notice, are the mavericks that will not run with the herd, a law unto themselves. Maybe they are bold when the rest are shy, or vice versa. At any rate, we do not want to be seen so we stay low and avoid quick motions, for early in the game we learned that fish are difficult to approach and ready to take alarm. The clearer the water the more wary the quarry. The thing we want to know is what is that area where it is not possible for the fish to see us because we are not in the window.

If there is a slope 10° to the horizontal or 80 ° to the vertical, both being the same, the grade is 6 to 1. Anything under this grade is out of the window. That means that if an angler and his equipment is less than 2½ feet above the waterline at a distance of 15 feet from the fish, he is out of sight of the fish because he is out of the window. This is a direct progression, thus the figure is 5 feet at a distance of 30 feet, 7 feet at a distance of 42 feet, 10 feet at a distance of 60 feet, etc. Thus, one wading in the water can move closer to the quarry without being seen than one on the bank or in a boat.

There are times when the angler can screen himself by utilizing tree trunks, bushes, weeds, reeds, protruding rocks, etc. With such protection and a minimum of quick motion the angler may be able to fish successfully even though he is not beyond the limits of the window. In effect seeing fish constitutes a second phase of stalking fish. Guides are usually true experts at this. Of tremendous help is a pair of shine-cutting Polaroid glasses, either glass or plastic, the better style having large curved lenses. Such glasses can be considered standard equipment for those who seek Atlantic salmon in clear water and trout in the placid places. The most interesting angling of all is when one is fishing for a fish whose every reaction can be observed. But beware of the tendency to cast where the fish appears to be instead of where it is; that is, avoid overcasting!

One reaction that is readily observed is that of a hooked fish when it first has a look at its would-be captor. Usually the sight of the tormentor instills in the fish new vigor, which is transformed into violent action such as a combination turn, lunge, and run. Big fish of the species, though, seem to glare at the angler for a few seconds' appraisal before they turn tail to retreat.

Edward R. Hewitt, the dean of trout and salmon fishermen of his day, was particularly interested in how a fly appeared to the fish. He constructed a portable glass tank that could be taken down and reassembled, which was used in lecture work before groups of fly fishermen and through which pictures were taken to illustrate his book, *Secrets of the Salmon.*

To offset the refraction of light in its passage from air into water of the tank he made a sloping end 48½ degrees to the bottom surface. The eyes of the individual or the camera looked through this side from a perpendicular position. A fly, natural or artificial, above or in or below the surface could be observed or photographed, the assumption being that for practical purposes the fish saw the same thing.

It was demonstrated that as a wet fly approaches the surface, the fly and the reflection come together until they appear to touch and be double size. When the fly breaks the surface, little waves form a series of flashes. When a dry fly is floating outside of the window, the only part a fish can see is that which punctures the surface. But each hackle that breaks the surface makes what Hewitt describes as a "miniature lens which catches light." As the fly drifts into the window it becomes visible above the surface and is flattened in appearance. As seen from below, the hackles of a drifting dry fly act as light condensers and cause brilliant spots of light. "It seems to me," Hewitt concluded, "that the light effects of flies both at the surface and below are much more important in fishing than design or color of the fly." The same should apply to plugs, bugs, spoons, and spinners.

What is important is not what the angler sees in a fly or lure as he looks upon it in his box, but the color, shape, form, and reflection of light as these appear to the eyes of a fish looking from underneath the surface of the water. Few things can be more beautiful than a man-made fly or lure and certainly nothing more artificial, but anglers will never agree which are the most effective of the extensive lot. They may agree, though, with Mr. Hewitt who wrote, "Beyond dispute, fish have acute vision—often far too keen for us poor anglers."

# 5

# The Greatest Problem

Only the high spots and the low spots, the incidents that touch the vanity and the incidents that pierce the ego, remain in the memory of the inveterate angler. The routine and the mediocre pass on like flowing water over the dam. If one were to select the most confounding situation in all angling, if he were to put his finger on the one thing above all else that humbles him before his quarry, it would be the matter of fish coming short to his offering, the last split-second refusal, which some refer to as "the false rise."

This takes place in silent water that flows like molten glass and it takes place where a rushing surface shifts and sings. It happens with both the dry fly and the wet fly and it happens with attractor and deceiver lures. It transpires with trout and salmon and it transpires with other game fish. And too, it is incidental with lures, plugs, bugs, jigs, rigs, and bait in both fresh and salt water. Thus, this can be recognized as the universal angling problem.

There occurs what appears to be a genuine acceptance of the offering, "a take," but when the angler answers with his lift of the rod tip to what his eyes have told his brain is a bona fide rise, there is no contact, just an empty feeling. It might be compared with hefting feathers when stones are expected.

There are occasions when a fish will do this one time after another in quick succession and there are times when it is done in quick succession by one fish after another.

In either instance, as it continues it may seem that the load of angling misfortune is mounting. When there is no hooking in spite of rising, emotions pass from expectation to hope to frustration.

Human nature being what it is, coming short does not enjoy a good reputation and it is not welcomed by most anglers.

To an amazingly great degree, reporters on fishing have evaded the issue. As hazardous as the subject may seem to be, I choose to give it a try, so here goes.

The pertinent question is, what can one do about it? Maybe the accurate answer is, do two things, the one mental, the other physical.

First and foremost is attitude, the psychology to welcome the false rise and regard it as a tremendous challenge. Look upon the fish that react this way as saints, not sinners; then approach the problem with an analytical mind. There is an old adage among fly fishermen, "Don't run away from rising trout." Possibly there should be another, Give your all to those that have come short.

Second, change fly, lure, casting angle, leader tippet, and/or retrieve—anything and everything—in an attempt to show the fish something better to his liking. The goal is to bring about that wonderful transfer of feeling through the equipment into the body and mind.

There exists complete agreement that anticipation is an important part of angling. From out of the East to points far and wide is spreading the concept that opportunities are limited, so try to cash in on them as they are presented. When a fish advertises its location and manifests at least partial interest by coming short, there is real reason for anticipation. This sort of refusal should not be frustrating, rather it should be thought of as dynamic activity.

We might do well to turn to the philosophy of Professor John Crowe, author of *Modern ABCs of Fresh Water Fishing:* "The man who is ever alert and observant, always thinking and never gives up has something going for him which is more effective than technical skill. Skill can be developed; the other is a gift. Care and zeal are important parts of the equipment of the successful angler."

Possibly we concur in the thought that streams are more varied in character than people. Maybe we should agree that the same is true of fish; therefore treat each false riser as an individual problem. This approach is strengthened when one recognizes the fact that the moods of one stream escapade are never repeated in another.

Together let us consider possible equalizers that could convert a false riser into a willing taker. Be assured though that this is not a case of the arrogance of the vain boast, for even though I am a victim of the one-more-cast complex, some fish are too exacting for me to contend with successfully.

A starting point is the question, on what are they feeding? There are times when the answer is mere conjecture, but this is not always the case. As a matter of piscatorial protocol remove what was first rejected and in its place substitute something fabricated to suggest the food you know or suspect is being consumed. The best one can do in this respect is show the fish something in which similarities can be seen and hope that differences are overlooked, for the presence of a hook makes direct and absolute imitation impossible.

If this experiment is unsuccessful, the next step could be to cut back size, both that of fly or lure and the diameter of leader tippet. There exists a close relation between the two. Then, too, there is something else: the lighter the tackle, the greater the uncertainty, but the greater the reward—call it glory if you like. Could it be that something not just right has been observed by the quarry, hence the refusal? If such is the case, it can be minimized with diminution. Maybe, too, they are feeding on some winged mite that is hard to see.

A rest and then a fresh start often work their charms. However, there are two kinds of rest: the shorter one where the fisherman does not move, simply waits; and the longer rest where he moves elsewhere to return later. The tendencies, it seems, are to make the first too short and the second too long.

The bugaboo could be some unnatural pull, drift, or drag set up by the action of the current. This might be imperceptible to the fisherman but not to the fish. In many instances a new casting angle will eliminate the objectionable action.

Of course, too, there is the type of fly or lure, along with the action it might be given by the angler. There is the hand-twist-retrieve rate and the faster bonefish-strip movement. We can switch from dry fly to nymph, to streamer, to midge wet, or from surface bait to sinker. We can change from natural drift to slow draw, to activated dancing. Possibilities for trial and error are great.

When one's mind drifts over days on the streams, the picture of the false risers becomes hazy. Pitfalls blend with successes. If I had it to do all over again, there would be a written record of attempted approaches and results, for such an effort would establish sound percentages. Imitation, diminution, angle, and action constitute a wide range and variation in *modus operandi*. I am not sure what my score would be. Neither do I know what the best sequence of the trial-and-error offerings should be. Sometimes it has seemed routine to convert a false riser into a willing taker; other times I have canceled off the fish as impossible.

Angling will always be a part of you and me, for to us it is a matter of importance and dignity. Arnold Gingrich, author of *The Well-Tempered Angler*, writes of it as a sustained love affair. It is true that an angler lives in a world of his own because in the pursuit of his sport he is dependent upon his own resources. He receives his greatest reward in the form of personal satisfaction, and satisfaction comes from the solution of problems. One gets old in angling the way wine ages. The false riser presents the prize problem. So I like to think, and hope you agree, that if one does not give his angling all to the fish that come short there is a shortcoming in his angling practice.

# 6

# *Selectivity and Drag*

There is magic in the word *trout* and there is magic in the information that there are trout out there; but how much more magic is there in the knowledge that the trout out there are rising? When surface feeding is in progress, the dry-fly caster is presented with two intriguing problems, each of which has a fascination of its own. Failure on occasion to overcome either develops an even greater respect for sport fishing for an extra-fine quarry. The simultaneous solution of both problems results in the supreme reward in fly fishing for trout, personal satisfaction.

The two problems are different in that the one has to do with judgment, the other with execution. In matching the insects upon which it appears the trout are feeding, be they of the aquatic or terrestrial world, a choice from the fly box is involved; and even before that is a choice of the contents of the fly box, no matter whether purchased or personally tied. The other challenge has to do with ability to handle equipment so that a dry fly drifts naturally without being drawn out of course by a tight line and leader. Trouble comes in the form of refusal by the trout, and it is not always easy to identify the cause. I suppose there are more occasions than we like to admit when neither fly nor float is satisfactory. In any case, the fish and not the angler judges the matter. It is a challenge for a fly fisherman to be judged by a jury of trout.

The height of recorded selectivity was noted by an Englishman named Read Webster, who authored *The Angler and the Loop Rod*.

In writing about this character, Theodore Gordon, bless his memory, offered the following:

He was confident that his method was the only proper one. He fished nine flies on a 15-ft. gut casting line and sometimes his whole basket of 20 lb. to 30 lb. of trout would be killed on one fly of the nine. It is useless to dogmatize on matters piscatorial, but why endeavour to destroy a fine art?

In the face of this, it is interesting to speculate as to what might have happened had the right fly, or best fly, been utilized at each of the nine posts.

Gordon was a great believer in direct imitation of the natural, as witness this reporting:

I had a lot of flies dressed to one of my patterns and could do nothing with them because the hackle was not *exactly* like the ones I had used. I had no faith and probably fished them poorly. . . . The yellow dubbing is from a quantity of beautiful stuff I bought 22 years ago. Some of the most useful colors have been used up. I did not imagine that I would ever have another opportunity, but so it has been. I fancy that it is very fine wool or hair from a young goat. Never have seen anything just like it. It is fast color. . . .

The weather has been trying, hot as the hinges of Hades. Killed the rise of fly, except yellows in the evening.

(The above paragraphs were written to Skues in a letter dated July 10, 1912, less than one year before the passing of the ailing Gordon.)

The most selective trout I have encountered have been those feeding on tiny winged ants in low clear water of mid-August. The next most selective were those taking Japanese beetles in clear placid water. I have never fished for the consistent late-afternoon feeders emerging to tiny olive duns in October, but I suspect that this situation would offer the supreme challenge to an avid dry-fly angler. I intend to make it a point to intercept this fall hatch of olives, and this should be possible in the Catch-and-Release section of the Little Lehigh River near Allentown, Pennsylvania, where there is no closed season and the hatch is reported to be heavy.

It has been my experience and observation that selectivity builds as the season progresses and this seems logical. Normal early-season conditions are relatively high cloudy water in which visi-

Lefty Kreh casting to a rising LeTort trout. *Photo by Irv Swope.*

bility on the part of the fish is not good and where in the higher water a fly floats faster. Thereafter, as the weeks pass, the stream volume and rate of flow decrease as clarity and visibility increase, making possible a more critical inspection of our offering. Furthermore, as the weeks pass, the less sophisticated trout in unrestricted waters landed in frying pans, the fittest for survival being the hyperselective.

A major early-season hatch in most streams is the handsome, dark-winged Hendrickson dun *(Ephemerella subvaria)* with its prominent divided wings. In the cold environment the subimagos float long and far before being able to fly from the surface. Trout like them very much, the only deterrent being digestive ability. In 65° water a sizable number will be consumed by the individual fish, but in 52° water probably no more than half a dozen will comprise a meal. In cold water, where digestion is slow, a little goes a long way; but there is nothing slow about digestion nor lacking about capacity in a water temperature in the mid-sixties. Something tells the trout how much food can be digested under the varying temperatures. To a large degree the appetite of warm-blooded animals, man included, is affected and controlled by time, whereas with a body temperature the same as the element in which it is located, the control is temperature.

A #14 Dark Hendrickson tied with a dirty-yellow spun-fur body and hackle-wisp tail has been satisfactory for me, which really means satisfactory to the trout over which it has been fished.

A gray-brown caddis, generally known as the Grannom, occurs early in the season, often in what might be referred to as blizzard proportions. Emerging caddis bounce around the surface of the water; later they dive through the surface tension to deposit the eggs. Trout, particularly the smaller ones, take them and a #18 Adams has fished this hatch for me in a highly satisfactory manner. However, if some Hendrickson duns start drifting, the trout, in a selective temperament, will turn to the mayfly and away from the caddis.

It is too late now for anyone to be able to convince me that trout are not individualistic and that some are not more intelligent, more observant, and more shy than others. It shows up in their acceptance or rejection of our wares; it shows up in their feeding routines; it shows up in the homes they choose and defend; it even shows up in what they do when they are hooked. As would be expected, the stream-bred trout are better survivors and the superior in every respect to those hatched, handled, confined, tamed, and planted by man. The exception has to do with resistance to disease. Fishing pressure exerts profound influence upon them, particularly before they attain catchable size. With size and strength added to natural intelligence and experience, the challenge to the angler is ever increasing. Finally, some fish become too smart, too strong, too shy, and/or too well protected to be caught. These die of old age. In the instances where pollution has caused a fish kill in a good trout stream, more large dead fish are discovered than the regular fishermen of the stream thought existed. The same is true where a census by electric shocking is made. I hate to see this though, particularly as a periodic thing, because some fish are badly burned when touched by the hot metal wire. The scar is an ugly black mark and sometimes long. There should be no shocking in mineral-laden limestone water with AC equipment.

The pattern, its size, and the leader tippet to which it is attached are frequently critical for some trout, but there is something else that is critical for all. When a fly does not drift naturally, that is, when it is drawn into an unnatural course by the pull of line and/or leader, it is no longer attractive to trout. In fact, this actually scares some. Here is such an obvious wrong to a trout that it even creates suspicion in a newly stocked catchable. In an attempt to beat drag the caster makes the leader kick back into a snaky form or he casts in such a manner that the leader and line curve so the float of the fly may be better and longer.

An experience at Green Drake time in the big water of Penn's Creek will not be forgotten. At dusk two very fine fish were gobbling up spinners in their respective lines of drift. It was difficult to work into casting position so that both could be covered, but I made it. I would have settled for either fish in the knowledge that it would be the best of the trip and the best of another Green Drake season. I could hardly wait to see the fly float to the one to the right of the car-sized rock.

The pattern was George Phillips' time-tested Wulff-type dry fly—tail, rabbit whiskers; body, pale yellow spun fur; hackle, cream; wings, impala-dyed yellow-green.

The cast was so long that the float at the end had to start with a straight line and leader. In the failing light the float appeared to be good, but time and again the fish passed up the fly, although feeding to the naturals continued.

The casting angle was changed and the fly was shown to trout number two. Again the fly came through untouched but not the spinners. The distance was simply too great for a good kickback cast with its slack leader. I tried to wade closer for a better delivery, but it appeared that the water would be over wader-top depth. In another twenty minutes it would be too dark to discern rise forms. Because it seemed to be too late to look for another big surface feeder, the question was: should casting continue from the same place or should position be changed by backtracking and then approaching these fish from another angle? The latter was chosen in the hope that I might be able to wade into closer casting position from above. The going was slow, both getting out of the big stream and coming back in, but it was successfully negotiated.

The new position was at least 15 feet closer to each fish, but this time on the upstream side.

The husky pitch turned out to be a good one with a nice kickback of fly and leader in the right line of drift. Cockily the fly rode the slick surface, which in this light and from this angle had the look of pewter. Uninhibited by pull or tension it floated right into the window. The silhouette of the large fly looked good to me out there in the failing light, when suddenly it disappeared in a broken surface. The slurp was impressive. The rings were widening around the spot when the lifted rod tip telegraphed through the line and leader the electrifying message, hooked. Things work fine but not for long. The hook lost its hold and loose line and leader came back at me. There was a mental reflection about the bad holding percentage of a downstream dry-fly cast.

The first several casts for the second trout were off mark; then came a good one, one that would foster a good float at the right place. This time the hook held and the reward was a real fish caught on the Green Drake hatch—the making of the trip.

To me this was a convincing example of, first, how well drag protects a trout, and second, how one should have confidence in the proper delivery of the right fly. Skues might have put it thus: "The way of a trout with a fly is fascinating."

Selectivity and drag are totally different, but even so there are times when it is most difficult for the angler to determine which causes failure. A case of this nature involved a brown trout, Vince Marinaro, and me. The incident occurred in a small backwater, tight against the upper side of a clump of protruding grass. The spot had been adopted as home by a fish that chose to indulge in afternoon surface-feeding activity. There he would feed daintily in his unperturbed way, apparently impossible to deceive. Periodically on different days the fish was shown little ants and jassids on 7X, along with other less promising flies. This went on for weeks, and the trout remained untouched.

One day I walked upstream several hundred yards to the one crossing place negotiable with boots, then doubled back to see what happens to a Marinaro presentation aimed at this fish. Carefully I wiggled my way to the spot, then stretched my neck like a turtle to have a look. There was the trout about six inches under the surface in feeding position. In back of it was the root system of the patch of grass, and in front of its nose was a miniature backwater possibly 1 foot in diameter. Ever so gently the water piled up against the grass, then fell away from it into a slightly different water plane. A small live green jassid, trapped in the sticky tension of the surface, drifted toward the smooth backwater; but as it approached, its rate of travel diminished. It hung almost stationary about three inches in front of the fish. Ever so deliberately, ever so confidently the trout moved up to meet it; then the little green bug disappeared in a sip that barely broke the surface.

Vince cast his jassid above the spot on a nice slack leader. The fly rode directly for the taking place, then began to slow down in the bay. As it hung there the line and leader straightened, with the result that the fly was drawn sideways in an unnatural manner. The slight drag could not be noticed by the caster but it certainly was by the trout. We concluded that the primary problem here was natural drift and that it might be impossible to take this fish. During the closing weeks of the season that fish provided a lot of hopeful casting for a number of fishermen, but not for Vince and me, for we had capitulated.

I recall, and very vividly, a Japanese beetle eater I regarded as impossible to deceive. The spot was in midstream where the current funneled into a fast narrow channel. It was next to impossible to miss the spot with a cast, and the water was fast and broken, giving the fisherman the idea that neither drag nor selectivity would be a tough problem. Every time some beetles were thrown in upstream of the spot, they were channeled into the tight line of drift of a voracious feeder. If ever a fish appeared to be easy to hook on a dry fly, it was this one; but things didn't work this way.

It was possible to lie down on the bank twelve feet from the fish and observe all, while someone above threw in beetles and someone below cast to the fish. Always it was the same: the trout accepted the real thing and rejected the imitation. Marvel of marvels, in the closing month of that season that fish was fed beetles many dozens of times, it was fished over frequently by competent casters, and it was shown probably the finest assortment of beetle imitations any trout ever saw, yet the mistake of taking the fraud was never made.

I would have attributed failure to drag on the grounds that the funnel sucked hard on the line and leader, except for the fact that a quartering downstream or cross-stream pitch had no semblance of drag, yet it suffered the same fate. That leaves selectivity. Could it be that this fish would only rush a beetle after it saw the legs move; and in a slow cumbersome way, that is the way it is with live ones no matter whether they are back up or down? This particular spot is now gone, for the stream was rechanneled away from there, so there can be no more studies conducted at this particular place.

Problems are the real challenge, the backbone of angling. Pitted against each other are sophisticated fish and accomplished angler. When a prudent fish is surface feeding, it is safe unless the right man comes along. Always there will be fish that some individuals can hook and others cannot touch. That is the way it is, all because of selectivity and drag.

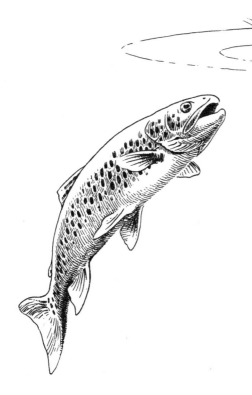

PART TWO

# 7

# *Intercepting the Hatches*

Man, with a certain element of doubt, thinks that events of his making and of his doing have a tendency to reoccur, as witness his adage, "History frequently repeats itself." There is no uncertainty, however, about repetition within the workings of nature, nor is there much doubt about their regularity and timing; in fact repetition is standard. Classic examples are the semiannual migrations of birds, the coloration of foliage in the fall, the growth of winter pelts on animals, the singing of frogs and the cicada in their seasons, the drumming of cock grouse, the strange love call of the bull moose, etc.—and the hatches of water-born insects, the last being the reason for this chapter.

The emergence of the aquatic insects from the water to shed skins in the foliage or their return to the water to reproduce, "a hatch of fly," as we anglers call both, are governed by the same stringent laws of Mother Nature that control the lives of all her children. So about the same time, in about the same place, year after year, there should be a rise of trout to a specific hatch.

Because rises of trout are of special interest to fly fishermen, good information about the hatches is fundamental. With solid background information the angler can expect to enjoy some success in intercepting hatches, then enjoy the interesting fishing they develop. Needed is a timetable for the stretches of trout streams the individual frequents.

A general national schedule is a guide, but it can be both confusing and misleading. Such a schedule does not separate the existent from the nonexistent hatches in your waters; neither can it segregate the wheat from the chaff in your waters, nor accurately date your hatches. It is concrete knowledge that counts.

Everyone can and should compile his own timetable, and he may choose to take the next step and create his own imitations of the naturals with which he contends. The sequence of the hatches is an interesting study and to imitate the hatches is an interesting pursuit.

In compiling the timetable, hearsay information can be just as valuable as eyewitness experience, for both serve as future reference. Regular fishermen of an area working together can compile their collective information to the mutual advantage of all involved. But mental notation does not seem to retain the information; it must be put down in writing to be captured, held, and then applied.

To the best of my knowledge there is no field book, fishing diary, or call it what you will, on the market into which entry can be made; so by necessity one organizes his own. Whatever the form, it is not only a valuable reference but, as time goes by, an entertaining refresher course.

In order that the angler can make an intelligent choice of fly, something must be understood about the drama that transpires before his eyes as one creature in cold-blooded nature wipes out a lesser aquatic life. It starts about the time of year when the evenings become comfortable and the surroundings attractive. It marks the start of a triumphant march featuring bursting foliage, the song of birds, and colorful blooms. In a general way too, it precedes the discomfort of summer heat.

Both the insects seen on the water and those seen above the water will determine which fraud should be attached to the leader for presentation to the feeding fish. Thus, both a study of insects and a study of rise forms is a phase of fly fishing for trout.

The first aquatic insects are gray in color, then along come the browns and finally the pale yellows. There are times when there is more than one hatch on the water, but the trout in their exacting feeding take only their preference. A common example of such selective-feeding activity is on emerging Hendricksons when there is also a veritable blizzard of caddis.

The rise form itself is a general guide in the determination upon what the fish are feeding. Generally speaking, a large natural brings about a noisy heavy rise, a medium-size insect a pyramid rise, and the midge foods an insignificant ring. When surface food is not plentiful, yet there are some rising trout, the fish feed from low positions in the water and their move to the surface generates a noisy take. On the other hand, when there is an abundant supply of minutiae, the trout assume high-in-the-water feeding positions from which they tip and sip. Furthermore, when there is a rise in progress of any of the three types, the rise forms of the larger of the feeders can be distinguished from the others because, by comparison, they are slightly heavier and deeper.

Each succeeding generation of fly fishermen talks about the current deterioration of the hatches. This reporting can hardly be questioned. Pollution is devastating; unnatural siltation is a vital factor, particularly on the egg hatch; widely fluctuating water temperatures and water volumes must take their toll. But a tremendously heavy hatch and a good fishing hatch are not one and the same. There can be too many flies for the best of fishing, but such a hatch in conjunction with a heavy rise is a fascinating phenomenon to observe. Light hatches can and do produce rises. Thus, the state of the hatches, so long as there are hatches, does not alter the approach of the angler; he can still fish the rise and match the hatch.

A diminished hatch often comes back well. Dr. Paul Needham was of the opinion that so long as there is a mating pair left on a watershed, that hatch can come back. Undoubtedly winds and waterfowl redistribute aquatic insects, even from one watershed to another.

What proportion of the trout of a stream section will surface feed? is a good question. Frank Sawyer, dean of the English river keepers, makes the following observation in his excellent book, *Keeper of the Stream:*

> The sport of dry fly and/or nymph fishing mostly has to depend on the odd fish here and there which, for some reason or other, has chosen to feed near the surface. But there are occasions when even the customary few are absent, when you can walk miles and miles along the banks of a fishery without seeing trout that would be worth the sport of catching.

Unquestionably competition is a factor. Some lethargic fish from the fly fisherman's standpoint may at times be induced to join in surface feeding when they see and hear others making the most of a temporary abundance of fly on the water.

The placement of the dry fly in relation to the position of the feeding station of a given fish is worthy of consideration. The general tendency seems to be to overcast. When the fly drifts to the caster's side, the leader tippet is inconspicuous, whereas an overcast fly shows lots of leader. It is a bad practice to skid the fly from the water when it is in the fish's window. Delivery should be well above the position of a dainty feeder, but a fly can be cast with good effect directly over or even in back of a slashing surface feeder. At least, that is how these things appear to me.

This approach to better dry-fly fishing got off to a great start. There is documentary evidence, particularly from the talented pen of one of anglerdom's most famous authors, Lord Grey of Fallodon, that a section of the Itchen was the site of the founding of the practice of matching the hatch. In what I regard as the finest written work about any sport, *Fly Fishing*, Grey writes about the wonderful stream that flows through the cathedral town of Winchester, England, where is located the boy's school, bearing the same name, which he attended.

It is here that the modern-eyed floater was developed and it is here where the hatches were observed and imitated. The water above Winchester was leased by Marryat and Francis Francis, then later by G. E. M. Skues and James Rodt. It appears that after it was learned how to make the wet fly float, the hatches of the Itchen were the main patterns to be imitated, the greatest competition coming from the Test and its fishermen, led by Frederick Halford.

George Selwyn Marryat of the Itchen, considered by some to be the greatest fly fisherman for trout who ever drew breath, was the guiding light for all, and that includes Halford on the Test. As a student Grey became acquainted with master angler, Marryat, then in later years wrote as follows about him:

> One could not say which was the more instructive, to watch his fishing or listen to his talk; no one had more information to give, no one was more generous in giving it, his knowledge seemed the result not only of observation and experience, but of some peculiar insight into the ways of trout. In the management of rod and tackle he displayed not only skill but genius.

*Hewitt Nymph.* Edward R. Hewitt is recognized as the greatest trout-fishing pioneer. Among other things, he popularized nymph fishing for both trout and salmon. G. E. M. Skues introduced this type of fly fishing on English trout streams by imitating about-to-merge flies, fished just under the surface in a natural drift. Hewitt took it up from there by imitating the natural swimming, crawling, and drifting larva. More often than not he would give them action by moving the rod tip. A favorite of his had a hard black back and soft yellow belly with sparse black hackle and tail. *Photo by James Fosse.*

Even in the beginning of this era of meticulous imitation, Marryat warned, "It is not the fly; it is the driver."

Marryat, who died at the age of fifty-six, did not produce a book, nor are there letters that can be perused; his fame comes from what others wrote about him; but Skues, a little farther down the line of famous Itchen anglers, who lived to be ninety-four, wrote voluminously and wrote extremely well. This keen observer gave his second but not his last work on trout fishing the enticing title, *The Way of a Trout with a Fly.* "Old Bardge" on the Itchen was his stamping ground and included was the war-torn period in history that he referred to as, "the disturbance of the twenties." So dry-fly fishing is a relatively young sport. The chief hatch and the one so dearly loved by all chalk-stream anglers was, and still is to-day, the Blue Winged Olive, "the B.W.O.," an *Ephemera.*

The basic concept was and is today in England, and elsewhere, to employ a counterpart of nature designed and constructed to deceive.

Embedded among feathers, fur, and nylon is the devastating part of the counterfeit, light wire steel, bent and well tempered with an eye at one extremity and with a sharp hollow point and a barb at the other.

The anglers of the Itchen, in the cataloging of their hatches and in the imitation of the natural, set a pattern that every dry-fly man who came after them would do well to follow for his stream stretches. Differences between them and most of us are that we fish more than one stream section and more than one stream, and we fish more months of the year than they; hence we experience variety and differences that show up in our more complex trail and calendar.

Some entomological studies by anglers have been made in this country and the results have been published. These serve as guides in the matters of identification and emergence dates:

> Preston Jennings, *A Book of Trout Flies*
> Charles M. Wetzel, *Practical Fly Fishing*
> _____*Trout Flies*
> Dr. Alvin R. Grove, Jr., *Lure and Lore of Trout Fishing*
> Ernest G. Schweibert, Jr., *Matching the Hatch*
> Doug Swisher and Carl Richards, *Selective Trout*
> Alfred N. Caucci and Robert Naftasi, *Hatches*
> Robert Boyle and Dave Whitlock, editors, *The Fly-Tyer's Almanac*

D. G. "Buck" Raunhorst of Slayton, Minnesota, has produced an excellent chart of the insects, their emergence dates, and their imitations; and it is printed on heavy stock and nicely folded.

Examples of studies on specific streams, published in book form, are Art Flick's *Streamside Guide*, which has to do with the aquatic life of New York's Scoharie; and Dr. Justin W. Leonard's handsome *Mayflies of Michigan Trout Streams*.

The type of trout fishing one enjoys is a matter of individual taste. Maybe the bait fisherman and the spinning-lure fisherman do not like a hatch and rise because they are unable to cope successfully with that combination, but for the fly fisherman that is something else. Here is the situation he forever hopes for, but, more important, this is something he can seek and find. The rise is the challenging enigma that pits fish and man against each other—a prudent and selective fish and a sophisticated and discriminating man. Fishing the rise with the dry fly is the pinnacle in angling for trout; that is a certainty in the game marked with uncertainty that we call fly fishing for trout.

# 8

# The Hatch of Hatches

There is a distinct similarity between cattle and casters in that
each regards the grass as being greener on the other side of the
fence. The following proves it in the case of a caster, one C. K.
Fox. Involved was the combination of location, hatch, and rise.

It was not by accident but because of accident that I was here,
this being about the only place I could get to in order to fish at all.
The nerve that runs down the back of the leg had been pinched in
an accident, making driving and walking painful, the getting into
and out of boots or waders a virtual two-man job, and contention
with current, mud, and slippery rocks all but prohibitive. Driving
time from home to this spot was a painfully long ten minutes; from
parked car to pool, a hard 2-minute walk, and from there casting
distance was 50 feet and less. This particularly convenient place
had been passed up before, the only reason being that greener
pastures seemed to lie beyond.

It did not feel good to settle down on the wooden shotgun-shell
box that had been brought along for that purpose, but it felt worse
to stand. Upstream 50 feet was a beautiful, 5-foot natural waterfall in the big brook or the little river, nomenclature depending
upon where you are from. In front was a flow of smooth water
about two feet deep beside a high stone wall crowned with a dense
growth of lilac. Fifty feet below was a low log dam with an interesting brush pile across the far corner. Actually the location
was directly in back of a house in a small town, but I could see no
one, or no house for that matter, from my low place under a
canopy of high foliage; and no one would be seeing me. There
wasn't even a dog around to protect his home against the crippled

stranger armed with a little fly rod. The tumbling and splashing of water was a soul-satisfying sound.

There had to be some trout in the deep picture pool featuring the falls and some more trout under the brush pile, and most certainly the surface feeders among them would know about the evening sulphur hatch and would have developed a feeding pattern to capitalize upon it. Maybe their feeding stations would be nicely spaced within my range between the tail of the pool and the breast of the dam. That is what I hoped for in my fishing from one spot, a sort of fisherman's throne. Enthusiasm was mounting. It looked so fishy and buggy and the stream stretch was so beautiful that a feeling of guilt crept over me for overlooking its potential in the past.

The sun was setting in a red west when the first sulphur dun appeared on the surface. The canary-colored wings were cocked skyward. There was a futile attempt to become airborne as the insect appeared to bounce on the water. For another yard it rode the surface; then again the wings were tested. This time the beautiful little fly could follow the dictates and intent of nature and climb slowly and unsteadily away from the water and into the waiting arms of the overhead foliage. There it would undergo a strange metamorphosis: the shedding of the skin and the sealing of the mouth. In an evening or two, and symbolically in the evening of its life, he or she would fly to the corridor over the water to perform the only remaining mission in life—but its most important—procreation.

There followed other emerging subimagos—first the break through the surface tension, the lift into the air, then the slow laborious flight into the foliage. Thus the evening hatch of duns was in progress. Now several could be seen at one time in the air and another just leaving the water.

Something else was stirring too. The imagos were leaving the leaves to mill about the high boughs of the trees, the tops of which were still bathed in sunlight. Now the flight in quest of mates on those cleared and strengthened wings was sure and fast. For every dun that left the water, there seemed to be a hundred spinners milling above, the difference in numbers being because the duns emerge slowly over a period of time whereas the spinners return in mass.

Before my eyes a dun riding on the surface disappeared in a

dimple. It was the first rise of the evening, a little fish in what I thought of as my stretch. Shortly there was another dimple, another slurp, and another casualty in the aquatic insect world. I sat on the box and watched. The rod set up and ready to go, sulphur imitation included, was propped up against a bush, but I did not reach for the equipment.

The spinners were pairing up and their quick, irregular flight was bringing them closer to the water. The tempo increased in their excited nuptial dance. Exhausted males would drop helter-skelter, some landing on the water, others on the land. Their normal passing, so unlike the normal death of the members of the animal kingdom, was one of ecstasy. The females carried on to deliver their precious cargoes of egg masses to the right place in the stream. Nature steered them to broken, well-aerated water. In a general way their irregular flight was upstream. Anytime a nymph becomes unattached, it is carried along with the current, thus the upstream flight of the fertilized females insures population of the entire watershed, otherwise in the course of time a hatch would work its way out of a stream.

Now in the failing light, there were duns, dead males, and spent female spinners on the water before me. Some drifting flies were traveling in every line of drift. And in every line of drift there was a feeding trout. The better fish were in the better places. This was obvious because of the variation in the rise forms and the sound of the rises. Within casting distance were approximately fifteen voraciously feeding fish, three of which appeared to be extremely good ones. The reaction of one Pennsylvania German friend to this would have been: "The fly is up, the rise is on."

Nature was staging a fantastic display. By the time the greens darkened and black velvet patterns melted into the silvery background of flowing water, activity was at its zenith. It was the lush time of year, the period before the hot-weather burn, and the most comfortable time to be abroad of an evening. As I sat there in the half light, not disposed to stir, I watched the flies in the air and the rings on the water. It was then I realized that this is the best hatch of all for me, therefore it should be my favorite. You may call them "Little Yellow Drakes," "Pale Watery Duns" or "Little Light Cahills," I call them "Sulphurs." In the days before Charlie Wetzel and Preston Jennings had produced their books relating to

*Mayfly Imitation*. The traditional imitation of the mayfly has upright divided wings. The above is an all-lemon-colored fly with hackle-point wings tied on a #18 hook made to imitate the important sulphur hatch or little yellow drake. The Pale Evening Dunn and the Light Cahill are common imitations for this hatch.

The sulphur hatch is of many weeks duration. Early in the season the duns emerge in the afternoon and the spinners return in the evening. During late June, however, both duns and spinners are on the water in the late evening only. *Photo by James Fosse.*

*Quill-Bodied Dry Fly*. Nothing imitates the segmented body of the smaller mayflies in a more realistic manner than the quill. Among the great patterns in this family are: Quill Gordon, Ginger Quill, Couchy Bondhu Quill, Blue Quill, and Black Quill. The standard patterns are tied with wings, but there are those among us who consider wings unnecessary window dressing. And, too, there are those who consider the quill-bodied flies best in limestone streams and the dubbed wool and fur bodies best in freestone streams. *Photo by James Fosse.*

*Spent-Wing Spinner.* After deposition of the egg mass, the female spinner drops spent to the surface, wing extended. Some dying males drop on the water in the same position. The logical imitation of the natural is the spent-wing tie.

Pictured above is an all-white spent-wing, wings being hackle points, tied on a #16 hook to imitate Ephran Lucon, the great August hatch on a few trout streams and many bass rivers. It is anticipated with glee by the fishermen of Pennsylvania's Yellow Breeches Creek. *Photo by James Fosse.*

the naturals and their imitations, Bob McCafferty and I were attempting to identify and classify hatches. In order to understand each other, in our fishing talk back and forth, we had to give insects names, and appropriately these were the "Sulphurs."

Thus this chapter has to do with what to my way of thinking is the most important hatch, the greatest hatch, the most interesting hatch. Involved are: stage setting, the actors, and the action. Let's start at the beginning.

In our trout world why do so many rave about dry-fly fishing? It is because everything about it is prolonged and much is visible. Things start before a fish is hooked, and there are times when hooking requires considerable doing. One sees the hatch, then the rise forms, then he attempts to match the hatch, then he delivers his offering, then he watches it drift into the window of the fish. Anticipation is prolonged, expectation is prolonged, execution is prolonged. If things are right, that is, if the fly and the float are right as far as the *trout* is concerned, the fly disappears in a ring and when the angler tightens the line there is a living throbbing resistance. "Electrifying impact" is appropriate phraseology to describe the contact.

Here is a unique hatch because it prevails over a long period of time. This not only establishes a feeding pattern on the part of the fish, but it makes for selectivity. In lowland streams early stragglers mark their appearance in late April. Farther north and in higher altitudes the date is deferred. On some streams the hatch is in full bloom by May 10.

Early sulphurs have a bluish wing and in my judgment the most effective size of pattern is #16. Duns appear on the water in the afternoon, and the fall of spinners starts before sundown. By Decoration Day, though, the flies are a bit smaller and the wings of the dun are canary yellow. The time of emergence of the duns is after sundown, and the fall of spinners takes place in the failing light. This situation continues for weeks on end, a real bonanza. A #18 fly now does a better job than a #16. Whether these two, which differ slightly in appearance and size, are separate and distinct species or whether they are different stages of the same species is academic. Only an entomologist by careful microscopic examination can identify the various drakes (mayflies), and the work must be done with male spinners—not duns and not females—it is that highly specialized.

There are at least two species of the same size and color, but I suspect more. *Epeorus vitrea* has two tails, whereas *Ephemerella dorothea* has three. Both become airborne quickly, the duns doing a minimum of drifting. The spinners furnish the bulk of the fishing.

Over the years two common and popular patterns have been employed to match these hatches, or if you prefer this hatch: Light Cahill and Pale Evening Dun. To this can be added two more standard patterns but not so well known: Tup's Indispensable (American version) and R. B. Fox (R. B. for Ray Bergman and Fox because the body material is light-colored belly fur from a vixen). To this quartet of workables I want to add two more specials, and therein lies a tale worth telling.

George Harvey, formerly of Pennsylvania State University, or more appropriately, of the central Pennsylvania limestone streams, and I engaged one winter in a little patter that went something like this:

H.  "I have finally come up with an improved sulphur imitation that works better than other patterns."

F.  "So have I."

H.  "The trout usually take this one with confidence and without hesitation."

F.  "Same with mine."

H.  "This pattern is the result of trial and error."

F.  "Mine too."

H.  "It has an off-color in it that to the human eye does not appear in the natural."

F.  "So does mine."

H.  "Funny thing, the odd color is bright orange."

F.  "Yes, bright orange."

H.  "You sound like Charlie McCarthy."

F.  "I'm serious."

H.  "Mine has two color of hackle, a few turns of honey, and a few turns of orange, intermingled; otherwise specs are same as Pale Evening Dun."

F.  "Here is where I get out of the rut. Mine has an orange gantron body, otherwise specs are same as Pale Evening Dun."

For my sulphur fishing I would not be without either of these two. Sometimes I start out in the evening with one, sometimes the other. There are times when one does not seem to suit a particular fish but the other will, so before I give up I prefer to show a discriminating fish both. For old time's sake once in a while I turn to a Pale Evening Dun, an R. B. Fox, or a Tup's Indispensable. Often they will produce but it appears that the trout like the orange jobs a little better.

Vince Marinaro has two special patterns, one for the dun, the other for the spinner. His subimago imitation has upright wings cut from duck feathers dyed yellow and his thorax-style tie of hackle, that is, hackle in the middle of the body; whereas he ties the imago with a body of ivory-colored porcupine quill, and the wings are hackle points tied spent.

Imitation has been called the sincerest form of flattery. The best imitation for a given hatch is the one that delivers the highest success percentage. And so it goes with pattern, always an interesting phase of matching the hatch with the dry fly.

There are two reasons why the sulphur eaters are hyperselective—a polite way of saying they separate the men from the boys. This is a late hatch, for the yellows come last, and by the time it comes along the suicide fish and the less discriminating fish have ended up in frying pans; and the stream is lower and clearer and the smaller pale fly is more difficult to imitate well than is the case with the bigger early-season dark flies.

The stream flats are of particular interest because they carry so many of the better fish and rise forms can be seen so readily thereon, but flat water makes for examination and discrimination by both trout and angler—the trout because there is more time for scrutiny and the angler because by rise forms he can spot the better fish.

How big are some of the surface feeders? The great Theodore Gordon answered that question in this way. "Fly fishing is more interesting where we know a few really big fish exist. They may be slow to rise, but give them a fair chance, they will take a fly occasionally." He also wrote, "In a low stage of water [trout] are very shy and secretive."

In reporting on the sulphurs and in writing about George Harvey and Theodore Gordon it should be pointed out that the latter fished in the home country of the former and he did so in sulphur time. The following was published in the old *Forest and Stream* magazine of March 14, 1903, under the name of Theodore Gordon and before the time of George Harvey:

> Many years ago I was fishing a fine large limestone stream near Bellefonte, Pa., in company with a native of that town, who was a most expert angler and who cast in a particularly graceful manner. The scene of one afternoon's sport was a rather shallow mill dam constructed only a few years before; this dam was full of brook trout of about a quarter of a pound each and they were rising steadily all over the water. We cast and cast, and compared the flies in our respective books. Finally in the envelope in the pocket of his book my friend found a small straw-colored fly closely approximating the fly at which the trout were rising. He put it on and in

half an hour or a little over, caught 42 trout. He had only one fly of the kind, so I was forced to play audience, nothing I could offer being tempting to the fish.

There have been years when a rise to the sulphur produced the highlight of the season. Such happened to be the case for me in 1965. My eye was caught by a widening circle in the silvery smoothness and my ear by a slurp; obviously it was a big fish. The location lent itself to a long and dragless float, but should the fish be hooked, 30 feet downstream was a large man-made brush pile.

After a few drifts the fish sucked in the Harvey Sulphur and sank back apparently unperturbed by the connection. There was no bolt, no jump, just smug complacency. In about half a minute some violent jerking occurred as though the trout were corkscrewing. In spite of the protective light tip of the little rod this was too much for the 5X strand of nylon.

Several days later Dr. Dale Coman of Philadelphia, author of the salmon book dealing with Maine's Pleasant Stream, visited me. He had enjoyed an interesting day with big fish on a sinking Black Ant, but knowing him to be a dry-fly man at heart I suggested at dusk that he accompany me in an effort to add icing to the cake. Upon our arrival at the scene of my recent catastrophe we saw that the big fish was at it again—same place, same way, and the hatch was fine.

The good doctor looked over the situation. He tied his choice sulphur imitation to the leader. The line was lengthened and the distance measured by false casting. The fly dropped lightly to the surface 5 feet above the fish. It drifted without drag, a perfect delivery. That which was hoped for transpired—the fly disappeared in a little whirlpool and the hook point became embedded. The fish simply settled back. After an apparent analysis of the situation it shook its head or twisted so violently that the leader could not take it. I knew exactly how the doctor felt and, too, what was going through his mind.

Subsequent evenings I watched for the big surface feeder but he did not show again. But something else turned up. One evening what appeared to be two excellent fish put up along the grassy bank across the way about 30 feet apart. It was dusk and both were busy eating sulphurs.

Instead of working into casting position below the lower of the two and trying for him first, I elected to do something unorthodox. After cutting back from 5X to 4X and attaching the Gantron Sulphur, I literally sneaked into a casting position so that one fish was up and across and the other down and across.

More often than not, upon being hooked with a dry fly, these big stream-bred browns bolt upstream, then jump, thus to increase chances for both it might be better to go after the upper one first in the attempt to avoid disturbance of the other. The stalk had been successful, for both fish continued to feed well.

Things worked fine. The upper fish took the fly, bolted upstream, jumped, then fought to hold that position. In due time it was landed without disturbing the lower trout. The fly was cleaned and dried by blowing on it, then pitched to fish number two with a quartering downstream kickback cast. Confidently the trout took the imitation. And so it was that I took two 18-inchers on back-to-back casts to highlight a season.

That troubled month, longer ago than it seems and longer ago than I like to think it was, I experienced some great fishing to rising trout from the shotgun-shell box along Cedar Run. Evening after evening and week after week sulphurs emerged and sulphurs returned, and evening after evening the trout rose. I know because I was there. None of these handsome fish was taken away from its beautiful place and some of them were caught and returned more than once.

By virtue of the duration of the sulphur hatch, its density, its consistency, its distribution; and by virtue of the activity it generates; and by virtue of the angling challenge it creates, here is the backbone for dusk fishing on many a stream for many a week. What a great fountainhead for rising trout are these wonderful sulphurs at the bewitching hour that marks the completion of another day.

# 9

# *The Hidden Hatches*

Picture a colossal aquatic hatch, his superexcellency, rising trout, and an expanse and succession of rise forms itching to be fished. The reaction to such a composite by the dedicated fly fisherman is, "Beautiful!" Would you believe it could be possible that there are long-drawn-out hatches of tremendous intensity and of considerable interest to the trout that occur on many streams unknown to all but a small segment of those who cherish fishing over surface feeders? These hidden hatches deserve special accolade because they can fire up fishing.

Both are tiny mayflies or drakes, but not too tiny to be insignificant to catchable trout, nor too small to be imitated. An appropriate angling name for one is "olive" because the body is olive in coloration and the fly is the same genus, *Baetis*, as the widely proclaimed and tremendously popular English chalkstream hatch, the Blue Wing Olive—the fabulous B.W.O. of English angling literature. The American, however, is much smaller than the Briton. The other minute drake is genus *Caenidae*, family *tricorythodes*, and because it has no hind wings, just one on each side, it could logically be called, "little single wing."

There can be three families of *Baetis* in the same watershed. Vince Marinaro caught floating duns, subimagos, held them until after molt, then forwarded the imagos to Dr. Banard D. Burks of the Illinois State Natural History Survey for species identification. In the group, which to the naked eye appears to be identical, were three families: *vagans*, *cingulatus*, and *levitans*. It has been reported that *vagans* has three life cycles every two years, but apparently one or both of the others have three or four broods each year. This would mean a nymphal stage considerably less than the usual one-year period for the majority of the Ephemerids.

Only a trained entomologist by microscopic examination could tell these flies apart. In the identification of mayflies the technical people work with the male imago, the duns and females not being suitable. Strangely, the chief distinguishing characteristic is genitalia.

Concerning the habits of *cingulatus*, Justin W. Leonard in his *Mayflies of Michigan Trout Streams*, 1962, reported that the habitat is gravel-bottomed streams of moderate to swift current, especially shallow runs and riffle areas. It may be that *vagans* prefers or requires slow water and weed beds.

Authorities agree that the nymphs are swift swimmers. I have seen tiny quick-moving nymphs in a tub of water in which the weed elodea had been shaken, which I believed to be those of the *Baetis* genus. Dr. Alvin R. "Bus" Grove describes these nymphs as "sprawlers" as opposed to "clamberers and burrowers."

The olive duns ride on the surface for a much greater distance than is the case with the sulphurs, even in the same water and air temperatures. Once the winged insect emerges, it can no longer feed, thus there must be great energy stored in the body by the nymph to permit the balance of the life cycle to be completed.

*Baetis* is taken from the Greek word meaning *enduring but a day*; thus the name itself is the clue to the brief existence of the insect as a fly. The molt comes shortly after emergence and soon thereafter the fall of spinners, which encompasses the acts of copulation and egg laying.

Eaton in 1888, Morgan in 1911, and Murphy in 1912 reported that the females crawl into the water to deposit the eggs. I have seen them on submerged posts, stakes, and the sticks of brush piles. In good light they show up well, for attached to each is a silver-looking air bubble. They do not remain transfixed in death to their submerged objects, which indicates one of two things: either they break away to pop up and float spent or they crawl out to return to the air to fly about for a short time before exhaustion and death. That bubble must have a use.

The facts that there is more than one brood in a twelve-month period and that there is more than one species mean that the emergence of the duns takes place at various times during the course of the year.

Frequently one sees heavy emergences of duns during the afternoon and evening but no fall of spinners, the indication being that they return after dark. Dead spent spinners seen in the eddies in the mornings and trapped ones in the cobwebs bear this out. There are occasions when the little olive duns, emerging in the afternoon, bring about a rise of trout. One effective imitation is a small Olive Dun dry fly, either with or without wings, another is a #22 Quill Gordon or Olive Quill.

The other tiny mayfly, genus *Caenidae*, family *tricorythodes*, "Black and White," is very different from *Baetis*, "the olives," in that it has one wing on each side instead of the customary two for mayflies and it is the spinner fall that sets off the trout instead of the emergence of duns, as is the normal case with *Baetis*. *Caenis* seems to pass from dun to spinner in an even shorter time than is the case with *Baetis*.

Shortly after daybreak on many streams from mid-July to mid-October, there is a great fall of *Caenis* spinners. Because the fly is so small in size and so fast in flight, it is a difficult hatch to see in the air, even though the quantity may be tremendous. They can be observed, though, in the direct rays of the sun against a background of dark trunks of trees or the darkest of foliage. First there is a great trading back and forth at an elevation of about 30 feet, after which the flight becomes progressively lower. About two hours after daylight the egg laying gets under way and the trout start rising to the spent spinners, which are difficult to see on the water. By 10:30 A.M. it is all over for another day.

Here is an aquatic insect that emerges as a dun, molts and returns as a spinner in a period less than half an hour in duration. The skin is shed shortly after emergence and shed skins can be observed clinging to some of the flies. Think of it, an early-morning hatch that flourishes unabated for one-third of the year, and during the part of the trout season when hatches are a rarity. The fish, which are expecting it and looking for it, are ready to do their part, at least those up to 16 inches or so.

The first angler I knew to become fascinated by *Caenis tricorythodes* was Bill Pfeiffer, a member of the faculty of the Pennsylvania State Forestry School. As a resident of Mt. Alto, he is a regular fisherman of wonderful little Falling Springs, which flows through Chambersburg, and the hatch on this limestone stream is extra fine. Bill met the challenge of identification, imitation, and presentation head-on, even before anyone else seemed to know about its existence. After considerable trial and error and observation he produced a productive procedure and pattern. His pleasure in tying and fishing his imitations reminds me of the adage "he who cuts his own wood is twice warmed."

The Pfeiffer imitation is as follows: hook, #20 short shank; tail, bronze-blue hackle wisps; body, peacock herl; hackle, bronze-blue; no wings. He says, "Maybe this does not look like this fly to a human, but so long as the trout take it well I'm satisfied."

Dr. Roebling Knoch, a very busy and important person, will set the alarm so that he can be up before dawn in order to travel 50 miles from his home in York, Pennsylvania, to be in time for the early-morning hatch and rise on Falling Springs. There he often meets Bill Pfeiffer. Roeb has found the hatch on Vermont's Battenkill and New York's Ausable. Dr. Leonard writes about it on Michigan streams. It seems fair to suspect that this hatch is both heavy and widespread.

Another great *Caenis* fan who travels to intercept the hatch is Frank Honish of Philadelphia. Fishing with fine leader and diminutive dry fly is his idea of fly fishing deluxe. Once he started operating on the Little Lehigh near Allentown, Pennsylvania, he revolutionized the thinking of some of the patrons of that great stream. One mile of this is regulated so there is no kill and no closed season, and this hatch continues there into October.

The radiant moments of a trout season for Jack Bosh are the times when his superbly tied tiny #24 Coachmen is sipped by a trout and he deliberately lifts the fly rod and feels that the fly has been accepted. His leader tippets are usually as fine as can be tied without breakage when knots are drawn tight. This is his concept of deceiver fly fishing at its best, and his favorite streams are Penn's Creek, the largest of the limestone streams in the East, and the Little Lehigh.

One day I came upon something either by accident or in desperation—it is so long ago I can't be sure which. There was a #20 Starling wet fly in the box, a Starling being in color about halfway between a black quill and a blue quill—a gray-colored quill, body, and hackle. I dunked it in the fly float, removed the excess oil with false casts, then let it go. The finely tipped-out 11-foot leader delivered the fly so gently that it did not break the surface tension. It must have looked good as it floated to a trout that was sipping the dainty olive duns, for it was sucked in like the real thing. Later I tried the same thing on Single-Wing spinners and it does well with them.

Although the idea of using a wet fly to simulate a dry lacks appeal of some sort, it actually works under this exacting and rather complicated situation, midge drake fishing, for time and again the same thing has transpired under the same circumstances. It is possible that some of the exhausted drakes tip over or are blown over so that the wings rest spent together on the same side making a form and silhouette like that of a floating fly tied to be fished wet.

There are the normal four stages of *Baetis* and *Caenis:* nymph, dun, spinner, and egg; but compared with the larger mayflies there is lack of conformity. But it is not always the ordinary processes that motivate anglers. The tiny, carefully chosen and well-tied midge dry fly in conjunction with a 7X or 8X leader works well with competent delivery. If there is to be pleasure and success, there must be a combination of knowledge and skill.

Once there is a mass of duns or spinners on the water, the availability of easy food stimulates surface feeding; but its very abundance results in selectivity and the smallness of the natural is challenging. The feeding is dainty and deliberate, the trout assuming positions about six inches underwater from which they tip up and sip. It is not a voracious binge like the feeding to the larger insects such as the high-water early-season Hendrickson or the big Decoration Day Green Drake.

How about their value to the fish of the stream? Mayfly nymphs are vegetarians, thus they conert vegetable matter into a form palatable to trout. Their numbers can be tremendous. One cubic foot of gravel has been known to contain over a thousand Hendrickson nymphs. Since the olive nymphs are very much smaller, it seems reasonable to believe that there could be many more of them in a given area than is the case with larger Ephemerids. Granted, a *vagans* or *tricorythodes* nymph upon hatching from an egg is microscopic.

*The Palmer Tie.* The palmer-style tie of dry fly, featuring many turns of hackle, is most useful in fast broken water where, with the aid of fly float, it does not submerge. There are times when a fish will flash to, but refuse, such a fly. Once the location of the trout is known, a follow-up with a more lightly dressed pattern is generally effective. Ed Hewitt tied this fly with a face of a few turns of a light-colored hackle and called it "the bivisible" because it could be seen readily by both trout and angler. *Photo by James Fosse.*

The pigmylike mayflies have their way of slipping by unnoticed and unheralded, but it should not be that way. The crowning satisfaction in fly fishing for trout is in locating a surface-feeding fish, an unheralded and unobserved approach into casting position, the delivery of the right imitation, the hooking, playing, and finally the landing of the fish. In the case of the olives and the single wing the combination of size and pattern is critical, thus making it a particularly interesting challenge and a fascinating problem.

# 10

# The Terrestrial Insects

The true greatness of Theodore Gordon (1854–1915) and his contributions to fly fishing cannot be overstated. This frail little man, who devoted and contributed his entire life to angling, had more than one new dry-fly idea. When he first applied the English floating fly to American brook trout streams, he, like his friends across the Atlantic who fished the chalk streams for brown trout, was imitating the natural insect. His first flies were mainly imitations of the many species of the great mayfly family. Then he observed different land-born insects fall on the water, and saw that these, too, became grist for the mill of the fish. Aside from the fact that both were insects, hence trout food, there was little similarity between the two types of insects. One was high-riding and translucent, the other flush-floating and opaque. Gordon then created his own imitations of the terrestrial insects, and described the new style of fly as being "tied neither to sink nor to float."

The aquatic hatches were so spectacular that for the next quarter century little attention was paid to anything else. Deceiver dry-fly fishing did, however, spill over into attractor fishing with the designing of the spider, the bivisible, the fanwing, and the parachute fly, American innovations for fishing the water as opposed to fishing the rise.

But all was not well on the trout streams. The once abundant aquatic hatches were diminishing in intensity and duration. As the importance of the aquatic hatches to trout and fisherman alike decreased, the importance of land insects increased. This situation was not limited to American rivers, for a similar report came from southern Britain. The English blamed the loss of aquatic insects on the tar from hardtop roads, the Americans on deforestation and siltation.

In the thirties, two of the greatest successors of Gordon entered into the fly-supplying business, a fortunate occurrence for us fly-fishing neophytes. Edward R. Hewitt listed in his circular a floating winged black ant and Ray Bergman advertised in his catalog a green cork worm. The Hewitt claim was that because of the acidic taste, trout prefer ants over any other food and will always turn to them when available. Bergman explained that the green worm was abundant in the East in May and June, and when present, the imitation was indispensable. And with those two imitations the development of the terrestrial fly came to a halt for the next two decades, and hatch matching remained the approved system.

However, in the last thirty-five years the pioneering work of Vince Marinaro and Bob McCafferty and their many close associates has provided the angling fraternity with many cogent observations that confirm the importance of the terrestrial insect as trout food.

In many streams nature provides a continuous but usually sparse string of land-born insects in all lines of drift. These insects, ranging in size from small to large, do not ride high and dry on their toes, as is the case with the aquatic insects. They bog down in the surface, trapped by tension in the surface film from which the only escape is via protruding grass, weeds, foliage, or brush. Only the grasshopper and cricket can make progress in the tenacious film, and it is slow and laborious at that. The bodies of all these land-born insects are opaque.

Rarely do they descend upon the water in such quantity that their numbers constitute what fishermen regard as a hatch, but they drop with sufficient regularity to collectively constitute a source of food for the trout—food of the most sought-after variety. Many pass the angler unnoticed. When trout appear to be "rising to nothing," it is frequently the obscure terrestrial insect that has brought about the activity.

Add to these land-born insects the nymph drifting in the surface film as the back is splitting and the winged insect in the process of emerging. Until the dun actually utilizes its wings, it rides on the nymphal shuck as though it were a raft, and it is then partly wet and partly dry—just as is the case with the terrestrials. The colder the weather, the longer the ride. An effective imitation of the splitting nymph in appropriate size is the Hare's Ear spun with fragments of yellow or gray wool, tied on the hook shank and ribbed with gold tinsel—no wings or hackle; a tail is optional.

We know what the terrestrial insects look like, and we know when they appear on the stream, yet the question remains, how can they be imitated?

The answer to this question lies, in part, in the future. However, in recent years there has been substantial development. We, as anglers, are still in the evolutionary period with terrestrial-insect fishing. Yet, as just mentioned, in the last quarter of a century many important advances within this area were made. Possibly never in a general way will the terrestrial fly replace the high-riding aquatic imitation as a trout taker, but it will enjoy its big innings when it reigns supreme; there will be numerous occasions when it outfishes the standard dry fly by a very wide margin.

The late Bob McCafferty tied flies on a commercial basis, and a terrestrial pattern he popularized that was in great demand was a sinker known as the Black Ant. The fly was drifted or drawn submerged.

It was inevitable that the time would come when the Black Ant would be tied with high-quality hackle to represent the insect for which it was named. From observation Bob arrived at the conclusion that the terrestrials and the hatched adult of the stream-born insect float unless they are temporarily sucked beneath the surface or have disintegrated into sodden pieces, the thinking of the patron saints Izaak Walton and Charles Cotton to the contrary.

It was also inevitable that a fly would be tied in a midge size with cinnamon body and ginger hackle to imitate the little red ant in the same manner as the larger black pattern simulates the carpenter ant, each in appropriate size.

These flies really came into their own when some hackle was trimmed away in the shape of a V from the belly part of the fly, thus insuring that they ride low—*in* the surface. In due time the tail wagged the dog; the floating partner of the submerged original became "the ant."

There are occasions during the course of a trout season when ants develop wings and this occurs during their mating season.

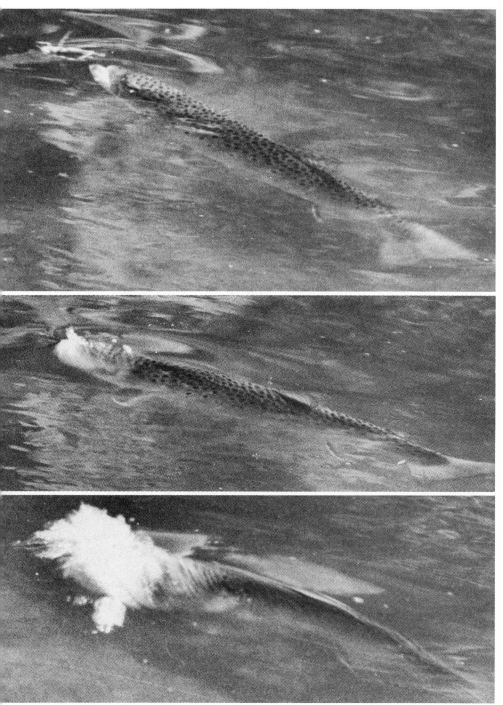

An unusual sequence showing a trout rising to and taking a grasshopper that
has fallen into the stream.

They are poor fliers with no apparent destination; consequently a substantial number find their way to the water, where they drift hopelessly mired in the surface film. There is evidence that flying ants are a special food favorite of the trout. If the water is clear, they most certainly will be consumed, and trout seem specifically to be on the outlook for them. On occasion I have seen trout pass up larger, high-riding aquatic insects in favor of the flush-drifting dead or doomed ants when both were readily available. Flying ants are present in greatest quantity during the month of August.

Vince Marinaro created two patterns by utilizing a novel tying trick—there is no tying silk involved! Nylon, about size 3X, is dyed either black or cinnamon. The back half of the body is built up by wrapping the nylon around the shank of the hook. The hackle is then tied into the middle of the thorax or upper body of the fly with the nylon. After the hackle is wound and anchored, the front half of the thorax is built up with the body material (nylon), then tied off at the eye, just as one ties off with tying thread. He also uses the guard hairs of porcupine as body material.

The usual practice is to tie the Black Ant on a #16 long-shank hook or #14 regular and the Cinnamon Ant on a #20 or #22 hook—both with the V trimmed out of the bottom. There is no tail, ribbing, or wings, the hackle forming impressionistic translucent wings.

A tremendously important minute land-born insect marks its appearance in quantity with the first hot days, particularly in the meadow reaches of trout streams. It is the little leafhopper—the jassid. Some are mottled brown, some pale green, and still others a dirty gray or brown. These are the little opaque insects that one disturbs with every step while walking through the grass or weeds. They look and act in a general way like baby grasshoppers. Once stranded in the water, they bog down in the surface, thus becoming difficult to see. Trout have a great fondness for these insects, taking many that are delivered to them by different tangents of the current. Always the rise form is of the very dainty variety.

Every here and there is located an incessant feeder—a trout that periodically makes a rise form on the surface much like that of a feeding fingerling. However, it may be a trout that could easily swallow a fingerling. This fish may not pass up any of the other terrestrials, but in all probability it is the jassid that is responsible for the bulk of his activity. Trout feeding on leafhoppers are among the choosiest, for they are very difficult to deceive with the standard dry fly. Almost every flat section of stream has some such feeders, and frequently in some quarters they enjoy the reputation of being impossible to catch. Such a thing, of course, is not the case with any fish on the feed. Any problem fishing is a wonderful challenge, and the jassid eater is one of the most interesting.

Vince Marinaro, who loves problem fishing, and I set forth with the express intent to find a solution to this situation. Straining the surface water with a special cloth disclosed that there was little present other than jassids. Carefully observing the lines of drift of feeding fish where the water was silvery (and consequently even minute particles were visible), we saw the jassids disappearing in tiny dimples. Obviously it was a matter of developing a suitable imitation, for it already had been discovered that diminution with standard dry flies was not the answer.

In a stretch of stream several hundred yards in length there were about twenty-five trout of varying size that spent every afternoon right in the same places, taking each leafhopper that traversed their narrow lines of drift. For one week Vince put up in the fishing hut in my LeTort meadow. When he was not fishing, he was either conducting a series of water tests or tying more flies, attempting to imitate this natural.

It was my custom to join him in the late afternoon to check on operations, replenish his diminishing larder, and to fish. About the fifth evening he was bubbling over with enthusiasm.

"I have a fly," advised the maestro. "Show me a jassid eater and I think I can hook him."

I immediately pointed out an incessant surface feeder with which I had a nodding acquaintance—as far as I was concerned an untouchable fish. He was taken by the new fly on the first perfect float. Then, Vince handed me three of the beautiful little imitations.

The previous evening I had played unsuccessfully with six regular feeders in an upper meadow, and the best I had been able to do was raise one once in a while, none actually touching the fly. Here was the perfect testing ground for the newly created Jassid.

Compared with results of the past, an extraordinary twist of

*The Floating Ant*. Over the decades older fishermen have watched the aquatic hatches deteriorate in intensity. There is a question as to why this is transpiring, but there is little question that it is so. The result is that the feeding of the trout on terrestrial insects increases in practice and in importance. The fly pictured above is a black ant, an extremely useful pattern when trout sip in a dainty manner in low, clear water and also when the carpenter ant develops wings in September and many get on the water. *Photo by James Fosse.*

*Jassid*. Leafhoppers abound in the grass and weeds beside trout water; and many, in their helter-skelter life, end up trapped in the surface film. Here they are opaque and flush floating. The jassid-style tie was developed by Vince Marinaro in the early 1940s and since has become world famous as an effective pattern for the daytime dainty feeders during the heat of summer. The first jassid had an orange body, ginger hackle clipped short top and bottom, and a jungle-cock top, flat on the back. Variations and other color combinations have been tied. *Photo by James Fosse.*

*Firefly.* Fireflies abound for weeks on end in the meadows, some dropping in the water, where they are trapped in the surface film and thus become trout food. The imitation should present an accurate silhouette. Various feathers can be used as the flat top, and the hackle color does not seem to be important. A long-shank hook makes for good body length. The wing of the above fly is a feather from a golden pheasant crest coated with lacquer and dried in trim form. This is a great last fly of the day. *Photo by James Fosse.*

*The Cricket.* The all-black flush floater, when ½″ to ¾″ in length, is one of the most effective floating flies that can be fabricated. Three materials are put on the hook: fur body, a feather wing on each side, and a hair wing with clipped head. This is a creation of Eddie Shenk, great angler from Carlisle, Pennsylvania. For some fishermen it has become their most useful floating fly. *Photo by James Fosse.*

events occurred. Each fish was promptly hooked. It took no more than half an hour to deceive trout that I previously could not touch and that were held in high regard as being ultraselective. Obviously, here was the answer to the most exacting trout fishing we had encountered.

Vince ties his Jassid on #18, 20, and 22 hooks, the middle size being his favorite. The hook shank is covered with colored tying silk, over which the narrowest of hackle is palmer tied. The hackle on the top is either trimmed out or parted so that a jungle-cock eye (or two of them) can be tied flat on the back. This is the one type of feather that is opaque. My preference is to place two mated eyes, concave sides together, on the top so that they appear as though they are one. The little roof forms a perfect silhouette of just the right shape. To complete the fly, a little V of hackle is snipped away from the belly part.

The original Jassid had orange tying silk and ginger hackle, but other combinations have since fished on a par with it: black silk and black hackle, pale green silk and honey hackle, and gray silk and badger or grizzly hackle. The formation of the fly and the way it floats on the surface appear to be considerably more important than the colors involved. As far as I am concerned, the Jassid is indispensable for meadow streams and the larger flats of mountain streams, and its usefulness commences each year with the first hot days and continues throughout the remainder of the summer.

There is a woodland infestation known as the oak worm or leafroller that hangs suspended from the fine thread it spins. It is extant throughout New England and the Middle Atlantic states and as far west as Minnesota and Missouri. Strangely, at least half a dozen species fit the description. Now and then a yellow one shows up. The adult moth lays the eggs on the hardwoods, the oaks being first choice, and that is where the larva feeds. In many forest areas it occurs in great quantity, with the result that a considerable number reach the water. Once detached from their silken strands, the oak worms fall to float in the surface layer.

The late Ray Bergman was the first to imitate this juicy morsel. His original pattern was cork, bound to the shank of the hook with tying silk, which gave a segmented effect. The whole thing, point and bend of hook excepted, was painted pale green.

George Harvey, the old fly-tying and casting instructor of

Pennsylvania State University and a well-known angler in his state, ties his oak worm with pale-green-dyed deer hair, which is then clipped. He and his fishing partner, Charlie Stoddart, attach great significance to this imitation.

The oak worm imitation is frequently difficult to cast. For extreme accuracy and for rod-tip casting to create a tight bow in the line and leader, it is often best not to false cast. By utilizing a snappy pickup from the water and a snap of the rod tip to release the fly, it is possible to negotiate a cast far under overhanging foliage and brush. The deer hair worm can be handled more easily than the cork imitation. As it cannot sink, false casting is not necessary to dry it. I have watched George Harvey and the late George Phillips attain perfect floats by slap casting the worm in lines of drift that appeared to be utterly impossible to fish. I am sure they have fished spots in hard-fished waters that are never touched by the dry flies of any other fisherman. Furthermore, in all probability they would not have been able to snake out some of the trout they caught on their green (oak) worms with a standard dry fly. This worm is usually tied on a #16 long-shank hook.

As Vince Marinaro was in the process of working out a solution to the problem of deceiving incessantly feeding trout, he experimented with ties of the common housefly, for he knew trout consumed them when available. This, however, is a terrestrial insect that is not as opaque as the others. The tie is: body, gray dubbing; wings, the tips of starling feathers tied split and flat; and the hackle, narrow badger or grizzly; on a #20 hook. A V of hackle is trimmed away from the underside.

The grasshopper is another terrestrial that is a favorite of all trout—including very large ones. A good imitation stands as fine a chance of taking large fish as its counterpart, the Green Drake, does in the comparatively short mayfly season.

Imitations of the grasshopper in the hands of many fishermen illustrate a wide variety of ideas, in fact, anything from a Muddler Minnow greased to float to the elaborate hand-painted quill hopper. My early favorite was a fore-and-aft style of tie on a long-shank hook. The hackle was ginger, and the body was yellow wool; the tail, a loop of red wool; and the wings, turkey. This imitation accounted for a reasonable number of fish, but there were many fish that would rise to it, inspect it, and then refuse it.

One summer day, Ernie Schweibert and I were on the LeTort, and our hoppers were not doing as well as we thought they should. He decided to tie up something that night for the next day that would involve a different principle. Instead of making hackle float a realistic-looking body, he would try a hairwing for the support. It was in the early days of nylon yarn, and he chose this rather than cotton or wool because it does not soak up as much water.

The proof of the pudding was in the eating. Next day the fly fished well and produced. To simulate the big legs he added turkey feathers. Appropriately enough this came to be known as the LeTort Hopper, and it is so listed in most fishing catalogs.

Art Neumann, the first executive director of Trout Unlimited, provided me with his version of the Hopper. This one is a tied dry-fly style on a long-shank hook. Hackle and tail support the long chenille body. A good dry-fly dressing is required, and this one fishes well.

A small black Hopper becomes a Cricket. Eddie Shenk, a fine commercial flytier and deputy warden for the LeTort, put this into practice, and it has become a great local favorite. To its credit is probably what at one time was the largest brown trout taken on a floating fly in Pennsylvania. This was a 9-pounder caught by Ed Koch of Boiling Springs from the LeTort in 1965. A decade later Bob Harpster caught a 13-pound brown trout in Spruce Creek on a Cricket.

There are places in the East where the Japanese beetle is found in such profusion that it can be picked by the handful from certain foliage. Like all the rest of the land-born insects, some find their way to the surface of the water. Once consumed by a fish, the digestive juices in the trout's stomach remove the interior of the beetle, and the collapsed hard shell is eliminated normally. A strange thing, though, is that only a small percentage of trout will touch them. However, those that do feed upon the beetle develop a genuine interest, devouring them in great quantities.

There have been a number of Japanese beetle imitations, including a coffee bean cemented to an old fly, clipped deer hair, cork, and palmer-tied flies. But the anglers who utilize the Jassid-type in a large size smile sympathetically at anyone laboring with other ties. Actually the insect appears in two sizes, the female being larger than the male, and the trout take both. I am of the opinion

*Hopper.* There are various imitations of the grasshopper, ranging from all quill to greased Muddler Minnow. A fine pattern is Art Neuman's, which encompasses the combination of hair wing and hackle to make it float. This fly, with its chenille body, must be treated with a good fly float.

The hopper is a required imitation for summer fishing in a meadow. It can be fished natural drift or jerked, for the hopper has a proclivity to drift then kick, drift then kick. *Photo by James Fosse.*

*Japanese Beetle.* In order to fool trout that will eat Japanese beetles, the imitation must be good. It should be flush floating, opaque, and form an accurate silhouette. Peacock herl is a good body material; hackle, black and ginger intermingled; wing, breast feathers from peacock or black feathers from neck ring of a pheasant cock bird. The wing should be two feathers sealed together with lacquer and trimmed for silhouette. *Photo by James Fosse.*

*John Crowe Beetle.* This easy-to-tie but frail little beetle was first made, then popularized, by educator and writer John Crowe. It is an all-hair fly and can be tied with natural bucktail or black. This great summer fly seems to work equally well on freestone and limestone streams. *Photo by James Fosse.*

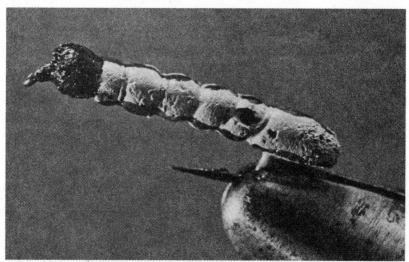

*The Oak Worm.* Some wooded areas produce a tremendous number of oak worms for some weeks beginning in mid-May. Where there is a trout stream, there will be great green-worm feeding and fishing. There are some streams where trout during the green-worm period seem to eat nothing else. The imitation can be cast upstream and fished natural drift or cast downstream and fished as suspended on the web. *Photo by James Fosse.*

that it is better to imitate the smaller one, thus reducing to a minimum any discrepancies between the artificial and the natural. I like a regular #16 hook, black tying silk, with either black or ginger hackle or the two intermingled, and enough of the jungle-cock eyes tied flat on the back to form the silhouette of the living creature. This has been very pleasant to fish and is a highly satisfactory imitation in every respect. If you can obtain the iridescent peacock breast feathers, two cemented together make a wonderful roof for this fly.

Aquatic hatches hit their peak prior to mid-June on most waters, and by and large they are notoriously poor late in the season. However, the fact remains that there is surface activity brought about by terrestrial insects, and the trout that have survived the spring campaign are superior fish in every respect. They have just completed their heaviest feeding period of the year when digestion is fastest and the food supply the greatest, in water from 60 to 65°. They are in prime condition and are as wary as trout can become. In addition, the waters are low and clear.

It is then that the supply of terrestrials is at its maximum for the year. To fish the water well, one must turn to a lighter leader to which is attached an imitation of an ant, a jassid, a 'hopper, or a certain creation that is applicable to the water at hand. By necessity the angler will be fishing in the surface—not on it or under it—with flies, as the great angler Theodore Gordon put it, "tied neither to sink, nor to float."

# 11

# *Trout Bugging*

When we examine the angling past we must conclude that the bug-type trout lure was produced with little or no study of the trout's diet; it was more an adventure at the fly-tying table. This type of lure, whether floating or submerged, captured trout as well as the fascination of fishermen, possibly because for both it was different. Those who employed them were the mavericks that broke away and would not run with the herd. Here was pioneering and that was good, a sort of American reaction to established English tradition. It is an interesting segment of trouting history.

Probably bugs for trout started with a nature-loving New York Stater by the name of Tuttle. In the thirties the old man tied hair bass bugs on a commercial basis; therefore it was a natural step for him to fabricate a miniature form for trout. His ingredient was natural deer hair, some of which came from a pet.

The Devil Bug, with some hair picked out and trimmed, looked like a floating batwing beetle. This was produced and sold in two sizes for bass and trout.

A second lure that proved to be more effective on trout would submerge. This one had a wad of compact hair parallel to the hook shank, and it was bound tightly in two places with wire instead of the then standard waxed tying silk. What looked like a mane came from the head over the back. The other end had the appearance of the tail of a minnow. This clumsy fly rode on its side. But when the mane was snipped off to look like the crest of a cedar waxwing, what was left was as good a bucktail as money could buy. Tuttle even painted little yellow eyes on it and usually used dark hair on the top half and light buck on the belly part.

My introduction to the Weber Akle family, a wet bug, was something like taking a pledge in the inner sanctum. The origin of the Water Akle is hidden in the dust of time, but its creator, the great old Weber Company of Stevens Point, Wisconsin, still flourishes. When animated with rod-tip action, the Water Akle was an extraordinary wet fly, and it would "skin a stream of browns," or so I was told. Out of respect for my benefactor, Don Martin, I treated it as a secret weapon until the cat was out of the bag, just as he had done.

The Water Akle came in a variety of patterns. The all-gray one happened to look like a watercress bug (sowbug). The fly had no tail. However, a piece of duck wing feather was put on first. Then came a fat wool body. The "tail" piece was then brought over the back and anchored near the eye. Ahead of this was added some soft hackle to complete the fly. The two local secret weapons were the all-gray and one tied with some peacock herl over a yellow wool background, plus ginger hackle.

A commercial flytier by the name of Stanley Cooper of Wilkes-Barre, Pennsylvania, had a different method for making a bug out of a standard wet fly. He took a good pinch of hair and made it stick out of the tying silk at the head of the fly like the horn of a unicorn. This was then divided into two slanting wings protruding backward from the tying silk like the wings on a Miramichi Butterfly. This attractor was painted by Dr. Edgar Burke and is pictured on one of the fly plates in Ray Bergman's book, *Trout*, published in 1938. Stan has demonstrated his craftsmanship for over fifty years and is still going strong. When he sold his millionth fly to Abercrombie and Fitch of New York City, they put it in plastic and hung it on the wall—and that was back in 1962.

Cliff Zug, the creator of the Zug Bug, resided in Reading, Pennsylvania, until his passing. He fished the wonderful little rivers of the Poconos. Cliff's creation was a juicy-looking sinker featuring a fat peacock herl body anchored with gold tinsel, plus throat hackle and tail and sometimes with a wing case.

One of the reasons I live beside the LeTort is so that I can fish regularly with a minimum of effort. Another is to compare notes with the interesting people who visit its banks. Thus, between fishing and listening, I feel well-posted on comings and goings and streamside doings. My ego was pierced with a barbed point when I saw advertised in a catalog that enjoys national distribution a floating fly bearing the name of this stream—a fly about which I knew nothing! This prompted me to order some LeTort Beetles, as advertised, from Paul H. Young. (It was the same year that marked the untimely passing of this dedicated and talented fly fisherman and rod builder.)

Back came a box of little black hair bugs, not the clipped-deer-hair-body type, but rather the old Weber Akle style of tie, where the material is tied in at the bend, then brought to the front in symmetrical arrangement and there tied off and cut to fancy. Because of the tubular hair, this fly floats flush and opaque, whereas the Weber Akle series was made of feather and wool on heavy hooks to sink and to be fished wet.

One glance at the contents of the box and a bell rang. Here was the same thing I had seen Bob Runk of Pittsburgh use to fool, on the first cast, a sophisticated surface feeder that for several weeks had been too much for me. Bob had no name for the fly, but he told me it was a favorite of Chauncy and Marian Livly, a distinguished husband-and-wife fishing team.

In due course the Livlys put in an appearance in the meadow, and I learned from them that it was the conception of their friend John Crowe, who had written about it in his work, *The Book of Trout Lore*. The fly worked well on the LeTort, so in talking to Paul Young about the bug, Chauncy referred to it as "the beetle good on the LeTort," hence the catalog nomenclature.

The beetle in black, like the lady in red, appeared attractive and soon took its place in my chest kit beside the old established jassids and ants to be shown to the dainty daytime feeders. I am not so sure but that in the flats of freestone mountain streams it is the most valuable of all floating flies when one does not have a hatch to match or the presence of green worms to imitate. A strike against it is the fact that it is a very fragile fly.

The date was Friday, May 13, 1966. There is nothing significant about the date except that after completing a job near Allentown's Little Lehigh River I could drop in on my way home to put in three hours of fishing. Dr. Jim Marcks, my successor as state president of Trout Unlimited, had strongly recommended I try the new catch-and-release trout area that he and the Allentown fishermen had brought into being.

There is one type of trout fishing that to my way of thinking is the finest. It is when trout are rising in smooth clear water and can be watched. One sees every movement as the fly is drifted to the fish. Acceptance is always thrilling, and rejection can be, too. Experience has demonstrated that when a trout moves to a fly then drifts back with it, keeping it under close inspection, the fly and the leader are not far from being right. You have almost fooled him. Here may be a potentially willing taker that deserves concentrated effort. Some, of course, are more difficult to fool than others. On this day in front of me in the Little Lehigh I had the cherished setup.

Those incessant and dainty surface feeders were first shown my favorite Jassid on a #20 hook (body, peacock herl; hackle, black and ginger intermingled; wing, two dark feathers from the neck of a ringneck cock, sealed together, clipped, and tied as a flattop), but although the fish would swim under it and look it over, the Black Jassid drifted untouched. A second special favorite, a little Cinnamon Ant (body, orange seal fur; hackle, blue-gray tied thorax style) suffered the same fate. Then on the leader tippet went a #18 John Crowe, black, deer-hair Beetle. In quick succession three fish that had looked over the Jassid and the Ant took the Beetle. It seemed so easy now. For the sake of comparison I removed it and in its place tried a Jassid with jungle-cock wings, but again only interest, no takers. Following this the Beetle took several more fish. Then I switched to another old standby attractor of mine, a small Black Spider with a gold tinsel body. The same thing happened—nothing. This sort of thing continued for about three hours; the Black Beetle was the only fly the trout would touch. It was convincing evidence that the fish there knew what they wanted. By the process of trial and error I had learned that answer.

Before and after that date there were in spots great concentrations of March flies, both near and away from the water. A March fly looks something like a small termite, but as far as I know, it does no damage. The body is black and symmetrical, not shaped like an ant; the legs are rust colored. The flies plaster the windshield of a traveling car. Many drop on the water. The report came through that the trout of the Pocono Mountain streams were "jam-packed" with them. The trout of the Little Lehigh, the stream of Allentown's famous fly fisherman Big Jim Leisenring, took the Beetle because it simulates the March fly. The same was true over 100 miles away on the LeTort, at Falling Springs above Chambersburg, and on the Yellow Breeches at Boiling Springs and Brantsville. In effect the early part of the '66 season was John Crowe Beetle time, a veritable one-fly period. Even after the sulphur hatch broke, the trout seemed to be conscious of and on the lookout for the March fly, and they were responsive to at least one imitation. A second pattern was quickly improvised for this "new" terrestrial insect by Johnny Alevers and Ernie Schweibert at Henryville (body, black fur; hackle, ginger; wing, white duck tied flat).

It would be false to give the impression that the LeTort Beetle is and has been an early-season-only offering. August is a big month for it, with such terrestrials as winged ants and Japanese beetles in abundance to set the stage for all the flush-floating opaque bugs. Certainly this black hair Beetle is a general pattern.

March flies appearing in quantity in May could become a regular thing. The insect world may be changing. This may seem contradictory, but it appears to me that man with his widespread use of pesticides is decreasing the number of creatures that control the culprit sought by the spraying. It seems incredible that in every place where widespread spraying is done prey and predator in the food chain decrease in the same proportion. Should the intended job not be done, there are bound to be species of insects that proliferate at the same time that others deteriorate in health and numbers.

Songbirds have decreased in number. Who knows much about the supply of other insect eaters such as bats, wasps, hornets, spiders, and the praying mantis? Nature out of balance could result in a different, if not strange, insect world. The next decade may prove or disprove man's ability to control and dominate insect life, which in turn will affect many different animal and avian species in the food chain that are dependent upon insect life. Therefore it would not be strange if there were a tremendous increase of certain insects and a substantial decrease in the numbers of others. And it will be noticed by those who are probably the most observant of the insect watchers—trout fishermen in general and the deceiver trout flytiers in particular.

The most elementary ties at the vise are Corkers, which float, and Honey Bugs, which sink. Whether or not these are legitimate flies was once more than academic. In regard to their use in the regulated trout waters, the Pennsylvania Fish Commission said no to the Corker because it is fibrous, but yes to the Honey Bug because the material before treatment may have come from a sheep. Apparently whether the ingredient was animal or vegetable was the crux of the matter. The commission has since reversed its stand on use of the Corker.

If someone who might be a potential fly fisherman has a hankering to catch a fish on something he has fabricated, place a hook on a vise and turn him on to a Corker or Honey Bug. Strange as it may seem to the classic fly fisherman, both are easily manageable, pick up easily from the water, and each in turn looks good to the fish.

Paul Burger, a Pennsylvanian, is the Honey Bug man. He treats and dies wool to be tied either alone or with some trimmings on a hook. He makes his appearance at the shows where he sells food for hatchery trout and body material for Honey Bugs. This treated wool, wormlike on a hook, has the reputation of being a devastating thing on newly stocked trout that are still concentrated and, by necessity, experimenting in their feeding. Maybe a scent is incorporated; I don't know.

Corkers are nothing more than cut rounded lengths of cork tied to a light wire hook, then hand painted. One day I was fishing with Ron Kommer. He gave me a partial handful of sundry wormy-looking objects attached to hooks, with the explanation that his dad makes these and swears by them for trout. That was my introduction to them, and I must say I was not impressed.

However, one day I showed a regular feeder an Ant, then a Jassid to no avail. As I gazed into the open fly box, a little green object caught my eye and seemed to beckon. Every fly fisherman can understand that! Well, the trout took the Corker on the first drift over it. Thereafter I experimented with the lot of them. The one that the trout seemed to like best was the small green one, but

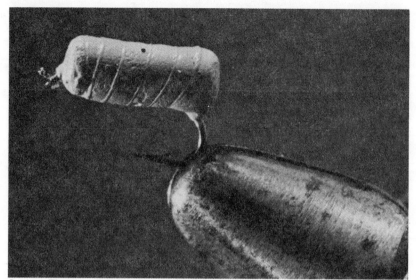

*Corker.* The tiny corker, tied and promoted by Bill McIntyre, is amazingly effective. Here is a floating fly that does not have to be false cast. It seems to be at its very best in light-green color. Never discount the effectiveness of this little bug. *Photo by James Fosse.*

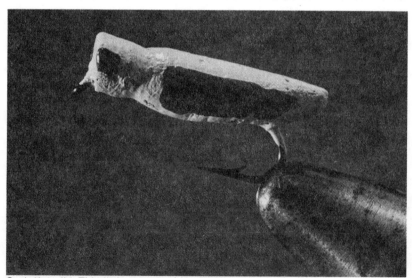

*Cork Katydid.* This little cork creation was fabricated and colored by Bill McIntyre. It looks good to bass and large bluegills as well as to trout. The beginning flytier would do well to work some with painted cork, and the beginning flycaster would do well to have a look into bass and bluegill fishing. *Photo by James Fosse.*

they at least took a good look at larger ones and striped ones. No question about it, Corkers were, at the very least, achieving partial success.

More recently I met Bill McIntyre of Pittsburgh at a Pennsylvania State Trout Unlimited meeting and he gave me his "Tote-a-Lure" pinup of Corkers he has on the market imitating worms, hoppers, beetles, and bugs.

The trout bug, in all its varieties, wet or dry, attractor or deceiver, simple or complex, has moved in to take its place in showcases and fly boxes. It is one more American fishing innovation to be attached to the business end of monofilament, which is just as American.

# 12
# The Last Fly

Advances in the assembly, style, form, makeup, and size of the fly have continued without abatement in America since World War I. Consider the following:

Patterns designed to match the hatch stemmed from Roy Steenrod, Ray Bergman, Rube Cross, Preston Jennings, Charlie Wetzel, Art Flick, and a host of others. There's the easy-to-see and easy-to-float Ed Hewitt Bivisible. Messenger, a West Virginian, and Tuttle, a New Yorker, perfected clipped-deer-hair bass bugs and trout flies. Jack Knight and George Harvey created the Fish Finder, a dry fly that often makes a trout show but is usually refused. However, it sets the stage for a follow-up small, dull taker. Hewitt came up with his exciter, the Neversink Skater fly, and Charlie DeFeo developed a clipped-hair version of the same. Bill Blades introduced the tube flies and tied realistic dry flies with detached bodies. There are streamer flies by Herb Welsh, Edson (his first name is lost to me), Ray Bergman, Sam Slaymaker, and others. Along came the nymphs of Clayt Peters, Ray Bergman, Ed Hewitt, Dave Whitlock, Ernie Schweibert, and Wayne Leonard. Vince Marinaro produced his little Jassids, Ants, and Beetle forms and the thorax tied on dry flies. It seems certain that Bill Pfeiffer was the first to attach great significance to the little drake, *tricorythodes*, and successfully imitate it. George Harvey initiated a special night wet fly. Ernie Schweibert developed his hackleless Hair-wing Hopper and Eddie Shenk, the Cricket. George Harvey and Dick Henry pioneered imitation oak worm fishing. Al Troth has a great little wet freshwater shrimp and a good sowbug. Doug Swisher and Carl Richards introduced their Polywing Hackless dry fly, an imitation spinner. Bill McIntyre has his hand-painted corkers. Dave Whitlock ties a superb freshwater sculpin. Somewhere along the line came the Spider, the thin-winged large variant, and the parachute fly with its hackle parallel to the surface. Then too, there is the fore-and-aft floater and the sinking Woolly Worm.

And so it goes. Has everything been covered? Maybe not. There was something I needed badly, but nothing seemed to fill the bill. No matter what available fly I tried as the final one of the day to pitch to a surface-feeding fish when there was no apparent hatch of aquatic insects, the result was usually disappointment and frustration. For the most part this happened on the LeTort, close to the house, but it transpired elsewhere, too. I watched and talked with different anglers and always the story was the same: "Those big night surface feeders are plenty tough."

My house is 120 feet from the stream. Close by is swampy meadowland. On slightly higher ground is grass and weeds. Beyond that are two 100-yard hedgerows, one of multiflora rose, the other of autumn olive. Close by are a woods and a patch of pines. This topography is typical of this valley and also of the edges along many other little rivers. The key to the problem might be the most readily available food or foods. So I removed the yellow bulb from the porch light, which my wife had placed there because it was advertised that this particular color would not attract "pests," and in its place went a standard bulb, which would look good to insect friends and associates.

Observation over a period of time showed that two distinct insect types gathered around the light. One was a tiny *Diptera* in great quantity. This is a member of the true fly family and too small to imitate. I ruled it out on the grounds that most of the evening risers were too big to be *Diptera* eaters. There were three different crane flies: the large, brown whirling one; the medium-sized orange; and the small yellow. It did not seem likely that these got on the water in sufficient quantity because they like to settle on mud. There were a few green gauze wings but not in sufficient quantity for the number of risers. There was a small hard-bodied, longish brown fly in good quantity. I had never seen this insect before, and it appeared to be a nocturnal terrestrial variety. Then there were some millers and now and then a moth. The aquatic insects, other than *Diptera*, were conspicuous by their absence, which ruled out night hatches not seen by the angler because of the failing light.

It did not seem possible that anything around the lights at the house could be the insect that spurred some good trout into surface feeding. By the process of elimination, that left the possibility that whatever the trout were taking on the surface was not attracted by the light. It appeared there could be but one answer—fireflies. This little valley is a veritable fairyland on summer evenings for many weeks on end. From the first of June into September, each lightning bug, in his or her own time, turns on and off that mysterious lantern about which we know so little. Apparently many, like the ants, the jassids, and the 'hoppers find their way to the tenacious surface film of a stream.

It was at this time that Dick Clark of Philadelphia and Alfred Miller of New York together paid the LeTort a visit. I told them about my recent conclusion, not yet knowing whether or not it was sound. Dick Clark had been the fishing partner of the late Jim Leisenring, the flytier and wet-fly authority from Allentown, Pennsylvania, and Big Jim had been Dick's mentor, particularly in the field of fly tying at which Dick long since had become adept. (Together they wrote *Wet Fly Fishing*, one of the early American books on wet-fly fishing and fly tying.)

Several days later there came in the mail a small parcel containing Dick's concept of an imitation firefly. Aside from the differences that there was a hook built into it and the fly's light would not go on and off, it was most realistic. I never attached it to a leader, for it seemed to be too elaborate to subject it to any kind of hazard, and I lose my share of flies. As things turned out, it may be that this was the last product from Dick Clark's vise.

Dick Clark idolized Jim Leisenring, and Jim's passing was a great shock to Dick. Some admirer of Big Jim painted, or had painted, a portrait in oil of Jim. It somehow came to hang above the bar at Charlie's Place in Analomink, located on the Paradise Branch above its confluence with the grand Broadhead. Charlie's Place was one of the chief spots in the country for the gathering of the fishing fraternity. It was from there that some of the finest stream stretches in the East were fished. At Charlie's, fly fishing for trout was the chief subject of conversation, evening after evening, week after week, for many a season. When a dam was constructed at the head of the stream with an overflow outlet only, ultimately the water temperature in the lower reaches increased. The trout moved out of the 75° water to find cooler water conditions. That was the body blow for Charlie's Place and Analomink. The famous rendezvous changed hands and became just another beer joint for the local imbibers. The new management removed Big Jim's portrait and substituted something more enticing, something like a lounging Cleopatra.

A Mr. Hoffer of Virginia knew that the health of his old friend Dick Clark was failing. He realized that it would be a meaningful gesture if he could obtain Leisenring's portrait and give it to Dick. So one day he handed his son Bud a roll of money with the directive, "Go to Analomink and bring back that picture."

Bud experienced some difficulty with the wife of the proprietor. She knew nothing about the portrait except that every now and then someone would inquire about it; therefore, she suspected it was worth big money to someone. Bud prevailed in the end. She went to the attic and brought down the painting.

The next job was to induce the ailing Dick to leave his room and join a group of anglers at a dinner spot. When the presentation was made by Mr. Hoffer, Dick wept, then wheezed his heartfelt appreciation. Often the catching of trout is not the greatest reward of angling.

Charlie Most of the federal Fish and Wildlife Service must have known of my proclivity for orange-bodied flies, for he once gave me a patch of seal fur dyed a burnt orange. There is the orange-bodied dry-fly-tied thorax with blue-gray hackle, which my fishing companion of old, Lew Kunkel, called his Robin; there are sulphurs with orange in them, either body or hackle; there is the orange Fish Hawk, one of the most effective of the myriad of wet flies; and there is the old optic bucktail with the juicy-looking orange body, named Poison by the late Fred Everett.

In my amateur way I tied narrow ginger hackle on a #16 long-shank hook, then added a dubbed-on rusty-orange seal-fur body. I trimmed the wrapped-around hackle from top and bottom, leaving it protruding on the sides only. The roof for this one was a beautiful V feather from the crest of a golden pheasant. The ¾-

inch-long feather was first coated with feather glazer, making it opaque, and then stretched into a slender form so the shape corresponded to the silhouette of a firefly. (I wanted to remain consistent with Vince Marinaro's theory that a trout cannot distinguish the lack of depth when a flat opaque top is attached.) The finished product looked good, although not in a realistic way—it was impressionistic.

I knew precisely where to launch this fly on its maiden voyage. There was a fish that made impressive rise forms in front of a brush pile. I had watched and unsuccessfully cast to this trout on different evenings.

The new fly was promptly accepted; its first fish was a handsome 17-incher. The following evening it accounted for another about the same size. I did not press my luck either time, as anytime I get a good one at dusk, I call it the end of a perfect day lest anything else prove an anticlimax.

There is a situation that fits hand in glove with the evening fly. When one takes advantage of it, the result is a bonus for the dry-fly fisherman in the form of a possible extra half hour of fishing.

In the evenings, at times it seems that casting is toward a surface that has the appearance of molten pewter, and sometimes it looks more like an even plane of tarnished silver. In either case the ring of the rise is visible, although your fly upon the pale water may not be.

The requirements for the additional-time setup are stringent. First, there should be holding water, the kind that harbors some good fish that come out from their hiding places to surface feed each evening as the light fades. The water must be smooth and the skyline low with no trees, shrubs, or high bank in the immediate background. The angler must be facing due east or due west as he peers across the flat water. When there is the ring of a rise in the estimated vicinity of your fly, a lift of the rod tip divulges the situation. Either the lift is met with the resistance of throbbing life or there is a feeling of emptiness.

Two such great places existed where I frequently filled out the quota of daily fishing time. They were reserved for this special situation, in essence a taste of angling dessert. The fishing was not the frantic type typical of the violent rise to a heavy fall of spinners. Rather it was the intense kind that involves at the very most a few fish.

The two sites were on different streams, and the streams were different in nature. One had its native population of brook trout, the other browns. At the one the angler faced the west, at the other the east. The one was a large open pool with a fast run and a big protruding rock at the head. The other had a beautiful deep backwater in front of a submerged ledge.

Sadly, fishing at both spots is no more; each has been ruined by man. The one lost its native population of brookies when a large hatchery was constructed not far upstream; now the flat is unbroken by surface-feeding activity. The other was eliminated when an arrogant highway department took out the east-to-west flowing stream bend, to make a north-to-south shortcut under a bridge. This was not because of need but because of policy.

Another excellent place for this kind of evening fishing is in the flat water tail of a big pool, which always holds some good fish. A favorite feeding location is that area near the lower extremity where the bottom starts to slope upward into the fanned-out shallows before spilling into the next riffle. In some such situations the angler can operate from a bank on the east or west; in other cases he must carefully work his way into the tail of the pool as he watches facing directly east or west.

There can be various versions of a good evening fly for fishing to the rise on a silver sheen, the proof being effectiveness. I like that first model off-color orange Firefly, partly for a sentimental reason and partly because nothing succeeds like success.

# 13

# The Minnow-type Fly

Nature in the rough is seldom mild. There is a plan to dispose of weaklings, cripples, and sicklings. As though fearful they may become breeders and as such water the stock, nature makes them vulnerable to attack so that they are likely to be struck down. This is the law of the survival of the fittest at work, and this is what brings about evolution. In the aquatic world the large prey upon the small when capture is not difficult; and the weaklings, the cripples, and the sicklings are most readily caught. Therein lies the reason for the long minnowlike fly, no matter whether it is tied to deceive or to attract or whether the wing is vibrating streamer, waving maribou, or breathing hair. Streamer-fly fishing is exciting, interesting, productive, and easy. It can captivate and fire the fishing imagination.

This is the most elementary fly fishing because it is downstream fly fishing. The pull of the current straightens out line and leader and makes the fly swim. The flow of water away from the rod eliminates a buildup of extra line that must be picked up, then extended for the next delivery. Later one can turn about, cast upstream, and follow the other methods that bring to light the errors. In all types of angling, however, mind and muscle are engaged in the business at hand. The finest starting point for the neophyte fly fisherman, in my judgment, is streamer fishing. In addition to trout, included in his quarry are bass, bluegills, the whole pike family, tarpon, shad, and the salmons.

Great as fly fishing is, there is a hazard. It is the possibility that at an early stage the beginner will become trapped in a bog of indecision and doubt to the point that he is confused and uncertain, with the result that he gives up. The key to continuation is education. There are different ways in which one learns. Some are fortunate enough to have a companion who is a fine teacher. Then there is the slow but thorough trial-and-error approach. And finally there is the reading of what others have to offer.

Once one realizes that it can be done and he is doing it, there follows a lifetime of pursuit. Once there develops the persistent and passionate attempt to improve technique and enhance knowledge, the rudimentary matters take care of themselves. Ultimately there develops supreme confidence and optimism. Each cast is expected to produce. Angling has become the combination of experience and experiment and the difficulty of catching fish has become a fascination.

Most of us who took up fly fishing in the decade following World War I were induced by the writers who contributed to the periodicals of that time to give the new "bucktail fly" a chance. I clipped such an article by an anonymous writer, probably an editor, pasted it in a loose-leaf notebook, and this became the modest beginning of an angling library. The term *streamer fly* had not yet been coined but *feathered minnow* had. This time it was not an English contribution but the concept of Americans, and contemporaries at that.

Development took place in Maine, the reasons being big brook trout, "Square tails" and salmon, "landlocks." Early flytiers and their respective ties that gained eminence were Herb Welch with his Jane Craig and Welch Rarebit; Joe Stickney who developed the Supervisor, Lady Doctor, and Warden's Worry; Carrie Stevens and her Grey Ghost; A. W. Ballou and the white maribou, his "Special"; Bill Edson and the Light and Dark Tiger. Other famous New England flies included Mickey Finn and Nine-Three. Most of them were streamer flies in the feather sense, however Mickey Finn had a wing of dyed hair.

It was in the thirties that we saw ads and looked at pictures of this American-born fly type. That was the era, too, when many anglers discovered it was fun and practical to tie their own and create their own. Hence there were flies and effigies of flies and pure creations of fancy to tickle the human fancy. Many patterns were ornate. Some looked good to the trout and some not so good.

In the Midwest William Kidder, world-traveling angler, designed patterns for eastern brown trout, sea-run brook trout, and black salmon to be tied by the Weber Lifelike Fly Company team. These were among the first, if not the first, to be pictured in a catalog.

The tendency of the steelhead and trout fishermen of the Pacific coastal streams was to shorten the wing in order to produce a fly that could be cast farther and with less difficulty—less air resistance on wide water.

The best-known minnow-type fly on the eastern slopes of the Great Divide is the Muddler Minnow. Dan Bailey, retired schoolteacher and proprietor of the famous tackle shop near Livingston, Montana, is largely responsible for its claim to fame. Oddly enough this hair-wing wet fly, when greased, becomes a fairly good imitation of a floating grasshopper. It was this fly that gave the late George Phillips, founder of the Phillips Tackle Company, the idea of how to tie hackleless floating hoppers. On the other side of the Divide, steelhead flies, to a large degree, are hair-wing versions of standard trout and salmon wet flies. The Far West has been hard hit by the bucktail binge, but most of the flies are tied with hair other than that from a deer.

Colonel Joe Bates has preserved for posterity much history and many fly specifications in his definitive work on the subject entitled, *Streamer Fly Tying and Fishing.*

In recent years Sam Slaymaker popularized the tiny long-wing fly called Streamerette, so named by the dean of Pennsylvania trout fishermen, John Wise. There are three generations of fly fishermen in this family bearing that name and no doubt Jack Wise number four plays in his crib with fly-tying material.

Two miles from my old home there flows an amazing small limestone stream, amazing because it was such a rich natural reproducing stream. This was the scene of my bucktail campaign, the laboratory. Enjoying the vigor of youth, I kept after the brown trout there with unremitting energy on the premise that he who catches the most devotes the most time to it, and success crowns efforts. It was a real binge involving all the angles—the big and the small, the bright and the dull, the slow and the fast, the far and the close, the early and the late—everything in my modern adventure in old-fashioned wet-fly-fishing enjoyment.

Once and for all, my angling system was blown up as thoroughly as guns blew up the feudal system. It was demonstrated here so conclusively that artificials were more effective and more fun for me. I will forever be thankful for the exciting sinking fly with the long wing that, in the main, was responsible for the turn from worms and minnows to hair and feathers and from tossing to casting.

Day after day Cedar Run had an evening hatch of sulphur duns and at the same time a great fall of Sulphur spinners, which resulted in a heavy rise of trout including some real fish. This lively period was limited to the short duration of dusk; prior to that the stream appeared to be dead. As things turned out, though, it wasn't dead for a good streamer fly or bucktail drawn just so through the right places. It became my custom to arrive at the stream about seven in the evening, fish my way downstream with the new wet fly, then shortly before dusk substitute a finer leader, attach to it a dry Pale Evening Dun, dry and grease the line and await the occurrence of the dependable rise of trout to the hatch. Developments demonstrated that this was a potent combination or routine, the explosive wet method followed by matching the hatch with a good floater. There were times when one was more rewarding than the other, the determining factor for thrill usually being size of catch.

Both the streamer-fly apprenticeship and that of the dry fly were unusual in that each, in that wonderful little laboratory, was trial and error, there being no supervision by a craftsman. The experimentation continued weeks on end and in one season after another.

There follow a few words about some of the things that I now believe contribute to successful streamer-fly fishing:

The swing of the swimming fly just as it slows down to turn upstream and into the current is the major taking point in the retrieve. If the fly is cast to a spot so that it will swing into and slow up at what salmon fishermen refer to as a "lie," so much the better. The minor taking point in the retrieve is near the point of splashdown as the gradually accelerating swimming fly moves away from the target area. Hence a knowledge of water and fish is essential.

Although you are not able to follow the course of the fly as it passes through the rougher water, the trout are able to see and take it. There are times when a fish raises to it but nothing is felt by the angler. Missed or refused, I believe it is always the latter. But a raised fish is a fish to fish to and a fish to fish for, right away and maybe later too.

Striking with a short line is quicker and surer than it is with a long one. The answering strike with a high rod often results in just a nip because the point of the hook does not penetrate over the barb. It is easier to connect when a low rod tip follows the course of the fly. The fact remains, the feel of the moment of contact is electrifying, a kind of comforting jolt.

Trial and error divulge some secrets of fly action too. The streamer, tied with feathers, fishes best in relatively big jerks—in what might be described as rhythmic darts. The bucktail, hair-wing type has been most effective when worked in small jerks. The third type, the willowy maribou, seems to look best to the trout on the slow steady draw. The regular hand-twist retrieve is a part of the competent manipulation for all three.

Unseen, unheard, and unheralded by the quarry, that should be the position of the angler and his equipment. The fly should be out there for the fish with nothing related to it. You do not want to fish water where the fish have already been put down by someone else, either.

A baseball player has either good or bad hands. So has a man playing a hooked fish. Strains should be evenly applied so that there are no jerks. Jolting snaps leaders, whereas even application of give-and-take protects them. A slowness of reaction makes for slack so that a fish can take it up with a jerk. Keep contact with a tight line and a high rod.

The concept that the use of the streamer fly should be limited to the usual early-season conditions of high and cloudy water and in the periods during and after summer rainstorms should be challenged. These flies work early and late in the season and during the course of the day. Start them with the whiskey weather when the clouds rush overhead like blown snow and you may find that their use will continue into other seasons and spill over to other situations and with species of game fish other than trout.

A subject of special interest, of course, is the matter of the most effective patterns. Out of all the trial and error, five favorites emerged for me. Two happen to be similar bucktails in style of tie

*Optic Bucktail.* The early thirties ushered in the bucktail era, and a woman exerted growth on both practice and popularity. Carry Manning tied her Optic Bucktails in several sizes and a variety of patterns. This was the time when fly rods with backbone were making antiques out of the old standard buggy-whip type. And when one angler after another was discovering that a bucktail fished down and across moved fish. Some of the "takes" were more strike than rise. Here, in fact, was an ideal method for the beginning flycaster to pursue. *Photo by James Fosse.*

and size, if not in color; one, a streamer fly in several sizes, and two very different maribous in every respect.

The Optic Bucktail was the craft of a woman, now gone, who for decades tied for Cook, Newton, and Smith of New Haven. The product of Mary S. was superb in every respect. There was a large series of patterns attached to cork blocks on attractive display cards. In due course they were all given a chance in Cedar Run. One pattern tied on 8s and 10s reigned supreme. Fred Everett, the great nature artist, came to like it so much he said, "This fly deserves more than a number; it must have a name." Henceforth it was "Poison," and Poison it still is. Part of its appeal may be because it looks like a large stone-fly nymph.

The specifications are as follows: tail, red; body, loose orange wool held in place with gold tinsel ribbing; wing, dark natural bucktail; jungle cock shoulders; big head with painted eye.

In view of the fact that Poison with its fat juicy-looking body seemed to lead the Optic parade and it was the only one so designed, I requested some similar ties in different colors. Ultimately one took its place with Poison, and somewhere along the line it became known as "Pestilence." There are instances when the watershed with its native population develops the pattern; there are instances when the flycaster develops the pattern; but I know that in the case of Poison and Pestilence it was the pattern that developed the angler. In an attempt to improve effectiveness, I went to the extreme of greasing the hair to make it shine and glisten, but I suspect it was a case of gilding the lily.

The specs for Pestilence are: tail, orange feather; body, loose yellow sheep wool held on with gold tinsel; wing, yellow polar bear or bucktail; jungle cock shoulders; built-up head with painted eye.

For about three years I was a two-bucktail fisherman; then Ray Bergman changed that when he wrote, "A maribou is the most exciting fly I have ever used." Reference was to the big white one, the Ballou Special. Then the late Bob McCafferty, like Bergman, a professional flytier, introduced the direct opposite of the Special. His was short and black as opposed to long and white. At first there was much secrecy about the source of the maribou feather and some substituted the softest downy feathers from the underside of a turkey. Later we learned of the African maribou stork. These flies will move their share of trout, particularly when fished slowly with a steady draw.

The late Gene Craighead regarded streamer-fly fishing as artificial minnow fishing, nothing more, nothing less; therefore his one and only fly in this general category was a direct imitation of the natural, a pointed-nose dace made of feathers. The chief characteristic reflected in his fly was a dark lateral stripe on a light side over a silvery underpart. Robed in its spawning cloak, this minnow sports some orange and yellow so Gene went all-out to imitate it at its finest and added orange and yellow.

The materials that make up the Craighead streamer fly are: tail, orange maribou; body, silver tinsel; wing, two brama (badger) feathers; hackle, yellow.

Some streamer-fly, maribou, and bucktail incidents may prove to be of special interest because they throw light on this type of fishing.

*Craighead Streamer Fly.* Gene Craighead, a member of the well-known Craig-head family of naturalists, developed, tied, and fished his imitation of the common trout-stream minnow, the pointed-nose dace. He fished his fly fast and with a series of rather violent jerks.

The wing is a white feather with a black lateral stripe down the middle (Broma feather); the body is silver tinsel; added to this are a few turns of soft yellow hackle, and usually Gene gave the fly an orange throat and orange tail. *Photo by James Fosse.*

The Pennsylvania stream of Big Spring, in the judgment of many of the fishermen who have fished it, was the best brook trout run or river, as you please, in the East, south of Maine. Jim Chesneys, who was born and raised near the Big Spring source, discovered how to catch its largest fish, provided the fish could be spotted over the clean gravel in the crystalline water. Carefully and slowly he moved into casting position above and away from the fish, then cautiously he cast a small streamer fly so that it could be drawn in front of the fish. Usually the sequence was this: The trout paid no attention to it for a while, maybe ten minutes, but the angler continued the mechanical casting with as little effort and commotion as possible. In due time the fish usually manifested interest by slight movement under the fly. This was normally followed by a chasing stage. Finally the fly was taken. When Jim set out to win the brook trout division of the Harrisburg Hunters and Anglers big fish contest, he could usually, in the course of a season, come through with a brookie weighing between 2 and 3 pounds caught in this manner.

It had been my fortune to locate two big trout in big water of the Yellow Breeches Creek located about 100 yards from each other, thus making it possible to fish for two big ones for sure on one escapade. Both had been raised on Optic Bucktails but neither could be induced to take the fly. On a subsequent trip the upper of the two darted out from a log beside the heavy water and snatched a #8 Poison. This fish turned tail and went down through some heavy water, but was landed without difficulty in the eddy below an island.

This was a 4-pound trout, but I figured fish number two was the bigger. This second fish chased the same Optic but refused it, then refused some more flies too. Intermittently there was fishing for and the resting of the trout, but it did not show again. Finally I tied on the big white maribou and tossed it right over the spot where the fish had risen. The soft fuzzy feathers drifted dry-looking like a prostrate powder puff. The rod tip was given a twitch which ran down to the feathers to make them in turn twitch. There was a sound like a boot being pulled out of the mud as the big fly disappeared. Immediately the brown swapped ends, tore down through a shoot with a brush pile along the bank below it, and promptly demonstrated how a smashed leader silences a screaming reel.

About the town of Hillsgrove, Pennsylvania, on the Loyalsock Creek is some heavy water known as Ludie's Riffle and below the town of Barber's at the old August Beck camp is a big picture pool. For three days Lew Kunkel and I bided our time between these two beautiful spots. The only fly that took a fish was a #10 Pestilence and, when the last one we had was snatched away for keeps by a fish, we jumped into the car and scurried off to Williamsport in a vain hope of finding more, or at least a yellow hair fly.

A New York State tier of the thirties by the name of Tuttle had an oddly tied bucktail he advertised in the magazines as the Devil Bug. It looked as much like a floating bass bug as a bucktail, but it would submerge on the retrieve. Strange to say, the stubby compact hair body was held together with two copper wires, and eyes were painted on the head. Normally this fly had a big loose crest of white hair over the back. The one tied to the leader had the crest snipped off, leaving about a third of the normal Devil Bug. Midway in the sultry afternoon a storm broke, and a noisy wet one it was. In due time I emerged from cover to fish a stream that was clouding and rising. What happened to me and the Devil Bug in the next two hours is wonderful to recollect. It was the greatest catch of sophisticated brown trout I have ever made, the Kingfish among them checking in at 4¾ pounds.

The minnowlike fly makes a fellow big-fish conscious. I was hoping for a big one when this one "took." A Pestilence was snatched from the Slate Run water after it had become a part of big Pine Creek and tore away in the darkness toward the bridge. This happened right off the lawn of the Slate Run Hotel at the town of Slate Run, Pennsylvania, in what is big primitive country for the crowded East. For those who like to fish for trout, or hunt bear, or shoot a buck from hillside to hillside, or follow a grouse dog, my nomination for the host with the most is Don Williams.

The placid LeTort, now my home stream, has been a tough nut to crack with the minnow-type fly, and like other streams, it seems to have a best pattern. Here the preference is for a little black maribou about 1 inch in length cast into hiding places and slowly drawn out or away with a slow, smooth action.

It was a sense of gratitude that led Simon Leepervaun to advise me of the location of a mammoth trout that had broken him. You see, it was becoming more difficult and less convenient for him to secure minnows and he appreciated the bucktails and maribous I gave him; and he was getting along well with them too. This was the year after my fishing partner of old, Don Martin, broke the Pennsylvania record with his 15½-pound brown trout, which he regarded before and after catching as the biggest trout in the state. Simon and I figured, that being so, we had found the number two fish and that it might even be longer than Don's but probably not as heavy. Both of us had had a good look at him.

The second time Simon hooked the fish he was employing the Ballou Special, the white maribou. The spot was a picture pool below the waterfalls from a dam in a big trout stream. Apparently the feeding position of the fish was smooth water between two trails of white water; at least that is where he took the minnow the first time and the fly the second time Simon connected. The complication was that on both occasions the fisherman was above the dam and the fish bolted for the twelve-foot hole 150 feet downstream. This time the fly line broke and the trout disappeared with the fly, 7½ feet of leader, and about 30 feet of line. We never again saw or heard of this trout.

Whenever there is a summer afternoon thunderstorm and a clear-up before dark I try to roll a big one with a 2-inch Craighead streamer fly in the rising and clouding water. Unquestionably such conditions bring out from the hiding places large fish that ordinarily do not forage before dusk or dark.

The rise to fame of the minnowlike fly during its relatively short life has been spectacular if not downright sensational. There will be no fall. It can take its place with other American innovations such as hot dogs, baseball, and fast guns.

A twitch can set up a tingle of excitement. There are times when one finds himself making the rod tip wag like the tail of a cat as she closes in on an intended victim. Usually the fly is taken in an impetuous manner, maybe in a welter of foam.

Eyesight is trained to read water and catch motion. One gets to know individual fish, the old alumni of the stream that have a way of reappearing. Visions of explosions come rushing back. In the lull between seasons the confirmed addict keeps in mental shape by telling stories at Sunday school, at cocktail parties, and across the poker table. There is a haunting question, though—what constitutes luck and what constitutes skill when fishing the minnow-type fly?

PART THREE

# 14

# *The Slow Draw and the Fast Rod*

The line of demarcation between wet-fly fishing and nymph fishing is a nebulous sort of thing. On the one extreme is the classic down-and-across cast with a winged and/or hackled attractor and the hand-twist retrieve back and up; on the other is an upstream delivery and the natural drift back of a realistic-looking fabrication. Beyond the shadow of a doubt the first is wet-fly fishing (as practiced by our ancestors) and the other is nymph fishing (as practiced by contemporaries). But neither of these has been nearly as effective for me, and some others I know, as two other underwater approaches unlike the basics. Whether either is wet-fly fishing or nymph fishing is academic, so therefore unimportant to all but one—me. The trouble is I do not know how to title this chapter.

Credit for one of these approaches to subsurface fly fishing for trout should go to the late Bob McCafferty, the other to George Harvey—two tremendous fly-rod men who had the good fortune to know each other and who even fished together on at least a few occasions.

The McCafferty Ant was a sinking, hard-body, wasp-waisted affair with a few turns of soft hackle tied in the midsection—later named thorax style of tie by Vince Marinaro. His regular Ant was black and tied on a #14 hook. It did not take him long to learn that the most effective method of fishing it was to cast slightly downstream, or straight across toward cover, then permit the fly slowly to draw away from the hiding place or feeding station. Any motion given it by rod-tip action or any speedup because of rod lift or hand-twist retrieve detracted. This he discovered and passed along to others such as me. Simply cast, then permit the pull of the current on the line and leader to draw the fly—precisely what one would not want to happen to a dry fly.

In the early days of the "Fisherman's Paradise" on Spring Creek near Bellefonte, Pennsylvania, before the number of fishermen outgrew the size of the regulated stretch of stream, the Ant was the most effective fly most of the time when in competent hands. It became Bob's practice, and that of his friends too, to match the hatch with a dry fly when there was surface feeding, but at other times to turn to the sinking Ant, unless there was some experimentation to be done. No doubt for some years it was the most productive fly in the Paradise.

This was not the only place where it performed admirably. The popularity of the Ant grew and its fame spread to all parts of Pennsylvania, then beyond. Annually Bob tied them by the hundreds of dozens. Those who did really well with them employed the slow-draw-from-a-hiding-place system and a silk-worm-gut leader tipped out to 4X, which in those days was considered light.

Behind the scenes in a little fly-tying shop something else was developing. When the McCafferty Ant was not being tied on a commercial basis, experimentation went on at the vise. They were tied in different sizes, in different colors, and even in different styles. There were two-toned ones and quill-bodied ones.

I reveled in fishing with him, for not only was he wonderful company and a great storyteller, but so much practical fishing information could be learned when one watched and listened. That inquisitive mind could be satisfied only with a sound explanation and that perfectionist attitude demanded a creditable performance.

"Try these," he would say as he handed over a little box containing a fresh assortment of experimental Ants. "That #14 Black Ant can't be the best one of all all of the time."

And it wasn't. We hit upon a #18 Ginger Ant. What this did in the limestone streams was a revelation, maybe a revolution. At first we liked gray because it was the color of sowbugs and scuds, but once we had light brown ones, they outfished the natural-looking gray.

So long as I can fish, I'll never forget one spot. It is the only place I ever angled where one could successfully wager even money—and come out ahead—that one cast would produce a trout. Here was the most dependable thing imaginable in angling, but part of the requirement was and is a #18 Ginger Ant attached to a fine leader.

In front of the one side of a stream-improvement V dam on Big Spring was a large submerged rock. When one cast the Ginger Ant between this rock and the far wall of the V dam and permitted it to draw away from there across the open V, a brook trout was sure to move for it. The only question was, would it be caught or just nipped?

Early in the season when the trout are not surface feeding, I often fish the #18 Ginger Ant on the LeTort or Big Spring, only now since the days of Bob McCafferty I do something that might not have met with his approval. The cast is not fished out completely as a thorough and patient McCafferty might have done it. I cast it across or slightly downstream to an obstruction, let it draw away a yard or two, then pick it up for the next cast. A minimum of time is spent on each retrieve and casts are concentrated on the best of places. Bob, I think, would have said, "You are not fishing the water well," to which I could only give the greedy answer, "When you can tell milk from cream, don't bother with the milk."

The opposite to the action given the sinking hard-bodied Ant is applied to the Horse-collar Midge. Instead of the slow draw, this is an animated jiggle.

George Harvey's creation has a hackle, wisp tail, a silk body, and a chenille collar—no wings, no hackle. Hook sizes are #18 regular and #20 short shank, the latter fly appearing to be about half the size of the former.

In the day when a #18 fly was a Midge, 4X was a light-gut point, and a 7½-foot rod a short one, we watched George combine these and, when the setup was right, hook trout after trout. Of course, there were certain requirements, but he did this time after time. In the last hour or two of the fishing day he would hook and land more fish than most of us caught fishing throughout the entire afternoon.

His testing ground was also the old fisherman's Paradise, and what a convenient place for him it was. During the day George, in the capacity of a fish commission employee, gave individuals free fly-tying lessons or demonstrated fly tying to groups at the check-in booth. Here many of us got our start in fly tying. When fishing pepped up late in the afternoon, he fished. Thus he was offered an opportunity to experiment with patterns and styles, then he had the opportunity to test his wares. Usually he operated with one of his Horse-collar Midges and almost always it was before an unofficial gallery. This Midge was developed in an effort to cope with the heavy feeding activity to minutiae that occurred about dusk.

Athletic George, fresh out of Penn State where he captained the track team and was Eastern Intercollegiate Cross Country Champion, moved over and around the rocks at the streamside like a cat. Invariably the midge was cast downstream on a short line into special spots. He passed up much water, his preference being smooth areas beside broken-water runs, downstream of wing walls.

Pulling the small hook away from the mouth of a fish resulted in an abnormally high percentage of ticked but unhooked fish; no doubt the steel hitting nothing but a tooth. Fish came so readily, though, that some missed ones made little or no difference.

It was the white Horse-collar Midge that enjoyed a reputation at first. The warden stationed at "the Project," the late Art Snyder, was a competent fly fisherman, as is his brother, Ken. In those days the large head of fish in the stream section was fed finely ground frozen fish to supplement the natural food supply of Spring Creek. It was Art's supposition that the white Midge simulated particles of ground fish, but this theory had fallacies. In the first place, to be effective it had to be fished with broken lifelike action; and, in the second place, it was most effective when the trout were busy feeding on something alive.

After the white Horse-collar Midge came other colors—black, yellow, gray, brown and, what became my favorite, olive. Soon the Horse-collar Midge enjoyed success in various and sundry trout waters ranging from fast streams to beaver dams and from silted creeks to new limestone ponds. This, of course, eliminated the original concept of the imitation of hand-fed ground fish.

There was an incident that will illustrate the potency of this odd-looking fly. One day some two decades after the conception of this fly, along with the way to fish it, I guided a girl on a riffle of Big Spring. In her case she tied flies before she ever cast one.

Among the recommended patterns for her construction was an olive Horse-collar Midge, which to her was "the little green bug." This being choice number one this day, it was tied to the 6X tippet.

The instruction was that she cast as best she could down and across and, after the current had straightened out the line and leader, pull the fly into the quiet area beside the fast run to be jiggled with a high tip. To guard against breakage she should strike from the reel; that is, not touch the line with the free hand until it was time to skid the fly from the water for the next cast or time to reel in a fish.

I figured she would get along fine on her own—with the left hand out of the picture no fish would tear off a fly, and with her standing in one place, she would not scare fish. Having received her master's degree in English I said, "You learnt good, now git to it; you're on your own," and with that I started upstream to fish dry between her and our mutual friend, Doug O'Hanley.

I wasn't 15 feet away when her reel screamed and she let out a squeal. I retraced my steps, then netted and unhooked for her a beautiful brook trout. "Nice going," I said, "that was quick work," and I again started upstream pleased with results.

About half a minute and fifteen steps later the same thing happened, so again I did the same thing. "I like fishing better than fly tying," she observed as I detached number two.

Her third trout set off Doug upstream. "Hey gilley," he yells down, "you better say right there on the spot." He understood perfectly that my rod wasn't for looks and I had come along to fish.

After number four was unhooked I pinched down the barb with a little tweezers carried for that purpose. Maybe now fish would flip off.

The farthest I could get away between fish was fifty feet. On practically every cast there was a willing little brookie waiting to take a pass at the green bug; it was only on about every third cast, though, that one was hooked; and they didn't flip off that abbreviated hook.

"Why do so many get away?" she asked.

That train of thought was broken when I retorted, "You are doing very well, now it is time to learn to unhook them."

"Oh no! I can't touch slimy things like—" and she hesitated—
"like snakes and fish."

So that was that.

By this time Doug was down where I had expected to fish. "You
have no use for a rod, better take it down between fish, then rush it
to your car between other fish." He laughed more heartily than I
had ever heard him laugh before, and by nature he was a laughing
man.

I unhooked some more brook trout, then Doug showed his hand.
"I'll unhook them for a while so you can get in some fishing," he
volunteered.

The girl caught on faster than I. "No you don't, she says. "This
is our secret weapon—just the two of us." That sure solidified the
togetherness I was trying to divide.

It was getting dark but she did not want to quit.

"You really like this?" I queried.

"Yes," she answered. "I want to catch two more."

"Why two more?"

"I have been counting; I want to achieve a goal."

"A goal," I murmured.

"Yes, silly, like the number of candles on a certain birthday
cake."

Strange how things change. After I married the girl she did her
own unhooking, but almost always it was unhooking a brook trout
from the "little green bug"—with the barb pinched down, of
course.

I have been very fortunate to have met, talked to, and fished
with some of the greatest American anglers of our age. Some
enjoyed national reputations because they were writers, or
talented flytiers, or rod builders, or casting champions. Others
shunned notoriety but were masters of their craft—our craft. Some
of their know-how rubbed off. What made each in turn so interesting was a dedication to a beloved sport. Time, the great destroyer,
has taken its toll of these enthusiasts. In the group, the two who
had the greatest influence on my wet-fly practices were Bob
McCafferty, who provided us with the sinking ant and the slow
draw to make it effective, and, George Harvey, who originated the
midge nymph with the chenille collar fished with a fast broken
action.

# 15

# Casting the Wet Fly

The booted angler fishes primarily for trout in little rivers and brooklets, the one in a canoe fishes mainly the big rivers for salmon, and the flycaster in waders fishes the middle-sized rivers for trout and salmon. The pools of the mid-sized streams are normally large and challenging, often mysterious. Frequently, the angler is faced with a situation where he needs to cast far and often in order to make precious fishing time count the most. Furthermore, it helps to cast with a minimum amount of effort, not only to save energy, but to protect the skin of the casting hand, the muscles and joints of the casting arm, and one's general well-being.

There are two specialized casts that accomplish these things in such a manner that the one who employs them should do considerably better with his hooking and catching than the one who does not use them. The reasons are both simple and logical: during the course of an hour, a day, or a trip, this angler will make more and better casts and thereby show his fly to more fish than the other fellow who has considerably more to learn about the art of casting.

It might be broken down this way: If a man makes one-fourth again as many casts as his counterpart, his fly should cover at least one-fourth more fish. Suppose he casts with considerably less energy. That might mean he fishes more hours or fishes without breaks. All else being equal, this makes an even greater difference in the respective catches, which in this situation are controlled by casting prowess.

The component parts of equipment are rod, line, leader, and fly.

*Wet Fly.* The age-old wet fly has changed little from the days of its creator, Dame Julianna Bernes, until the present time. In no other way can a fly be shown to move fish than by casting it down and across and permitting it to swing crosscurrent in a sweeping arc. The quill-bodied flies may be the most popular and attractive—Quill Gordon and Ginger Quill in particular. Most wet-fly fishermen utilize the hand-twist retrieve in conjunction with rod tip manipulation. *Photo by James Fosse.*

The idea is to coordinate them into a single efficient unit, and there is satisfaction, reward, and charm in so doing.

The one specialized cast can be made only when a right-handed caster is located on the left side looking downstream. Because of the direction of the current in relation to the pickup of the fly, it will not work from the right side for a right-hander. Involved is no false cast, yet the line shoots extremely well and casting is next to effortless.

Instead of picking up the line from the water and stapling it over the right shoulder, skid it off the water and up and over the left shoulder; make the rod tip travel high above the head in a half circle to the right; then thrust the rod with extended arm straight across the stream. When this is done, the line will have traveled in a plane parallel to the surface of the water, not perpendicular to it, which is the usual path. The result is amazing. It is so easy and just a matter of simple timing.

The hand-twist retrieve, like the bonefish strip, imparts broken action to the swimming fly as the noncasting hand recovers line, usually several yards of it. The skidding pickup sends it on its way to a high semicircle. The thrust of the rod to the right speeds the line and shoots the excess across stream as straight as a clothesline. A comfortable position is to stand braced in the water facing downstream. Following the pickup the cast can be made directly across stream. The usual thing is slowly to progress down the pool as the fly thoroughly and carefully searches the water for a willing taker.

My knowledge and use of this cast sort of grew like Topsy. Often I fished early and late at our camp pool on the Little Southwest Branch of the Miramichi River in New Brunswick. Frequently I cast there while breakfast or dinner was being prepared. Given a five-minute warning I could peel off waders, wash my hands, and be at my place at the table. This sort of thing makes for frantic fishing, when time must count. At this point the river follows its melodious course from west to east; the camp was on the north bank. That meant, when looking downstream I was on the left side.

In the heart of the concentrated water was a large protruding rock, our "watermark." At low-water stage, the front was about 18 inches above the surface, the back about 2 feet. Around it was some 5 feet of water at the low-water stage. Apparently this was gouged out in winter and kept free of rubble by the violent flow of water under the ice, which was held in place by the large rock. In front of the rock was a glassy-smooth backwater in the shape of a V, apex upriver. This was the taking place. It was only an odd fish that was taken below the rock, although at a glance that appeared to be bigger and better holding water.

The pool could be fished in ten minutes, providing a fish was not hooked and played or one did not spend some of that time climbing out of the water and up on the bank to unhook his fly from the cantankerous black alders. Therein was the rub. Even had the bushes been cut, there were weeds and stones on the sloping bank. It was not an easy place to fish.

A good high lift for a good high backcast was a necessity. Somehow, I discovered that it was easier to staple the backcast, when the fly was lifted from the water, over the left shoulder. Then I found that the line could be made to circle above the bushes without dipping down the way it would in the normal backcast over the casting shoulder. The push of the rod away from the body propelled the line wonderfully. The whole thing was a revelation.

It was at this pool, because of the circumstances, that I was able to perfect a specialized cast. But when I got to other pools, bushes or no bushes, looking down from the left, the old "camp-pool pitch" came into play. I like it so much that I employ it a great deal. In fact, either by necessity or by choice, the majority of the salmon pools I fish are fished from the left side. And it was a natural step to apply this cast to wet-fly trout fishing when using either the riffled hitch or submerged flies, by day or by night. Hence this cast, which involves no false cast, is my common practice. By the way, it does well in the wind.

About this time something else developed from the other side of the river, the right as one looks downstream. This, too, is a specialized cast which I also regard as indispensable. The casting is either straight across stream, eighting or quartering down, as one chooses. For good measure let us assume that distance is desirable.

This time the pickup following the hand-twist retrieve is a lazy one, almost like the start of a roll cast, and the fly comes out of the water and goes low by the caster's right, which is his downstream side. When the fly is in back of him, the rod is pushed hard forward and down, just like a roll cast, the line going forward in a wide loop. As it extends out and over the water, a small amount of line is permitted to slip through the thumb and forefinger of the left hand. In essence this is a baby shoot. Once extended over the water, the second backcast is made; but unlike the first, this one has plenty of authority. A little more line, about one yard of it, can be permitted to shoot backward. Then comes the powerful forward cast with a good push of the rod butt, the tip just riding along. As the line speeds out above the water, the rest of the excess line is shot. At this instant one puts in a quick and short double haul by easing the line in the left hand, then jerking it down. This, directly before release, at the least insures a straight line and leader, if not a bit more distance.

On paper, this may seem complicated, but actually once the feel of it is experienced, it is all very natural. This cast has one easy backcast made with authority, which means there is a minimum expenditure of time and effort. I do not like to see much false casting in wet-fly fishing because this is an unnecessary waste of time and effort.

These two specialized casts apply to both trout and salmon wet-fly fishing. Normally, greater distance is involved than is the case with dry-fly fishing and there should be much less false casting.

Good fly casting is beautiful to behold. Everything is coordinated through gradually accelerated motion. Each motion, each direction, flows into the next. Shoulder, elbow, wrist, and hand and rod, line, leader, and fly appear to be component parts of a single unit and the motion of them fluid.

I don't think one sees as many good casters on our rivers as should be the case, which is unfortunate. Some seem to rely on equipment for the job at hand. Great emphasis is placed on rod, line, leader, and fly and not enough on shoulder, elbow, wrist, and hand. The two greatest casters it has been my pleasure to watch have been Joe Brooks and Lefty Kreh—both poetry in motion.

There are two factors that, as the future seasons come and go, will increase the amount of and the interest in the big-stream wet-fly fishing. Each is brought about by man, one incidental, the other by design.

There are and will be more new sections of big-trout water below new impoundments that have deep taps. With low-flow augmentation, cold bottom water, which is trout water, is drawn from a lower depth of what is regarded as a warm-water impoundment. Because of high surface water temperature trout might not be able to exist above the dam, but because of low water temperature they can thrive below the dam. Two outstanding examples of this situation are below a massive dam on the White River in Arkansas, where there are 40 or more new miles of big trout water, and below a dam on the Delaware River in the vicinity of Hancock, New York.

The other factor has to do with the prespawning migrations of redistributed species of salmon from the Great Lakes and the Finger Lakes into various feeder rivers. The species are silver or coho salmon and the giant king salmon—and probably in due time landlocked salmon, which in reality are planted Atlantics. The last species survives spawning to return to the big water in preparation for another run, whereas the others die in the river after spawning.

# 16
# The Silver King

What about the lore and the lure of salmon fishing, particularly for the avid trout man who never gave it a fling? There is a perfect union in angling: a trout fisherman, fly rod in hand, and a pool on an Atlantic salmon river. It is my firm conviction that the rabid trout fisherman who has not fished for salmon should give it a try. This is based on the fact that marked simularities exist between the two types of fishing. However, salmon fishing is on a grander scale, particularly in the matters of the size of the water, the size of the fish, and the handling of them when hooked.

First of all, it is pool fishing. The fish travel through shallows and gather and loiter in the pools. Four to 6 feet of water is ideal taking depth, but some fish can be induced to move to a fly from deeper water.

There is a special charm in playing a good fish on a fly rod, and by way of comparison, there is no greater and more interesting game fish than the salmon. Things are often terrific and they can happen suddenly. In the melee that follows hooking there is often a smother of foam, and there is sheer power in the runs, lunges, and cartwheels. The speed can be so great that the cutting line erupts a spray of water and sings an intriguing little song of its own. In the early stages all the angler can do is hang on without exerting influence on the fight of the fish. It is clear that he is dealing with a powerful captive possessing a maniacal desperation. The thrill of having such a fish connected to a fly rod is great.

Is fly fishing a stereotyped and mechanical game? Some anglers fish as though that were the way it is supposed to be. I cannot concur. There is great opportunity to be innovative, to exert forethought, to be observant, and to experiment. I believe in changing a losing game. There are the frustrations and irritations, but these enhance the satisfactions and successes.

This may sound strange to some and heresy to others, but the poorest practitioners I have watched in action are natives along the river, and the best performers seem to be those who live farthest away. There are exceptions, of course. By necessity the trout man from faraway has become observant, analytical, and an experimenter. It is my opinion that there is a great deal to consider in presentation, size, and style of fly, and it is important to be not only a fine caster but also a keen angling thinker.

The only time I use a standard dry fly is in water at a temperature of more than 55° when either the fish can be seen or when I am reasonably certain of a fish in a specific resting place. At other times in warm water I use the riffled hitch by day and the skater fly from sundown till dark. In either event, the fly is moved on the surface so that it can be shown to the greatest number of fish, which is not the case with the limited path of the natural drift for the standard dry fly.

In the case of the skater fly, I keep ready a greased leader tipped out to 0X, so the fly can be lifted directly from the surface on the pickup thereby maintaining stiff hackles. Sometimes the skater is taken in a welter of spray by a charging salmon, at times from below and at times from above. I like very much to cast the skaters downstream for a natural drift on a slack line and leader following a kickback cast; then when the fly is about to drag, it is skipped from the heavier water to slower side water in a series of jerks. Thus the fish are presented two totally different actions and impressions on each cast of the fly.

Make sure to use the proper hook for skater-fly fishing for salmon. It took three different fish on one trip to teach me a lesson. I was using a skater designed for trout fishing and given to me by Ed Hewitt. The problem was that the light-wire #16 hook would straighten out. I bent it back for the next three fish, then was ever so gentle in playing them. For the next trip I had some well-tempered short-shank #8 hooks supplied by Ray Bergman. That was in the days prior to World War II. Now I would not be without them.

When the water temperature is under 55°—and this is typical of

*Skater Fly.* When Edward R. Hewitt contrived his skating fly and the method of fishing it, he created something spectacular for fly fishermen after trout and salmon. A sturdy hackle that will create a large diameter is anchored with slippery tying thread (unwaxed). The thread is advanced partway up the hook, then several turns are made of the hackle, which has concave side forward. With thumb and fingernail, the whole thing is jammed back. This process is repeated three-quarters of the way toward the eyes. A second hackle is tied in the concave side facing the bend. After a few turns it is tied off. The result is a compact fly with tips of hackle coming together. *Photo by James Fosse.*

*Clipped Deer Hair.* It seems apparent that the clipped deer-hair bodied dry fly first appeared on salmon rivers under the banner of McDougal—one Rat Face McDougal. His fly was different and effective. Somewhat later, in smaller size, it was applied to trout. On the little rivers it was given a more lofty name, the Irresistible.

This is a worthy style of tie to serve as a fish finder in fishing the water and as an imitation of a large mayfly such as *gatulatta*, the green drake. *Photo by James Fosse.*

morning fishing—I stick to standard wet flies, but adjust them to fit the nature of the water in the pool section at hand. The game plan is simply this. In very heavy water, like a chute, which often exists at the head of a pool, a big fly cast downstream holds best in the torrent. As a matter of fact, a double hook hangs in there better than a single. As the water fans out and slows down, a little farther downstream, I switch to a smaller fly, usually a low-water tie on a #8 cast quartering or eighting downstream. At the tail of the pool I like to drop down—or is it move up?—to a #10 or 12 on a stubby double hook, cast across stream, and retrieve as fast as this can be accomplished comfortably.

Some of the finest salmon fishing I ever enjoyed was during a high tide in a tidewater pool that looked as much like a lake as a river. The only way two of us could move these fish was with a little fly and a fast retrieve.

Maybe there is a point in time and an event in the life of a salmon fisherman when he becomes an angler, not just a caster. I like to think so, and do so with reason. I'll never forget my initial successful experience with a midge salmon wet fly. I was walking by a location that had a combination of ledges and loose stones under about 5 feet of flat water. This specific stretch did not even enjoy the dignity of having a name. I had just unsuccessfully fished the oxbow pool and was taking a walk upstream, partly to enjoy the solitude and partly to see what was around the next bend.

Since there was no fly attached to the leader, I opened the box and my gaze fell on the smallest thing therein. It was attached to the leader. I waded in at what appeared to be a slight dropoff at the upper end.

The action that transpired between then and nightfall is unforgettable. Obviously the place was loaded with fish, mostly grilse, but not all. Most of the times I drew that little fly sideways and fast in this stretch of river about 150 feet long, action of some sort resulted. There were many wakes, some false rises and swirls, and every so often a hooked fish. My two camp companions thereafter referred to the spot as "the Fox Hole" because, it seemed, I was always anxious to get back to it. Today this particular section of the Little Southwest Miramichi is within the boundaries of an Indian reservation and difficult to get to fish, but, they tell me, the Indians still refer to it as "the Fox Hole." That big afternoon was important because it was then I got the idea of drawing a small fly directly across smooth water.

The leader tippet must be a consideration. I think the lightest that one can employ and still hold on to a fish is 3X; however, with that kind of terminal tackle, fish, even grilse, cannot be beached. They must be met out in the river with a net. In our camp we beach ours because we like to make the catch without help; and 10-pound test or a slightly heavier monofilament tippet has served us well in low clear water. If the river is high and cloudy, we step down to 8/5 or even 7/5, the latter testing 13 pounds.

Small wet flies, the riffled hitch, and the Neversink Skater fly have become indispensables for me. The same is true of the fast cross-stream draw with the midge wet fly in the tails of the pools and the slack-line, downstream cast of the skater combining natural drift with skipping to the side. When the riffled hitch is employed, my preference is for a low-water #8 fly, preferably hair-winged.

A word of warning: Should you cherish late-afternoon and dusk fishing, as I do, or should you insist upon solitude now and then, as I do, avoid the rivers of New Brunswick. Current regulations in that province are such that it is not only necessary to hire a guide; he must also be located within talking distance of you, and guide hours do not usually extend till dark. In other Canadian provinces one can be on his own when he so chooses.

# 17

# *The Art of Diminution*

There comes a time in the trout season when fly fishing becomes a completely different type of challenge and the answer is to fish small and light. I call it the art of diminution, but maybe Carlisle's great angler-flytier Eddie Shenk says it better with his expression "fishing with next to nothing."

Midge fishing is the newest phase of fly fishing for trout, and to date so little has been written and spoken about it that this dimension of angling is still in the formative stage. It is the only remaining operational frontier, for it seems that everything else has been well taken care of before our time. The door to minutiae was barred for our illustrious ancestors because of tackle restriction due to manufacturing limitation. Now that tiny, light-wire, eyed hooks can be produced, nylon strands that caliper as little as .0039 are on the market, and light rods with cushioning tips are available, a new phase of fly fishing is growing.

In this brief treatment of the tiny-fly, fine-leader, light-rod game let's start with the rod-and-line combination, then consider the leader, and finally take a look at the fly, all of which are closely related.

Imagine that the time has arrived in the fishing season when, in spite of the fact that there is no aquatic hatch, there are some rising trout. It is obvious that in the lower, clearer, flatter water the rise forms are different. Now there are dainty dimples made by fish feeding in a deliberate manner instead of crystalline sprays

This chapter is reprinted from *The Anglers' Journal*, Number 1 (Winter 1969), with the kind permission of the Anglers' Club of Philadelphia.

and pyramids formed by the trout that come up from the bottom and snap and snatch.

It does not take much fishing to determine that the heretofore dependable #14 Light Cahill on a 3X tippet won't touch these fish. Neither will the next step down, a #18 Adams on 5X. They continue to feed, yet there appears to be no fly on the water. What is happening is that these fish, and there are some good ones among them, are taking a position of watchful waiting about six inches under the surface and having the current deliver their food to them, that food being minute land and water forms that are not easily seen by the angler. It is up to the angler to adjust to the situation, because such feeding offers a challenge and presents a fascinating problem.

The first thing in order is a switch in rods from the standard 8- or 9-footer with the normal tip to a different rod with a thin sensitive tip of delicate action. By necessity this rod is shorter because a long one with a thin tip is so much of a buggy whip that it will not hold up a back cast. A short rod with a sensitive tip will function in a satisfactory manner in this vital respect. So fishing for the remainder of the season will be done with a lighter and shorter rod, but do not be surprised if the little "stick" operates so well and is such a pleasure to employ that it becomes the general-purpose rod, eventually replacing the heavier one.

A DT-5-F line (the old HEH) will probably be the right line for the little rod. However, if most of your casting is short you may prefer a #6, which shoots better at close range.

To the line you may choose to attach a new concept in leaders, one with stiff nylon in the butt and midsection and limp nylon on the front quarter, thus making three-fourths of the leader stiff and the last two strands limp. This makes for good casting and a nice turnover. Since the length of the leader overall and the length of the individual strands are not critical, the leader can be tied by guesswork rather than by careful measurement. The Joe Brooks taper could work out something like this: 24 inches of 20-pound, 18 inches of 12-pound, 12 inches of 1X, 12 inches of 3X, 18 inches of 5X, and 18 inches of 7X.

Now comes the most interesting part in our campaign of diminution, that handsome barbed fabrication at the business end. It is my belief that there are four indispensables, two to imitate terrestrial forms and two imitations of aquatic drakes. To these four can be added a Midge Coachman as a happy compromise and a tiny Black Spider with a gold tinsel body as the lone attractor midge.

There is a difference of opinion about the minimum hook size. Vince Marinaro and I set it at #24 in the belief that anything smaller does not possess sufficient bite to hook in a satisfactory manner. I became gun-shy of the #28s when I felt eighteen fish in a row without hooking or landing a single one. There are others, however, including Eddie Shenk, who believe #28s to be practical. There is no real concern about holding once the hook catches skin, for they are tenacious things. In fact, a tweezers is a fine thing to have handy as a removal instrument. Often just a snick is felt when the angler answers the rise by tightening the connection. This is probably the hook hitting only the teeth. Hooks with turned-up eyes increase the bite, which in turn increases hooking chances.

If you stretch a piece of cloth in a good line of drift, as Vince Marinaro does, or if you watch the water with a pair of field glasses, as Dr. Albert Hazzard does, you will find that there is a considerable amount of food floating adrift *in* the surface film. These are mostly land forms, and they are opaque; the great preponderance are jassids and ants. By comparison, the aquatic insects are translucent and, in the subimago form, high riding— that is, *on* the surface film.

Ernie Schweibert attaches great significance to ants as available and choice food. Ants, the most common of all insects, vary in size and color. Some drop, helter-skelter, from overhanging foliage throughout the long season, but there are August and September afternoons and evenings, during their mating season, when the winged ants, the breeders, literally pepper the surface of the water. If this is not the special food favorite of all trout, it certainly must be one of them.

The ant eaters assume a position in a good line of drift about 6 inches under the surface from which they tip and sip. The rings are dainty, and frequently the dorsal fin and upper part of the tail break the surface. The feeding tempo can be fast, that is, one dozen or more rises a minute per surface feeder for several hours.

Ernie Schweibert's favorite imitation has a black seal's fur body and blue-gray wings. Vince Marinaro likes a body built up by winding porcupine guard hairs around the hook, and he places the hackle in the wasp waist midpart. My daughter had a red-tailed pony in a streamside enclosure, and a considerable number of hairs from the filly's plume found their way, indirectly, to trout taking cinnamon-colored ants. A #20 or 22 Ant tied to a 7X tippet and cast so that it drifts naturally over a feeder is what Vince Marinaro calls "pretty fishing."

Closely related to the ant fishing is fishing for the jassid eater. In fact, when a trout is feeding on the one and the other happens along, that too becomes grist for the mill. In actual fishing, one sometimes encounters ants so small they cannot be imitated. Under such a condition I switch to a Black Jassid, and it has worked well.

For the most part I like my jassids on short-shank, turned-up eye, #20s. There are various color combinations that seem to attract fish on equal terms. The first one that its originator, Vince Marinaro, tied had an orange tying-silk body, ginger hackle, and a jungle-cock roof. The orange was followed by the Black Jassid— black body and black hackle. Then came other versions, including a pale green; but the first two are hard to beat, particularly if the jungle-cock eyes are the oval type, as opposed to the long trim ones, for the necks vary.

Some years later I tried a miniature Japanese beetle that can be considered to be a jassid—#20 hook, peacock herl body, black and ginger hackles intermingled, and a flat-wing top of two trimmed black feathers from the dark ring of ringneck pheasant, sealed together with feather glazer to make the flush-floating fly opaque.

This is half the story of minutiae, the land insect half. The other half deals with two interesting aquatic hatches that have passed by pretty much unnoticed in the exacting game of meeting the challenge of the hyperselective feeders that tip and sip. All parts of the equipment are specialized and related. Together, this type of feeding and this type of equipment provide a variety of fly fishing that is very special. To many fly fishermen the art of diminution has become the most rewarding of all the types of fly fishing for trout.

# 18

# Competition

The more fish, the greater the competition. And the less food, the greater the competition. These two factors complicate matters for the trout and simplify matters for the angler.

Concentrations come in two forms: regulated areas where there is a minimum of killing in order to protect both native and planted populations and in the put-and-take spots for the chasers of the fish truck. The former insures a consistency in angling opportunity, as well as a supply of brood fish for the stream. The latter is strictly a temporary proposition for man and fish, unless the fish, for some unforeseen reason such as a storm or flooding, are lucky enough to escape the impending slaughter.

The downfall of newly stocked trout is the necessity to feed in the face of competition. This explains the effectiveness on them of corn, doughballs, canned vegetables, pink salmon eggs, gumdrops, and all manner of spinning or flashing hardware. On the other hand, a protected mature population has no real downfall other than the natural causes of death.

The following experiences are the result of competition of the first type and each resulted in great personal satisfaction, which is the reason for angling. So this is a look back over the fleeting seasons.

It was 9 o'clock on an August morning and the Falling Springs hatch of the little drake was in full bloom. Spinners were performing their nuptial dance above the surface as duns were leaving the water. The trout were ready and willing, partaking of both. In good weather they had been taking this fly in quantity every morning for the past five weeks, and they would continue to do so until October 15—what a duration! Although the fly is very small, the hatch was heavy and unquestionably many of the trout partook each day of a large breakfast. They would only stop eating for the day when capacity had been reached, and then they would not feed again until the following morning.

The morsel was small but the majority of the trout in this regulated stream section were not. Give trout, which have a strong inclination to surface feed, a chance to survive and they remain surface feeders. This place with this hatch proved that, small as the fly actually was.

I call *tricorythodes* "little single wing," for there is but one wing on each side of the body instead of the usual two. However, the wing is relatively long for the length of the body. It is an oddity in the ephemeroid world in that it emerges, flies about, sheds its skin, and mates in the course of a morning. Locally this is referred to as "*Caenis* fishing."

As the trout tipped and sipped, taking the upright-wing duns and the spent-wing spinners, they were adhering to a law of nature: eat the most readily available food. But with all this activity, there was a fishing challenge. These fish inspected a fly ever so carefully. Experience had taught them to do this. The leader tippet had to be 5X to 7X and the fly a good imitation. After weeks of this type of feeding in the face of hard fishing they were as difficult to deceive as trout become. Mike Cohen of Freshet Press described this fishing to me as being "frustrating."

But there is a saving grace, which comes in the form of an appeal to greed. Pick a flat water area where the fish are visible; then look for two feeders close together. Cast your imitation in such a way that it comes to them in a perfectly natural drift, and watch. There are times when one trout makes the slow move to inspect the approaching fly and this triggers off the other into quickly moving in and taking over. Usually—but not always—it is the second to move that gets himself into trouble, but the first fish sometimes lets his guard down and becomes grabby.

This is the game Vince Marinaro and I play on the hatch of single wings once the separate fish have become most difficult to fool. The key to it is flat clear water where the fish are readily spotted. I have seen Vince pick them off there when other anglers were experiencing difficulty even with worthy imitations.

Playing the game of spotting pairs of rising trout while matching the hatch had its start for Vince and me in the forties. It was probably his idea. Many a time in the sulphur season, which is a long one, we went together to nearby Cedar Run, a stream with a fine native population of brown trout and a superb sulphur hatch, the perfect combination. At dusk, there was an emergence and a return of the little yellow drakes, which transpired evening after evening for many weeks on end with the result that the trout not only looked for this food supply but many depended upon it. Very likely there were some fish that ate nothing else once the evening hatch became established. Rises of various trout were seen day after day at the same spots.

Early in the sulphur season many hooked fish were returned or lost. They became progressively more difficult to deceive. A difference could be noticed from one week to the next. By July the fishing was exacting.

Then we hit upon the plan of pitching to two fish located close together. Maybe the initial idea was that this doubled one's chances. At any rate, the final thought was that when two fish are close together they resent each other, but neither will abandon the favorite position. Territorial integrity is a powerful influence in the world of wildlife, and trout are no exception.

It is common belief that trout are more readily deceived in the failing light of evening, but I can't say that experience bears this out. We know they have great vision at close range, and we also know they can see to take a fly on a dark night. Probably it's a mistake to compare their vision with our own, the two are so different. At any rate, it came to the point that it was no accident, but design, when an imitation sulphur was drifted down the alley where two trout could see it at the same time.

Of all the trout I ever caught, the one that provided me with the greatest satisfaction was one of a pair of big sulphur-fly eaters located above a massive brush pile on Little Cedar. The experience is as vivid in memory now as it was in fact the evening it happened. On different occasions I had lost flies to both of these fish, for upon being hooked each, in turn, would dive back into sanctuary in a treasure-house of snags. Now they were not only all but impossible to land but, to make matters worse, they had become most difficult to hook. This challenge haunted me.

On the memorable evening the hatch was heavy in the fading light. The hordes of spinners were going through what angler Richard Blackmore, author of *Lorna Doone*, referred to as "giddy dances and fervid waltz." Some were dropping spent on the water. Although the water warriors themselves could not be seen, the great dimples they made on the silvery sheen, close together and sometimes simultaneously, were both conspicuous and impressive. Six feet downstream was that menacing brush pile. I knelt in my casting location in the grass, imagination fired up.

The first job was to hook one of these fish, the next was play it and keep it away from the brush pile and finally get it into a net. A game plan developed.

The first move involved a study of the feeding rhythms of the two fish so that the cast and drift would come at a time when they were both looking. That meant waiting for simultaneous rises, waiting while they settled back and swallowed, then making the pitch and hoping that the line of drift was above the fish and was free of naturals. The hope, if not the expectation, was that one would move a little to inspect the fly and thereby trigger the other into taking it.

If that was subterfuge, the rest was skullduggery. I had placed several rocks in the grass beside the spot at which I knelt to make the downstream cast. The idea was to lift slowly and gently when the fly disappeared, then quickly to shift the rod to the left hand and with the free hand throw a stone in back of the fish in an attempt to induce it to bolt upstream.

A Hollywood script could not have made things work closer to plan. When the stone hit in back of the trout with the fly in its mouth, he spontaneously bolted upstream away from the sanctuary of snags. As the fish passed by me, I jumped to my feet and hurried to the head of the flat caused by the jam. For maybe thirty seconds the trout hung there, then swapped ends and tore downstream toward the brush pile. The reel screamed. A trout can run so far and no farther on the first run, and not as far on the second. This one could not make it to the brush pile. When I lifted the net with the trout's head deep in the bag, it was time for rejoicing.

It broke what had been a sulphur dry-fly barrier for me, a fish better than 20 inches. There was the additional satisfaction of a successful culmination of my plan.

This incident reminds me of a similar one, but one that involved just luck and no plan.

The late April Hendrickson hatch on the Yellow Breeches is good in a 15-mile stretch and poor or nonexistent above and below this belt. Most of the fishing, and certainly the best of it, is with the daytime emergence of duns, as opposed to the evening fall of spinners.

I was at a section we called McEddie's, because it was located between Harry B. McCormick's and Eddie Jones's property. This is rather big wader water, and at this point the stream flows through a wooded area. Every here and there is overhead cover for the trout in the form of a fallen tree or brush pile.

High water had undermined a small streamside elm, which consequently fell, then held perpendicular to the flow. The backwater from the damming effect made an ideal feeding position on the upstream side of the trunk, and the line of drift was good and narrow because it flowed over part of the trunk but was diverted by a brush pile at the branches.

Located in this narrow path about 1 foot under the surface were two forms, which looked like torpedoes when my sunglasses cut the glare. Obviously the fish were in a surface-feeding position. One had to put up with the invasion of his sanctuary and feeding position by the other, I thought. Maybe the invader would be the more greedy of the two. There were some Hendrickson duns making their long floats before becoming airborne. Unquestionably these two fish were aware of them.

I could not get at the two from the bank above, and it was too deep to wade into a casting position from midstream at this section. But it was possible to cast across the log from the bank below. Either one of these trout was too big and strong to be directed, at first.

My special Hendrickson with the dirty-yellow body was set into action. The kickback cast dropped it lightly to the surface about 3 feet in front of the two trout. Cockily, the dark wings started on their downstream path. I could see everything. The trout on the left moved to its right to come under the fly in an upward slant.

The trout on the right broke to its left in order to beat the other to it. I did not see the usual dimple; instead there was a boiling surge.

When I lifted the tip, it was met with a throbbing resistance. For me no sensation in angling equals this. The hooked fish responded by jumping out of the water. Then, in a frenzy it lunged downstream over the shallow water that flowed over the log.

I did not have to force the fight in this eccentric battle—in fact, I couldn't have. The lightninglike bolt carried the fish downstream, away from trouble and past me. This was not a case of skilled management; it was sheer luck! The trout could no longer tear into the heart of trouble. There was no terrific climax. The heavy fish was readily netted. It was the best trout I ever caught on the Hendrickson hatch. By all rights it should have been one of the most difficult to land, but instead it was among the easiest.

The competition of feeding sometimes takes another form. Now and then I have fished a well-managed stream section that flows through a wooded area. Those who have developed it left no stone unturned to produce the best possible angling. They have even gone to the extremes of drilling wells and pumping water to increase the stream volume, and in the coldest weather they pellet feed under the ice when food is scarce. The pools are stocked periodically from adjacent propagation troughs. Only brook trout may be killed; the browns are reserved for sport.

The typical pool in this stream has a deep channel on one side where, in spots, the bank is high; there is an edge of shallow water on the other side where the bank gently slopes to the water's edge. Home for the trout is the deep channel where they line up, but because of the number of trout resting there it is a poor feeding location. When it comes time to feed, each fish, usually one at a time, breaks away from the chain and assumes a feeding position away from the rest, off to the side in the shallows. In this location they are vulnerable to an artificial ant, jassid, or floating green worm, even though it is difficult to tempt a fish in the lineup at the same time. The difference may be an alert, feeding fish as opposed to lethargic, slumbering ones. Just because fish can't close their eyes does not mean they don't sleep. After all, as humans, we can't close our ears, yet we sleep.

This breakaway-from-the-pack type feeding can be seen in the regulated section of the Little Lehigh near Allentown, Pennsylvania, particularly in the upper half, when the water is clear and visibility is good. I would rather take my chances with the singles in the shallows off to the side than with the concentrations in the deeper water, tempting as the latter may be.

# 19
# Night Fishing
# for Big Trout

Normally it is a watershed or a stream that is responsible for the development of effective methods, rather than the other way around, the fishermen; but there is an instance where a single pool was responsible for this. The famed Goodsell Hole of the Allegheny River was illuminated by the street lights of Coudersport, Pennsylvania. The town pool spawned the most sophisticated night-fishing methods imaginable; it spawned flytiers; it spawned dedicated anglers who cast night after night; and over the years it may have produced the greatest tonnage of big trout in the fly-fishing history of any pool anywhere. Here was the exacting feeding grounds where night fishing experienced its most severe growing pains. The day when the dictates of some engineer were followed and the place was altered beyond recognition some strong men literally shed tears and figuratively cried out in anguish.

Still living are two of the group of old-time regulars, plus a fellow townsman who fished with them as a boy. Left are some pictures, an angling diary, some news clippings, and a glow in memory lane. The youth has grown into a competent writer and outdoor authority who is torn between two loves, grouse hunting and trout fishing; and, if I may be the judge, the warmest spot in his heart is reserved for night fishing for big trout.

Lack of knowledge and experience disqualifies me from writing on this subject, for my total catch of big trout taken on night flies can be counted on the fingers of one hand, yet the subject commands a nook in a trout book; thus I have asked the expert, Jim Bashline, a graduate of the Goodsell School, and the person I regard as the foremost authority on night fishing, its history and its tradition, to contribute this chapter—his chapter. The sections in parentheses that follow are quotes from the old diary of R. H. Pinney or remarks attributed to him by other fishermen who knew this pioneer, after-dark, fly fisherman for trout.

## THE NIGHT WATCH
### *By L. James Bashline*

The sun was down. The light which illuminated the huge clock in the court house steeple was turned on. From several directions came figures carrying fly rods, already strung up, with jiggling wet-fly droppers dancing in cadence with each step. For this group the evening meal was over, any important worries had been laid aside for tomorrow, the important business was coming up.

The script might change a bit this night, but the stage setting would not. Mr. Grennels was the first to arrive and he would take his place at the flagstone wall on the Mill Creek entrance to the pool. Bob Pinney would make his appearance on the south side of the Allegheny, survey the pool momentarily and then carefully wade across the slick tail water to his driftwood bench on the opposite side of the stream. P. C. Cauffiel, the angling lawyer who never, or hardly ever, fished could be counted on to show up just at dark to offer his advice on all and sundry questions. P. C. lived nearby and through the years became known as a sort of Goodsell Hole gillie emeritus. Others soon followed and their appointed locations were occupied with a minimum of conversation. Darkness would come with finality, and while other fishermen were reeling up, this silent entourage prepared to play the deadly game that was their specialty. Trout, big trout, was what they sought, and frequently their search was not in vain. The pool they fished, known as the Goodsell Hole, was made for night fishermen—or was it the other way around?

Night fishing for trout undoubtedly was practiced in other parts of the United States and the world prior to 1918 but conversations with historically inclined fishermen lead me to believe that Coudersport, Pennsylvania, was in this respect a most unique fishing town.

In the center of this maple-shadowed little village, which is located near the New York State border, the headstream of the Allegheny River and another stream, with the overused name of Mill Creek, joined forces. The pool formed by their junction has been known as the Goodsell Hole since 1865. During that year a carpenter and builder, Nelson H. Goodsell by name, erected a planing mill at the edge of the pool. A splash dam and a series of water locks provided hydraulic power for the operation. Exactly what year the mill ceased to operate is not certain, but it was lost forever in 1928 as the result of a fire. Nelson Goodsell did not know what would be in store for the pool which would bear his name, but he was a fisherman of sorts. Old newspaper records reveal that he did catch a speckled trout weighing 2 pounds 10 ounces in June 1876 in the pool behind his mill. Brown trout being an unknown creature in this country at that time, his fish for Pennsylvania waters was certainly something to talk about.

("Father, used to do some night fishing for speckled trout before 1900 and he made out alright. Wasn't much point to it though, the brook trout were so plentiful at that time a man could catch any amount of them during the day on wet flies.")

The exact date that brown trout first appeared on the Pennsylvania angling scene is difficult to establish. Some private ponds and independent trout culturists had small numbers of them sometime before they were stocked in any quantity by the conservation agencies. But it is generally accepted that about the period of the First World War the big dark-spotted fish started to make their appearance.

They were viewed with a great deal of suspicion by most trout fishermen. They seemed to reproduce well, they grew fast, they fought hard—but, they were much more difficult to catch than their brook trout cousin. Three small wet flies cast haphazardly downstream was standard procedure for the average-sized 10-inch brook trout. These brown fellows, it was quickly discovered, would have no part of this approach. Of course when the dry fly took the country by storm a few years later and the anglers were spun around to fish upstream, some browns started to wind up in the creel.

It must be admitted that the bait fishermen soon learned how to fool the brownie. Big minnows, night crawlers, and soft-shell crabs were all found to be good brown trout baits. The bigger trout particularly were found to be fond of these meaty offerings.

The fly fishermen were disturbed, however; they just could not interest the larger fish with their feathers. To be sure, an occasional big one made a trip to the surface and committed the fatal mistake. This was, however, all too infrequent to be satisfactory.

("The first brown trout that we saw here in this part of Pennsylvania were handsome fish. An array of X-shaped black or dark brown splotches dotted their sides and the little red spots looked like flecks of blood.")

As the numbers of brown trout continued to increase in the Allegheny (they were reproducing exceptionally well) a strange phenomenon was observed. Beginning about the tenth of June, trout would commence to move out of the deep holding meadow pools of the Allegheny and begin an upstream migration of sorts. (Experiments with tagged fish later proved that some of these fish traveled at least 22 miles for two consecutive seasons.) Many theories have been offered to explain this migration, but perhaps the best one is that a lack of oxygen in the more morose pools that lie downstream from Coudersport force the trout to seek better-aerated water. There were several pools on the way to Coudersport that would hold trout for a time, but the Goodsell Hole was the principal "way station." The whirlpool action in the center of this junction was to the trout's liking and here the fish would pause before making another upstream dash.

Doctor Phillips, a sometime practicing dentist and an incurable angler, was most interested in this trout migration. Doc was a good fisherman. He had caught his share of the native brookies that were so abundant in the many mountain streams of the north central area of Pennsylvania, but these brown trout were most curious indeed. He caught one of them from time to time, but not with the regularity that he wished for.

Doc, as was the style of the day, fished with a string of three #10 or 12 wet flies. We cannot be certain whether it was by design or by chance that he stayed on one night and gave an honest try with these little wets. Whatever the circumstances, he did persist, and a few seasons of serious after-dark experimentation proved to the doctor that night fishing was more than simply a way of losing sleep.

The idyllic part of Doc's fishing life was that his wife was a most accomplished flytier. She did not fish herself, but Doc more than made up for her lack of practical information. We can only assume the private conversations that took place when a new pattern was being developed.

Doctor Phillips' "secret," his fishing technique for taking brown trout at night, was discovered by the local angling talent in due time, and a page of angling history in America began to be written.

("Doc Phillips caught a lot of fish but I can't ever recall of him catching a real whale. Plenty of 16- and 18-inchers, hundreds of them, but I don't believe he ever caught a 2-footer. Of course, Doc never got to using the 4s and the 6s. He liked the smaller flies, I think 10 was as big as he used. Most of the big trout, that is, fly-caught fish that came from the Goodsell were taken on 6s.")

For the next thirty years, the Goodsell Hole probably outproduced any similar area of water in the United States. The fantastic concentration of trout, the select dozen or so night fishermen who were developed there, and the ideally laid out pool created a combination that yielded an annual harvest of several hundred trophy fish! We are talking about fish above the 20-inch mark.

The conformation of the pool changed a bit each year as the result of high water and shifting gravel bars, but seldom was the pool ever more than 75 feet in diameter. From season to season the pool generally retained its circular shape. The pair of incoming streams averaged about 20 feet across, and the escaping tail-water formed a flow that to many would be termed a "brook." During the peak of the night-fishing season, this tail would seldom exceed 30 feet in width. Depth of the pool in its center was accurately sounded at just over 12 feet, although this did vary somewhat from spring to spring.

I wasn't fishing the Goodsell during the early night-fishing "experimental days," in fact, I wasn't even born. To make up for this oversight on the part of my parents, Lady Luck arranged for me to become friendly with some of the Goodsell "greats." That I became friendly with this group of specialists at the outset is not really a true statement. This process took some years, and the initial barrier to bridge was convincing the regulars that I was sincerely interested in fishing. To prove this and to be accepted it was necessary to come to the shrine night after night after night. I count those apprentice years as among my happiest, for, as a teenager, life itself meant fishing.

The most skillful of my mentors and a continually studying post-graduate himself was Robert N. Pinney. Bob had remained a bachelor, for he sincerely believed that anyone who enjoyed fishing should not be distracted by anything so trivial as marriage. His almost photographic memory (he could quote verbatim whole chapters from Skues) could have secured for him a most profitable place in the twentieth-century business world. This too would have interfered with his fishing, and he chose to remain a night clerk at the local hotel. This position did not pay too generously, but it did make possible an ideal fishing schedule. Every afternoon and evening were available. Bob made wise use of this time from his standpoint, and it is most doubtful if any living man ever knew a single piece of water as well as Pinney knew the Goodsell Hole.

("Wives that get along well with fishermen are hard to find. I never took much time out to look, so I didn't find one.")

Although he grew to prefer big wets after dark, he was equally skilled in the use of floating feathers by day. He was probably the first angler to cast a dry fly, that is, one tied for that purpose, on northern Pennsylvania waters. He obtained his first floaters from Hardy of England during the early twenties. Following this initial experience with floating flies Pinney evolved into a split purist—dry flies would be fished during the daylight hours, and large wets would be used after dark. He never deviated for the balance of his life.

As in most pools, trout of the Goodsell Hole had two preferred feeding stations. A few trout took up position at the two inlets of the pool and the remainder drifted toward the slick tail glide as evening approached. As a rule the daytime bait fanciers preferred the inlet locations, while Pinney and others who cast the big wet flies found the tail water better suited to their talents.

It would be entirely possible to fill several volumes recalling famous catches of trout that came from this tiny trout factory by means of Pinney's fly rod. But the simple truth is that such episodes sound preposterous. I would find them so myself if I had not had the opportunity to fish this piece of water for nearly ten years. During that period I observed Pinney successfully land over fifty trout which exceeded the 20-inch mark, and several hundred under that length. In addition to these fish, six other permanent or semipermanent regulars at the pool were chalking up similar tallies. Did such a place exist in Pennsylvania? And if it did, why wasn't the news widely broadcast throughout the East? Two big reasons form the answer. The Goodsell devotees were not about to share their fishing with the crushing mob (they probably wouldn't have had to anyway, which leads us to reason number two) which is, there are very few fly-rod owners who have the required temperament to stick out the fishless nights until their efforts are rewarded. Even the mighty Goodsell Hole, which was a night fisherman's paradise, spawned but a dozen case-hardened veterans. But what a dozen they were! Innovators all, each one developing and constantly improving on his favorite method of capturing big trout.

While the Goodsell was their first love and the home base for most of them, all of the disciples did on occasion fish other waters of the area. An authentic-sounding rumor of a big trout in a certain pool of the Oswego, Sinnemahoning, or the Genesee was often reason enough for one of them to forgo an evening at the shrine to have a go at it elsewhere—at night, naturally. But no matter how strong the lure of exotic waters and faraway places, the Goodsell Hole commanded their strongest attention. And why not? On any June or July night they could be positive of casting their flies over twenty-five or thirty 2-footers. And if they were fortunate enough to remove some of these fish, the following night would see several more take their places. Trout-rich as the Goodsell was, it was most decidedly true that these fish were first of all *brown trout*. And as brown trout are everywhere, they were not caught with impudence on each and every cast. Nor were they always certain to strike on any given night. They reacted as anglers the world over expect brown trout to act—selective, sophisticated, and unpredictable.

It was my extreme good fortune to list Robert N. Pinney as a close friend. Hours spent with this angler in fishing and talking about fishing must number in the thousands, and each of these hours is carefully catalogued in my angling treasure book. Anything I have said in the past about night fishing, or will say in the future, is heavily laced with Bob's thinking. It is most unfortunate for anglers that Bob Pinney was not inclined to set his thoughts in article form; there were a diary and pictures, though, to which I have access. Forty years of fly fishing at the Goodsell Hole and other waters of north central Pennsylvania would have produced good copy for today's reading. Pinney is with us no longer. The Goodsell Hole is gone too—in its place is a concrete chute to control floodwaters. But trout still feed at night, and there are some anglers who will search the blackness for them. Let's pursue the subject further.

The willingness of trout and especially big trout to strike large wet flies at night cannot be explained entirely. There are times, of course, when nocturnal hatches of mayflies create a natural feeding condition. *Ephemerella guttulata* is a sometimes night-hatching insect, and so are some of the big *Hexagenias.* June bugs, various types of moths, and several hard-shell insects are also "night runners." This miscellany of surface food satisfies most anglers when attempting to explain the surface rise at night. If no surface food is available and trout are in a feeding pattern, they will search out underwater prey, which takes the form of crayfish, minnows, hellgrammites, burrowing nymphs, and whatever else is available.

The combined experience of many thoughtful night fishermen causes me to wonder if food is always the motivating factor for the rod-banging type of strike that occurs quite frequently at night. Autopsies performed on dozens of large night-caught brown trout revealed that their stomachs were practically if not entirely empty. Natural food was there for the taking, but they would have none of it, and seemed to be waiting for that colorful wet fly to drift close by.

("Last night we took about a dozen big trout from Goodsell's, same kind of night tonight and nothing stirring. I'm sure the moon has something to do with it.")

When considering the flies used in night fishing by the somewhat opinionated artists of north central Pennsylvania, there cannot be a more thought-provoking subject. The patterns that have been proven as effective missiles cannot be considered trout flies in the usual definition that prevails today. A popularity poll of night flies during the era of the Goodsell Hole would have turned up such names as: Montreal Silver, Governor, Silver Doctor, Hardy's Favorite, Professor, Grizzly King, and an assortment of salmon flies with their full regalia of exotic plumage. The famous Yellow Dun would have undoubtedly topped Pinney's list during the early days, but alas its body-material formula has not been duplicated for at least twenty years.

("Mrs. Phillips' Yellow Dun was hard to beat. I don't think there has ever been a fly like it. I tried for years to get Ernest Hillie to come up with the right body material. So far we haven't got it. Maybe we never will.")

This is probably a good place to reflect for a moment on this so-called lost pattern. Much mystical significance was attached to this fly. Some of this legerdemain was justified, for many fishermen who knew of it swore by all that was holy that it was the greatest wet fly ever concocted. That it originated in the vise of Mrs. Phillips is not known for sure, but it was her tie on the leader attached to her husband's rod that won the creation its initial fame. His astounding catches of brook, and later brown trout at night, made such an impression on local fishermen that his wife spent little time tying any other pattern. The fly consisted of lemonwood duckwing, a dark ginger hackle, a snatch of black and white wood duck for a tail, and a fleshy pink-hued fur body. The fur was the secret ingredient, and while many suspect it to be dyed mohair, no one to this date has laid his reputation on the line to absolutely declare it! When dry, the fly might be taken for any ordinary pink-bodied attractor. When wet, the mystic quality became quite evident. The body was pink, and yet it was not. It was a bloody swatch of something alive. Anticipating the day that Mrs. Phillips would no longer be tying this fantastic fish producer, Pinney (and others) laid in a good supply of this pattern. Following her death the storehouse of Yellow Duns was gradually used up. I used a few of these originals myself, and I must admit that it was a most amazing fly. But unfortunately, according to the style of her day the wet flies that the dentist's wife prepared were tied directly to genuine gut snells using eyeless hooks! The gut deteriorated on most of these, and it is doubtful if many of these flies exist today. I managed to salvage two of these original ties, and count them among my most treasured possessions.

("Jimmy, if you could come up with a yellow dun that would match the old one you would become famous. Of course, we couldn't just let everybody have the pattern.")

The bright tinsel-laden flies, such as the Silver Doctor, Professor, and Grizzly King, might possibly be taken for small minnows. The darker patterns, more closely resembling a real insect, can be more easily explained, especially when there has been some surface activity before darkness has completely descended. As with emergence charts, which the daytime anglers dearly love to fool with, there is a preference pattern of sorts that nightfeeding trout seem to follow. The darker, more realistic patterns like the Governor, Hardy's Favorite, and Lead Wing Coachman seem to be the preferred types during the beginning of the night-fly season, which in most eastern states commences about the first week of June. As the season progresses, the flies that produce most of the action become more brilliant. During the last week of July and all of August the silver-bodied flies will outfish the more conservative ones by a wide margin. There is an exception of course (as there must be when trout are concerned) and that occurs when a summer rain swells the stream to several inches above its usual hot-weather depth.

*Night Wet Fly.* In every trout stream there are some fish that have gotten by the anglers to become large, and large trout are mainly nocturnal in their feeding activity. Thus there exists the potential to catch a trophy fish from the hardest-fished streams, but there is a trick to it. The fly should be fished ever so slowly—just enough of hand-twist retrieve for the angler to maintain contact with the fly. The creator of the above juicy-bodied night fly was the late George Phillips, a tremendous trout fisherman. He tied it on a 4/0 hook. The body is orange wool and the wing is wood duck. *Photo by James Fosse.*

On certain nights trout show a marked preference for minnows or crabs, but even then they can usually be coaxed into taking a feathered creation. On most nights, however, if there has been some surface activity, or if the trout are casually fanning in that perplexing summer-doldrum attitude, the serious fly fisherman will be the top rod.

The methods of fishing the big wets at night are similar to those used during the daytime with the added requirement of *constant* attention to the rod-to-hand connection. The most productive routine is a slight quartering cast upstream and while the flies are drifting freely with the current, hand twisting the slack line into loose coils in your left hand. Unless there is considerable surface feeding at night, little fly action is necessary. As a general rule the slower your flies swim through the water the more effective they will be. As in daytime fishing, it is best to keep your rod pointed at the ten o'clock position. This will make it easier to keep in sensitive touch with what's going on at the business end of your cast, and puts your rod in a better striking position.

The rod used for night fishing should first of all have a sensitive tip. That "tip-in-hand" feeling is a most important factor when using flies at night. Weight and length of a good night rod is secondary to subtle tip action. A long whippy rod is not the answer, but rather one of the so-called modern dry-fly rods. These, if made by a good maker, possess resilient tip action but have ample power in the butt section. Not much false casting is done at night, but the weight of the heavier flies will quickly sap the strength of a less noble rod. An 8-foot rod will handle most situations.

The leader for night fishing should be a strong one. During the early days of the Goodsell Hole, and for that matter all American fly fishing, it was customary to use a level leader with dropper loops that accommodated the snelled flies. Some fine night work can still be done with this combination, but a short tapered leader of no more than six feet dropping quickly to OX or about 6-pound test is just about right. Even hard fished-over browns will not show reluctance to latch on to a bit of feathers attached to a heavy leader after dark. They just don't seem to believe that any fisherman is out to fool them at that time. Droppers with a leader of this type can be fashioned by simply extending one end of a blood knot at the midway point on the leader.

The use of a dropper will greatly increase your chances for success after dark. Depending on the type of water you are fishing, the dropper should be regulated at a distance from the lead fly so that it will gently "tickle" the surface of the water. It takes a bit of experimentation to determine just where this dropper should be tied on. The character of the water, the speed of your retrieve, and the length of your rod are all factors in deciding where to attach the dropper. About 3 feet up from the head fly is a good place to start.

With all types of trout fishing the outstanding fact that seems to emerge time after time is the inability of the fisherman to predict anything with any degree of accuracy. The vast bulk of my night-fishing experience has been practiced on the waters of the upper Allegheny and predominantly on the Goodsell Hole. After that wonderful place passed into limbo, the victim of progressive thinkers, I was forced to find some other waters that would provide after-dark sport. While nothing matched the Goodsell for sheer numbers of fish, lessons learned there have proved to be valuable in selecting other pools that might offer night-fishing possibilities. Fishing techniques that worked on the Allegheny have worked other places as well.

To generalize, we could observe that the best locations to night fish are the tails of deep pools and the intersections of small spring runs and larger streams. The primary reason that trout and especially big trout frequent the tail races is that food is more plentiful there and can be looked over with ease. The fisherman does not often spot big trout in these locations during the daytime simply because this position is much too vulnerable for them. In larger streams that are inclined to become a bit warm during the summer months, the small spring entrance to such waters is a natural. The lower water temperature, which means more oxygen, draws trout like a magnet. They too like to be comfortable.

All serious trout fishermen know the value of familiarity with the stream they intend to fish. Successful night fishing requires that you know the pools intimately. The depth of the water, the velocity of the current, and every snag should be memorized. The student night fisherman will still be hung up considerably—it's part of the learning process. To distinguish a snag from the strike of a good fish is learned by doing and no amount of words will ever explain it. When to strike back at night is probably the most difficult part of the game. At times the strike of a fish will feel like a gentle "pull" on the rod tip. This type of strike is most common when the flies are being retrieved slowly at a depth of 2 feet or more. Again, the strike may be described as a sharp "tap" on the line. This strike may be chub or shiner trying to tackle something too big for his size, and then again it could be a big brown sampling the bright feathers. The real earthshaker strike and the one that usually brings about the conversion of a nonbeliever is the slashing jab that occurs when the flies are being fished on or near the surface. This kind of strike usually occurs when the trout are doing some surface feeding and is usually done with such positiveness that there can be no mistake about what is happening. With any strike (or possible strike) after dark when using the big wet flies, it is good insurance to "give 'em the iron." The flies you use for this kind of business are much larger than the daytime counterparts and require a stiff jerk to be fastened in the mouth of a coarse-jawed brown.

("When the big browns are really taking after dark, they don't fool around. They hang on to the fly for a second or so and this gives you plenty of time to strike.")

It comes as a considerable shock to many dry fliers that trout, particularly brown trout, can be lured to such flamboyant concoctions as a Silver Doctor, a Professor, or the salmon tie of the Jock Scott. To these fellows anything larger than a #14 Light Cahill is regarded as saltwater tackle and decidedly not the sort of thing that a well-educated brown would be interested in. Some of the better night patterns do not remotely suggest any natural food. Why do trout take them after dark? It's fun to speculate—it may be out of hunger, sheer curiosity, or anger. But they do work with astonishing regularity. Twenty years of night fishing with the big wet flies has resulted in the theory that a good night pattern should contain at least one of three ingredients. These are peacock herl, silver or gold tinsel, and a bit of red. The red can take the form of a spray of crimson topping, a wool tag, or perhaps a red tail.

A rough-shod analysis arrives at these conclusions: peacock herl offers an iridescent sheen that is not available on any other feather. Peacock-herl-bodied flies have always been good daytime producers. It isn't too scientific perhaps, but the material just looks "buggy." Tinsel, of course, adds some glitter that might suggest small minnows. The red can be explained by the fondness that nearly all game fish display for the color of blood The color in nature usually means a wounded and helpless creature that can be easily captured. However, the trout apparently want their blood in just the right quantity, for an all-red fly seems to kill the idea. Have you ever caught a trout on the Scarlet Ibis?

("Next to the Yellow Dun, my choices would be the Silver Doctor, the Governor, and the Professor. The Professor was a great favorite of Eddie Cauffield and he took a lot of big trout from the Goodsell on it.")

In most places where trout are found today there is night fishing to be had. The most unique facet of the sport is that some of the very best of after-dark angling is to be had on the most hard-fished waters. Civilized waters take such a terrific pounding during the day that the larger and wiser fish have become acclimated to late-hour dining. The heavily fished eastern waters also become quite warm during the summer months and do not cool off until the sun-searing rays have passed behind the nearest hill. In water that reaches the 70°-mark trout tend to become sluggish and do not respond well to any offering. Darkness and the resulting fall in temperature often turns the switch for feeding activity, and the angler who sticks it out will often be pleasantly surprised.

This discussion has dealt completely with the use of big wets after dark. This undoubtedly has caused a bit of fretting on the part of some who prefer their feathers to float. I, too, enjoy casting the floater and at times their use after dark can certainly be justified. But the added problems of trying to keep a dry fly floating at night and the difficulty in even seeing it are indeed something to consider. The big wets are easier to control, cover the water better, and the combined experience of the Goodsell Hole clan leans heavily in favor of the sunken fly. Pinney, who probably logged more night-fishing hours than any fisherman ever has or ever will, operated under the assumption that big trout wanted a big mouthful; and that's just what the #4, 6, and 8 wets offer.

("I once took a 2-footer on a big #2 Fiery Brown salmon fly. It was a whole handful of feathers but that big brown trout took it just like he ate one every day. Did the same thing on a 1/0 brown Palmer. Of course, this isn't the rule. I like #6 best of all.")

Fishing after dark has an aura of mystic charm. Nighttime

adventures always seem to offer an extra bit of excitement and flavor—and so it is for the after-dark angler. It also has the special attraction of being uncrowded and, in these days of tank trucks and elbow-to-elbow fishing, loneliness while fishing is something to be sought and cherished. Not all fishermen have that extra unexplainable compulsion to seek their prey at night. It's a tough game that will never draw a horde of followers. The dedicated night man is a trophy fisherman. He fishes for the love of the game, and he seeks only to sink his hook into a fish capable of putting a bend of consequence into his rod.

# 20

# *Winter Fly Fishing*

In the spring, in the summer, and in the fall trout are individualistic creatures of nature. Tabbing their habits and food requirements with generalities is but to deceive oneself. There are
those fish that will surface feed at every provocation and those
that never or rarely feed on top. Some choose shallow water; some
like it deep. Some work at night; some by day. There were two big
trout that, while feeding, wiggled their way in and out of a dense
bed of weeds for months on end. There was another large one that
swam around a bend at the same light time each afternoon for
weeks. There are the Japanese beetle eaters and those that won't
touch them. After considerable trout watching for many open
seasons, either with or without a fly rod for company, it has been
demonstrated to me that trout are creatures of habit, but the
habits of individuals vary. But how about trout in winter? I knew
very little about winter trout fishing, but I *thought* I knew what to
do; and individual preference did not enter into my thinking.

Because of a change of state regulations in the stream running
by my house, I was enabled to indulge in some postspawning-
season trouting—winter fly fishing. Until the advent of regulated
fishing areas in which there is no closed season, I did not know
anybody who knew anything about such a practice. It simply was
not done in our parts, although this was not the case everywhere.
Some of us considered the very act of casting a fly in a trout steam
out of season as illegal, whereas others argued that so long as you
did not have a trout in your possession all was well. We never
heard of anyone being checked anywhere by a warden while in-

dulging in this questionable practice, but it would have been interesting to know what would have happened next. Possibly it would have varied with the individual officer. Had a so-called culprit been apprehended, the justice of the peace, no doubt, would have backed the warden, found the defendant guilty of something, and levied a fine and costs. The alternatives for such action are: pay or go to the expense and trouble of appealing the ruling in the county court. Locally there had never been a test case to establish a precedent.

It reminded me of fox hunting on Sunday in Pennsylvania. It is illegal to hunt in this state on the Sabbath, but it is legal to run dogs and shoot predators on Sunday, and the fox had been classified as a predator. In this instance, too, there had never been a test case, those concerned being satisfied with the status quo.

Each fall it had become my custom to do two things. First, I freshened up some trout spawning beds with additional river gravel; then I went musky fishing until the waters were locked up under ice. Until January of 1974, I simply waited impatiently for the trout season to open, the traditional Pennsylvania date being April 15—"New Year's Day." Henceforth it would be different. So I purchased a '74 license early in January and set forth.

My first and only inclination was to show the trout something big, bright, and heavy, so I fished slowly and deeply, even though to me this type of fishing lacks the appeal of the small-fly fine-leader game.

I went to the head of the meadow well above the house, intending to fish my way downstream half a mile, to the end of the regulated area, and I had expectations of moving some good fish.

Attached to the sinking line was a leader tipped out to 3X at the end of which was a Craighead streamer fly. I thought that the silver tinsel body in combination with the white and black Broma feather wing, lit up with the yellow hackle and red marabou tail, would interest the trout.

The first trout-fishing day of the new angling year was beautiful—clear, calm, bright, and above freezing. It was good to be outside and at it again. I wended my way upstream in order to fish my way through two long meadows.

The minnowlike Craighead streamer was highly visible in the

clear water and, when given a little rod-tip action, it appeared to be alive. I knew it would be seen by a good number of fish, including some big browns. Casting with the fly rod again was like coming back home.

Time passed and distance was covered. To my consternation and surprise, nothing was hooked and very little showed. In 300 yards there were two lazy rolls, and neither trout would come back for another look. I continued to cast and cast. Things were not going well. It was becoming monotonous. Obviously it was time to change a losing game.

I took off the bright Craighead streamer fly. In its place went one of Dave Whitlock's realistic freshwater sculpins. This fly, since its introduction here by Jim Bashline three years ago, had proved its worth, particularly for dusk and dawn fishing. It is a good imitation of the darter or miller's thumb, which abounds in this water. I fished it slowly and carefully from one end to the other of the second meadow, but this was not the time for this big deceiver fly. As I was working my way along, fish that were in shallow water over the weeds were being disturbed. They would see me before I would see them and away they'd go, leaving only their telltale wakes.

I stopped fishing, went back to the house for my polarized glasses and field glasses, then returned to walk and look—all of which should have been done in the first place. The main question was, what are these fish doing in the shallows over the weeds? Are they feeding there, or simply sunning themselves?

The stream itself looks different in the winter than in the other three seasons of the year. Beds of the water weed elodea are submerged in the winter, pushed down by algae and the constant flow. It was over these shallow beds that the trout were located. Close inspection revealed that they were on the feed. Invariably the tail came up, the head went down, and when they righted themselves, the gills would work as if they were chewing. Their food had to be either freshwater shrimp or sowbugs or both.

I did two things on the next rough winter day, which was not long in coming. I turned to my angling library in the hope, if not expectation, of finding information relative to winter fly fishing for trout, either in English or American literature. If it did not stand out big and bold, it could be hidden in the long shadows of time. The only thing that showed up in my search was accounts of wet-fly fishing for grayling in English chalk streams, with no mention of trout. It appeared that winter trouting over the generations had been taboo, although I did not know why.

Several years ago my friend Al Troth, a schoolteacher, flytier, and photographer from Montoursville, Pennsylvania, along the Loyalsock, had showed me a special creation, his conception of a well-tied wet shrimp. In the meantime Al had made the jump from the northern tier mountains of his native state to the spring creek section of Montana, where his shrimp had been responsible for hooking many large trout. Knowing that his address was Dillon, I sent forth my SOS. "Send me a couple dozen of your fine shrimp," I pleaded on paper, "and while you are at it, include your conception of a cressbug" (sowbug).

In the meantime I studied the trout and experimented with movement into casting position. Always it was the same. The fish would root in the shallow weed—head down, tail up—then pick up something and chew. These fish did not stay in one position; rather they slowly worked their way upstream about six feet, only to drop back and start up again. When one got too close to the next, there was a jealous chase, and the intruder was made to respect the territorial integrity of the established trout.

Now and then there was a fight between two brown trout of equal size. The two combatants would slowly swim upstream about 15 inches apart. Suddenly for no apparent reason there would be a wild swirl, each going for the other's tail. This occurrence was common in the month following spawning season, which was January. Apparently there is a shuffle of position after the trout leave the redds. Once a trout assumes a home base, it is jealously guarded against all comers of the same size and smaller. In the claiming of homes, size predominates, just as is the case with spawning mates.

The winter channel in this stream section averages about 25 feet in width, although it is not that wide in the summer when the weeds protrude. It was very difficult to approach within casting distance of the fish on the caster's side. In the shallow water they were both shy and observant. If the approach did not scare them out, the first cast usually did. Fish on the opposite side were something else again. They continued to feed as I slowly moved into position and then cast to them.

In short order the flies from Al Troth arrived and there followed weeks of fishing and experimentation. As long as it was above 32° and the line did not freeze in the guides and there was no wind, fishing was pleasant.

It became my practice to give the two Troth flies about even fishing time. They both fished best when cast to drift naturally into the feeding fish. If a trout would not take the first fly, it was shown the second. In due time I struck upon roll casting with a quick mend of the line. By so doing, the leader remained wet, the fly juicy, and there was a longer natural drift. Fishing was especially interesting because the fish could be spotted, then watched. Polarized glasses were a part of the equipment.

I had the time and inclination for experimentation, which is a fascinating part of angling. In due time two more flies, very different in style and in the manner of fishing them, were added to the winter fishing repertoire; and what may seem strange is that one is a dry fly.

George Harvey's #20 Olive Horse-collar Nymph has a ginger hackle-wisps tail and a chenille neck. When it is cast to a rooting fish on the caster's side, which is straight downstream, and the angler stays well back making a long cast, the trout take it when it is given lively action from the rod tip. Possibly in size, shape, and action it looks like a pair of hooked-up shrimp swimming upstream. (Some shrimp have the odd habit of clinging together all the time while others among them go their own individual way.)

The other winter fly that I have come to use is a tiny Black Spider, with a gold tinsel body and no tail. I discovered that if this is floated for a few drifts over a subsurface-feeding trout, about half the time the fish takes note and often sips in the fly. Possibly this is the counterpart of the LaBranche theory of creating a hatch.

The digestive process of a trout is controlled by body temperature, which is the same as water temperature. This means that in winter a trout will not eat as much or as often as it does in warmer water, thus eliminating large nymphs, crayfish, and small fish as a part of the cold-weather diet. I have not fished a freestone mountain stream in the winter, but from what has transpired in meadow streams it would appear that here, too, winter fly fishing for trout is a small-fly, light-leader game.

Nineteen seventy-four ushered in for me a new winter sport, much to my delight—one I hope to continue to pursue in the future.

# 21

# Maybe It Is Spring

The adage that one swallow does not make a spring is generally accepted, literally and figuratively. One thing, though: it is more convincing to one who sees the swallow than to the one who is limited to a hearsay report about one. Figuratively speaking, I have seen a swallow. The question is, is it a harbinger of things to come?

The '66 trout season had more than one month to go when I read the initial draft of Jim Bashline's chapter on night fishing. The great Pinney of Goodsell Hole fame had ingrained into Jim's young mind the concept that the dropper fly is the important one of the cast of two night flies and that its action should be to skim or cut the surface of the water.

In the waning part of a trout season my mind often wanders to New Brunswick or Quebec rivers where body and soul are located in the latter part of September for the big fishing fling of the year. When the salmon river is low, clear, and relatively warm, it has become our camp practice to show the fish a low-water, #8 wet fly tied to the leader with the Portland hitch. This odd connection makes a single fly skim across the surface just as Pinney in his day would have his dropper wet fly behave for trout. I got to thinking about trout and salmon and Pinney and the Portland hitch all at the same time. "Humm," was the reaction. In a stream such as the one I fish so much, one stands on one side and casts across to the grassy edge of the other bank. With the two-fly cast it is not possible to fish the important dropper fly in the tight zone against the opposite undercut bank and overhanging grass, but . . . "Hummm."

Obviously there are two possible things to be tried: fish with one fly attached to the leader with the Portland hitch à la Lee Wulff salmon fishing or throw the hitch on the tail fly to force it to skim the surface, too, the way the dropper can be made to do. How would it work? There was only one way to find out. However, in this stream, where there are weeds, a cast of two flies is an abomination when a fish is hooked.

Some years ago I had read about the Portland or riffling hitch in the writings of Lee Wulff but could not tie or apply it until Lee himself demonstrated to me exactly what must be done. After the fly is attached to the leader in the normal manner (Turle knot in my case) a half hitch is thrown around the tying silk at the head, then a second is put right in back of the first to act as a wedge. The pair of hitches is not on the top of the fly, nor is it on the bottom; it is on the side, and the proper side at that. If the wing is upstream and the hook point and bend downstream as the fly crosses the current, it is hitched up correctly. To accomplish the job I hold the fly, as I stand in the stream, just as I want it to ride on the surface, then from this position throw on the two half hitches.

The singular aspect implied in the name Portland hitch had at first thrown me off. Experience quickly demonstrated that a single hitch loses its hold and soon slips away to nothing. Later experience demonstrated that the double half hitch, on the other hand, holds indefinitely.

This method of presentation was a child of necessity born in Newfoundland. The story behind the Portland hitch as told by Lee Wulff in his great work, *The Atlantic Salmon,* is fascinating:

> No one now at Portland Creek claims to have been the originator of the riffling fly, but here is the accepted story. Long ago, warships of the British navy anchored off the stream and officers came ashore to fish. They left a few old-style salmon flies, which had a loop of twisted gut wrapped to the straight shanked hook to make the eye.
>
> Soft and pliable when in use, the loop enabled the fly to ride more smoothly on its course and avoided the stiffness and canting which accompanied any solid attachment of the stout leader to the eyed fly. But the gut loops grew weak with age, and many a good salmon, when hooked on an old and cherished fly, broke away with

the steel and feathers. To play'er safe, anglers often gave away old flies. To most recipients they were Trojan horses. Only to the Portland Creekers were they a boon.

Quickly realizing that a salmon hooked on a gut-looped fly was likely to break free, they made sure the fly would stay on by throwing those hitches around the shank behind the wrapping. The fact that the fly skimmed instead of sinking bothered them not in the least, for they were practical fishers of the sea. They fished the flies on spruce poles with makeshift reels or none at all. They cast them out and drew them back. And because they had no proper flies with which to fish they developed a new technique.

The first time out on a trout stream with the Portland hitch, I chose to start with a low-water #8 Black Dose attached to a 2X leader point and cast with a 9-foot heavy trout rod. If nothing else, I reasoned, this will be better conditioning for the wrist and hand prior to the long hard days of forthcoming salmon fishing than the normal use of the midge rod on trout. The initial start was in good

*The Riffled Hitch.* There is reason to picture a low-water Atlantic salmon wet fly in a trout book. When attached to the leader on the side of the head with two half hitches, so the bend of the hook is downstream while being fished, this becomes a great night fly for big brown trout. The hitches on the side of the head over the tying silk lift the eye and make the fly plane across the surface while being drawn by hand-twist retrieve and lift of the rod tip. This riffled hitch for salmon fishing was popularized by Lee Wulff, eminent angler. There are a few anglers now applying this to trout. *Photo by James Fosse.*

light, between sundown and dusk so there could be some visual trial-and-error experimentation before it was too dark to see everything.

The fly made a little spat when it hit the surface of the water beside the grassy bank some 25 feet away, then disappeared under the surface. A lift of the rod elevated the eye of the fly, making it climb to the surface where it slipped along like a tiny aquaplane at the apex of a little riffled V. Even though cast downstream, the course of the swimming fly was pretty much crosscurrent. For all the world it looked like a living, swimming thing. The way the fly surfaced and swam was attention getting and attention holding. So intent was I upon observing the lifelike action that the watery explosion at the fly was startling. That sort of thing was not anticipated until after dark. My answering reaction was received by emptiness. In spite of no hooked fish, here was something significant: the Portland hitch had attracted a trout, not scared it, and what I consider a sophisticated trout.

Shortly below this spot the Black Dose was lost in a willow limb. The fly used to replace the first one had a green hair wing, yellow hackle, and a silver tinsel body. Pinney might have approved of this, for he liked bright tinsel-bodied night flies.

By this time it was dark. Below the willow limb it happened again—the same kind of rise form, the same result. Like the first, this fish had come short and would not come back. When this fly was lost a little later in an unseen limb, I called it a night.

Normally at dusk the wakes of cruising trout are evident, a hallmark of this stream, and here was a good night for that. The time can be dated, for it was the last evening of the record-breaking heat wave of '66. It would be interesting to find out if the Portland hitch would produce when the cruisers are abroad.

I switched to a #8 Fiery Brown regular-style tie for the second try. The area fished for an hour was the stream section close to my house. Two fish took the fly in a rather violent manner, both being caught and each a little better than 1 pound. Thus, the ice was broken for me for trout on the Portland hitch.

Prior to evening number three of the experiment, there was a development. John Rex, with whom I was going salmon fishing in September, is a confirmed Portland hitch man for the very good reason that this method accounted for all of his fish on his first fling at salmon the year before. We had talked about a balanced tie, one with a wing on the top and another wing on the bottom. This, we agreed, when hitched should present a better silhouette than the standard wet fly; it should surface quicker and it should plane better at a reduced speed than the unbalanced fly. Thus he tied two Fiery Browns with two wings each, specifically to be fished the Lee Wulff salmon method, but for trout. He hitched up the one and I the other. That night he raised two fish, which slashed at his offering without accepting it.

From thence John introduced the two-wing hitched fly to stream smallmouth bass and assorted panfish. They liked it both by day and by night.

It was about the tenth try for me when something big happened, a fish that turned out to be a burly 20-incher, which after being hooked jumped three times. This brown pounced on the balanced version of the #8 Fiery Brown.

There followed a night when there were four rises to the same fly, three of which were takers.

In the subsequent weeks of the dying trout season it became my custom to fish a 100-yard stretch of the LeTort near the house for about one hour encompassing dusk and dark. A 9-foot rod was set up and kept ready for this purpose, and I stuck right with the two-wing Fiery Brown tied to a leader tipped out to 2X. Usually it would move one or two fish.

For me about sixty minutes of casting constitutes one night of fishing because, after that, excitement and expectation wear down; so I stop before anything depreciates. Furthermore, I have more faith in the first hour of night fishing, believing it to be the best.

I prefer the 9-foot rod to the customary 7½-footer I normally employ, because with it the swimming action of the fly is under better control.

This type of fly fishing is different from night fishing as I had known it. With the hitch one watches the swimming progress of the fly or its mark on the surface. There is a fascination to watching the traveling V with the dark blob at the apex as one slowly and carefully moves along. Take away this visual aspect and something good disappears with it. Stop moving and stand in one place and something desirable stops with it.

I must confess I care little for the mechanical casting of a big wet fly at the head of a pool and the painfully slow handtwist retrieve that is supposed to go with it. Apparently I am not geared right for this, but I am for one hour of slowly moving along and searching out a taker with a hitched fly that can be watched.

A pattern was beginning to form. Usually I could interest a fish or two each night but there was no such thing as a night when there was one strike after another. Four rises represented maximum activity for one session.

About half the time the action on the part of the fish was a surface-breaking pass at the fly but no touching of it; the other half was a business rise. Coming short was more prevalent when it was not dark, whereas the acceptance of the fly prevailed after dark. We learned too that more than just the big trout are looking for food at night, and the common concept was verified that some big fish move out at dusk to indulge in feeding.

Now the burning question is, has this swallow ushered in a spring? My reaction is, "Humm, could be."

# 22

# *Spin, Spinning, Spun*

You and I agree with the sentiments of the English angler, J. R. Harris, as expressed in his book, *An Angler's Entomology:*

> I venture to say that to seek the sportive trout offers greater variation of delights and thrills than can be found in any other class of angling. . . . Having used all kinds of rods, for many decades, I have no hesitation in stating that the acme of fishing is achieved by employing a fly rod for brown trout. . . . Again and again I have heard hard-bitten disciples of the fly rod express their sorrow that they failed too long in partaking of the thrills and pleasures of this alluring sport, so make up your mind not to postpone the happy day.

There are others, mainly members of a new generation of anglers who cut their baby teeth on the lob casting of lures from a fixed spool, who do not understand such feelings, for they know little or nothing of fly fishing. They could not know that the sensations that develop from the strike to a spinning lure and those from the rise to a fly are totally different. They could not know that angling's highest degree of satisfaction stems from deception and the use of the fly rod.

Why worry about the other person? Some are children of fly fishermen, others are friends of fly fishermen; that is why. You see, it does matter for those close to us with whom we want to share sport and whose company we want to enjoy to the fullest.

Since they do not know by experience that there is a more thrilling game than the one they practice and that it is a game that on many occasions is more rewarding, somehow someone should make the point that in desperation they give fly fishing a chance. After all, under certain conditions it is the only way certain fish can be caught, and in a general way the fly does its greatest work in low clear water and that is when the lure is least efficient.

Thus, this chapter is written for the spinning children of fly fishermen and for the spinning friends of fly fishermen, not for the fly fisherman himself. As is the case with nature, a seed can be planted, then at the proper time it will germinate, this to be followed by development and growth. Hence, there follows my effort to sow that they may reap.

## COME ON OVER

"What is one man's meat is another man's poison." On occasion, game fish are hyperselective in their feeding, having been eased into such a groove by the presence of a hatch of aquatic insects, schooled minnows, crustaceans in quantity, windblown terrestrial insects, in fact by an abundance of any available food. And there are times when the water is low and clear, and always under such conditions fished-over game fish become shy. And, too, these situations at times overlap. To some all of this is an intriguing challenge, but to others it is a frustrating curse. The truth of the matter is that under certain conditions game fish can only be taken by the employment of the closest imitation of the natural a craftsman can fabricate; there are times when the use of the finest of leader tippet is vital, and there are occasions and places where the combination of the two is a prerequisite of success.

Under certain circumstances a lurecaster can be the most effective operator of all. This is particularly true in the two fishing extremes: in primitive-area fishing for an unsophisticated quarry, and in civilized sections where the product of the hatchery has just been planted and by necessity there is experimentation in feeding activity. But on certain other occasions the lure situation is hopeless. Furthermore, there are places, such as salmon rivers and privately and publicly regulated waters, where the lure has been outlawed. Thus the spinning enthusiast can be plagued with hard times and bad places. How then does the spincaster meet the challenge of selectivity, the challenge of shy fish in low clear water, and the complication of equipment regulation? He has available a simple and effective remedy. He does it easily and readily, but he must work with about $15 worth of supplementary equipment as he effects a quick on-the-spot conversion.

A spinning rod can do everything. The same cannot be said of a spinning reel. All such rods will cast a fly line; all spinning grips will accommodate a fly reel; and any regular fisherman who has learned to cast with a spinning outfit can learn to handle the same rod in the same efficient manner, but as a fly rod loaded with a fly line.

Fish with an open mind. Selective game fish are a foe of compromise. If there is to be a rule in angling, it could well be the old Bill Tilden tennis maxim: "Always change a losing game." That is the reason for the rebirth of fly fishing after being buried under an avalanche of promotion of a more easily manageable substitute. Let it be assumed that you are a lure fisherman who is interested in the successful application of knowledge and you are one who is interested in improving and increasing ability to master the wide variety of situations presented by nature. Who doesn't derive satisfaction from accomplishment and who doesn't feel remorse at failure? To increase the amount of satisfaction and to decrease the depth of the remorse, you adopt the flexible position of shifting according to demand.

So you are faced with a hopeless situation—that is, hopeless for the lure with which you are casting. In spite of the feeding activity on the part of the game fish you seek, you are reconciled to the fact that your effort is worthless and useless. This is the time to change the losing game. Off comes the spinning reel with its fixed spool and monofilament line and on goes the single-action reel, the fly line, and the nylon leader. This reel goes on the end of the grip in such a position that when the reel is hanging under the rod the reel handle is on the right. The leader is threaded through the guides. The lightweight end strand of the tapered leader is much less conspicuous than the monofilament on the spinning reel.

There is a basic difference in the two kinds of casting. In the case of spinning, one casts the lure, its weight making the cast possible as the line rides along. In the case of the conversion, the line is cast with the fly-casting rod and the leader and fly ride along—totally different principles of delivery.

A 6-weight fly line will fit most of the spinning rods, but in the case of the very sturdy ones a level-8 would be better, and in the case of the lightest, a level-4. The floating nylon type is convenient and practical. Such a line costs approximately $2. Its storage place, a single-action reel, is available for $5 or even less. The 9-foot 3X leader, either with or without knots, plus a little plastic container of 3X nylon and another of 4X, costs about $2. The supply of flies can be very modest: four #14 Orange Fish Hawk wet flies, two #8 Little Yellow Bucktails, and four #16 Adams dry flies. Total bill for supplementary equipment—reel, line, leader, tippets, and flies—is about $15.

If you have a worthy casting instructor you will be doing fine in ten minutes; if you don't it may take twice that long to get the hang of it. The main points are: with gradually accelerated motion, skid, the fly from the surface into a high backcast; hesitate so the line has a chance to straighten in the back, then make the forward cast with gradually accelerated motion. If you care to do so, you can turn your head to watch the backcast. The small dexterities soon blend into each other and readily become automatic, all of which is fun and generates satisfaction.

The first fly casting should be down and across with one of the #14 Orange Fish Hawks or with one of the Little Yellow Bucktails. If perchance the cast is a poor one, the current straightens out the line and leader. The fly crosses the flowing water in an arc. In conjunction with this is a hand-twist retrieve, which is either automatic from the start or at first perplexing. Both my wife and daughter experienced difficulty with this, but I doubt if the majority would. This extra retrieved line is disposed of by shooting it into the cast, utilizing the simple expedient of letting go of the line at the end of the forward cast. The fly lands lightly when cast to a point above the water instead of at the surface.

As the fly makes its swimming swing in the current, the action can be steady or it can be broken into lifelike darts by rod-tip manipulation. The better method for a given time or fish can best be determined by trial and error. After the completion of the arc, the pull on the line by the current makes it easy to skid the fly from the water into a strong high backcast.

Another wet-fly cast can be quickly managed. This one is indispensable for crowded quarters where there is little or no room for a backcast, but is limited to short-line work. Thus it is both possible and fun to fish small waters and confined places where lure casting is well-nigh impossible. It comes in two simple forms.

When the caster wishes to cast quartering downstream while standing on the right side of bank looking downstream, he simply lifts the rod into a vertical position at the completion of the swing of the fly. As the line hangs downward in a lazy arc the rod tip is driven down with a forward motion, just as a nail would be hit with a hammer. In a fascinating manner the line rolls out and the leader turns over to deliver the fly across stream and down.

With the caster on the left side facing downstream, the roll cast starts above the left shoulder, the downstream shoulder, rather than the right. The motion of the rod is backhand, like driving the nail backhanded.

The casting of the wet fly is fun. The arcs that the fly travels cover lots of water, therefore the fly is shown to a maximum number of fish as one slowly works his way downstream. The expected acceptance of the fly comes unexpectedly. More often than not the rise is seen, either a mark on the water or the sight of the back of the fish as it rises to the fly.

A last split-second refusal of the wet fly or bucktail is all part of the game. The question of why is a matter of conjecture, but rejection is common. The general procedure is to show the fish the fly again and, if no sign of interest is manifested by the quarry within a matter of a dozen casts, rest the place and come back later.

In the main, wet-fly fishing is fishing the water, showing the submerged fly to as many fish as possible, a game of attraction by utilizing something made of steel, feathers, fur, and nylon. Most fly fishermen prefer dry-fly fishing; not because wet-fly fishing is not wonderful, but because dry-fly fishing is so very great.

The big inning for the floating imitation of the natural is the bewitching hour from sunset until rises can no longer be discerned amid patterns of black velvet on a silver sheen. That is when the egg-laying aquatic insects return to their river and provide a tremendous supply of protein-laden fish food. Under such a condition, trout are almost always hyperselective, no doubt the reason being because the abundant food is so fine.

But this is not the only time for rising trout. There are periods during the daytime of April and May when trout are given a chance to feed on the subimagos of aquatic insects as they drift on the water before taking wing on their maiden flight. Summertime features terrestrial insects including ants, jassids, beetles, true flies, hoppers, etc., which in turn find their way to entrapment in the surface film and thus become grist for the mill of his excellency, the rising trout.

A rising trout is one just itching to be fished for, but fished for in just the right way if he is to be taken. Just because dry-fly fishing requires more patience, perseverance, and practice does not mean that it should not be given a trial. It is more fun and more effective and it is a fact of fishing life that trout will take a dry fly in royal fashion when all else is refused.

Whereas the wet fly swims through the water in search of some willing taker, the dry fly drifts over the spot of a particular fish. By one method we fish for *a* fish, by the other we are after *the* fish.

With the dry-fly cast to a surface-feeding fish, anticipation is great and action is prolonged. The spot of the rise form has been noted and carefully marked. The fly is cast a little upstream of the taking place. It drifts into the window of the surface feeder. Only time will tell if everything is right; that is, right in the eyes of the trout. It is a thrilling sight to see the fly disappear in a dimple. It is another thrill, but no anticlimax, to feel live weight when the rod tip is lifted to sink the barb. It is fun to play a fish from a noisy single-action fly reel. Henry Van Dyke made note of the sound, for he said, "The Kingfisher angrily winds his reel as he flies down the river at your approach."

Dry-fly fishing is usually upstream fishing, whereas streamer-fly and bucktail fishing is downstream fishing, and wet-fly fishing as generally practiced is with the current. When one bucks the flow, a problem is created. As the fly is carried toward the caster, excess line accumulates that must be taken up. So as the fly drifts naturally in the general direction of the caster, he slowly strips in accumulating slack without disrupting the natural drift of the fly in order to be able to make contact with the fish when a rise

A 10-pound, 4-ounce trout taken by Terry Ward on a LeTort Streamer fly in the 1969 *Field & Stream* national contest.

occurs. He gets rid of this by shooting it into the next cast or false casts. False cast is simply casting back and forth in the air several times to dry the fly sufficiently to make it float on the next delivery.

Arthur Woolley, English fly-tying authority and amateur entomologist, states the psychological approach of the dry-fly man thus: ". . . to locate, even to select his fish, to observe it and determine the type of natural fly on which it is feeding, to offer an artificial pattern of that fly, and so to hook and land that particular fish."

There is something in angling for everyone. I have no quarrel with the one who likes to sit on the bank and stare at the point where a line enters the water, or watch an inanimate tip-up, or swing a bait toward a submerged log, or troll back and forth. I have done these things and have enjoyed them, but just because there will be no future repetition for me does not imply disapproval. It does not mean some types of fishing are not fine; it simply means that some suit some people better than others. In fact, it is fortunate that we all do not want to fish for the same species in the same manner at the same sort of setup. There is a place for all and there are some fish to provide some action for all.

Spinning is often wonderful. You should have seen my boy as a six-year-old, lobbing a surface plug into pocket water with his 3-foot rod and push-button reel as together we waded a beautiful small-mouth bass stream. When I got a strike and hooked something on my plugging outfit, we quickly traded rods; otherwise he was on his own. You should see my once-in-a-while-fishing spouse cast with her spinning outfit, but she employs one longer than that of our casting son. If it were not for this extraordinary mechanized equipment, neither of them could cast with lures. Just because I choose to operate with something that entails a little more practice and a little more skill does not mean that I do not think well of the mechanical approach for those who enjoy it or need it. I like spinning because it has been good for so many, my family included; I like casting with the fly rod and fly line and with the bait-casting rod equipped with the quadruple multiplying reel because they have been so very good for me. Presentation, the act of casting, is up to individual choice. The ability to catch fish is not the same as the ability to cast. Neither is the ability of one type of casting to take fish the same as the ability of another type.

Conversion equipment is simplicity itself. Every spinning rod, with the exception of the one with the reel built into a bulbous grip, now long gone, will accommodate a fly reel and it will cast a fly line. Because most spinning rods possess more backbone than the average fly rod, a slightly heavier one is required to bring out the action.

The habits of the trout have not changed since spinning became a common practice. They are still basically insect eaters. The only thing that has happened is that new anglers have learned to fish with lures and in so doing have overlooked flies, the normal natural food. There are times and there are fish that give the lure no chance against the fly. This is particularly true of stream fishing as opposed to pond and lake fishing. Every square yard of stream surface is altered by movement. Variation is from fast to slow and from broken white to smooth emerald. Variation is a demand on skill. There should be no frantic haste in any kind of fishing, but particularly not in fly fishing. Dry-fly fishing is the most deliberate of all. When carefully done, the fish and the fishing of others are disturbed but little.

Success may not be on a scale consistent with hope, but fishing should never be hopeless. Generally speaking, fly fishing is at its best when spinning is at its poorest, and vice versa. The single-action reel, the heavy fly line, the leader tapered to a fine diameter, and the fly are of inestimable value when the spinning fisherman finds himself on a stream when there is a hatch and a rise of selective fish. The angler may be headed for a rewarding experience when, under such a condition, he puts the fly to work in place of the lure. Selectivity in feeding on a fine available food supply is unchanged since casting began. Abruptly, successful fishing becomes a deceiver rather than an attractor game. Casting a fly can unlock some of the mysteries. When the time is ripe, come on over; don't whip a dead horse. Go forth with the spinning reel attached to the rod; return on occasion with the single-action fly reel on the rod grip—and with satisfaction in the knowledge that you fished well and effectively.

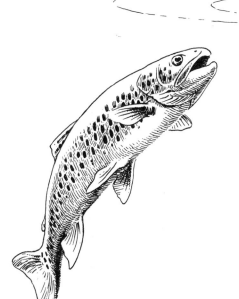

# PART FOUR

# 23

# *Old Trout Just Fade Away*

A fish is "it" until some angler develops a personal interest therein, then it becomes "he" or "him." Did you ever hear of anyone fishing for "it"? No, you fish for him. But gender will not be used loosely in this life story of a remarkable trout. Accurate reference will be made to "her," for she was neither he nor it. Our special interest in this particular fish is twofold: the great size she attained, larger than male brown trout ever grow; and how she lived dangerously on the fringe of urbanization in what men choose to term "civilization." She happened to be a fish with a high rate of metabolism, readily converting food into flesh. Her stream was rich, fertile, productive water where blocky trout put up violent resistance. Because of the interjection of man into her design for living she cultivated a degree of intelligence and prudence unknown in the primitive state. Finally, during the latter years of her life there was no chance of her being caught, for, in the first place, she was too smart, and in the second, too strong. Barring poisoning of the water, or some illegal practice such as blasting, she was safe from all but the ravages of time.

As one of nature's children she was a victim of a cruel pattern and law: hunt or be hunted, eat or be eaten. Man, who cherishes illusions of immortality, cannot help but wonder if mistakes have not been made with other creatures in making life so cheap in the scheme of checks and balances. The path of the mighty is strewn with successful pursuit and capture; then at last the fall of the mighty may be horrible. The story of a big trout is one of a glamorous past and an inglorious and tortuous future.

It was the period of year when the rock maples are flaming reds and oranges and the hickories are golden yellow. Well up in the watershed where the water runs clearest, the runoff is quickest, and the gravel is cleanest, was a redd laden with a precious cargo of eggs.

The hen fish that had deposited these eggs was a beautiful five-year-old brown trout measuring 18 inches in length, and her attending cock fish was one year older and one inch shorter. Judiciously she had chosen a good place and, being a strong fish, had worked the gravel well. It was amazing how large some of the stones were that moved when the powerful wrist of the tail was put through violent periodic contortions while the body was tipped sideways.

Now and then another persistent male muzzled in on her attentive cock fish, resulting in a fight and wild chase. While in pursuit of the new intruder he made the water fly, always moving back to the nest and his hen.

When the time came to start to expel the eggs, she dropped into the trough, which had been literally fanned out, with the gravel hump below it, so the anal fin and vent were down low. The cock fish took a position beside her. With bodies quivering and open mouths indicating muscular exertion, they arrived at the climax of their act. Pink-orange eggs rolled along the bottom to lodge in the gravel as milt spewed forth like a smoky cloud.

A myriad of the male's microscopic, wiggling, single-cell sperms were in search of eggs. They had but forty-five seconds to find the host before potency was spent. When one latched on to an egg, it bored through the elastic shell and into the liquid interior to give a start to a new generation of their kind.

The same thing happened at intervals until all eggs were deposited and fertilized. The hen moved a little more gravel with her tail to hide and cover a few more eggs. It was four days since she had started her work in the gravel and was joined by several competing males. Now that the most important job in his and her life was completed for another spawning season, the two brood fish dropped downstream, parted company, and moved into winter quarters, each to its own.

Some of the eggs in the nest were exposed. They might be eaten by small males that loitered at the redds. Other eggs rolled into the gravel to be well hidden and protected. Their future was not a certainty though. Should heavy rainfall occur and wash much silt into the stream, the eggs would be coated with unnatural solids in the water and some or even all would decay. Should the elements be mild or moderate, the rate of hatch would be high. Some of the little fish that hatched were doomed in a death trap, being unable to work their way out of the labyrinth in the gravel. With spring and summer would come hazards, for little trout are targets of hunters such as water snakes, kingfishers, ducks, and predatory fish including trout. But this is not devastating, for nature makes allowance for such natural losses; but nature has not made allowance for unnatural losses wrought by man, including siltation and pollution. Those trout that survived the first year would thereafter be sought by a new enemy, man. Life was uncertain, life was cheap, but at worst when conditions were adverse and the supply of trout low, the predators lay off, concentrating attention elsewhere on foods in greater abundance, a stringent law of nature.

There was one egg in particular in which we have a special interest, for it was destined to produce a very special fish, one that would be outstanding in various respects. This egg was covered with several inches of gravel.

The shell became harder as the weeks passed and a beady black spot developed therein. Then the whole interior began to exercise by wiggling. Even the bright sunshine reflected by the snow on the banks could not penetrate this aquatic cave in the gravel.

During the fall and early winter the average water temperature in the stream section was 50°, so at the end of thirty-eight days the egg opened and an odd, helpless little creature emerged. Had there been eyes to see, it would have appeared to be more like a grub than a fish. Safe in the gravel the wormlike fish, unable to swim, just wiggled as it lived off its relatively tremendous, translucent orange stomach. As the yolk was absorbed the sac-fry became increasingly mobile.

In one month the baby could swim in the open areas of the gravel pile and the egg sac had been almost completely absorbed. Then one day a slender little trout worked her way out of the stones and into a bright new world. As the strong flow of water carried the transparent tiny body away from the gravel pile, something told her to struggle to the shallows along the edge of the stream.

Here life was exciting and good. It was fun to seize, crush, and swallow microscopic zooplankton. The weeks passed and her progress was excellent because the supply of plankton suspended in the water was abundant.

Then the rains came and the stream became high and cloudy. The little trout learned to move off to the side with high water; she learned how to use obstructions as cover, and then to move back home as the water receded. She learned to stay quiet in a sheltered spot when the water became so muddy she could not see. She learned how to clean herself after the runoff on sparkling gravel. Just to live was a delight and she saw other little fish, some of them her brothers and sisters, also getting along well. They were an alert, quick-motioned lot.

Spring broke and, as the water warmed, the little trout and the big ones too had a desire to eat more frequently and in greater amounts. The higher water temperature accelerated the digestive process, the fastest digestion occurring when the temperature was in the low sixties.

The little trout was now an inch in length and the parr markings on her side began to show. Now and then a bigger fish raided the section, the intent being obvious, but the little trout was much too quick and fast in the security of the shallows. The combination of alertness and agility was her forte.

Then one day disaster struck, not to this little trout, but to one like her 10 feet upstream. She saw a quick motion above the waterline in her window, followed by a crashing splash. Up ahead under the surface a dark object swapped ends and skyrocketed back into the air through the mirrored surface to light on an overhanging branch. It cocked its head skyward, opened and closed its beak and gulped so the neck feathers ruffled, then smoothed. It was the end of the trail for a baby trout. Our little fish now understood that quick motion from above meant attack, but she did not know that the attacker in this case ate three times its own weight daily. Always thereafter while resting, her eyes looked upward; and with visual warning her speed and agility meant security. One day from a branch of the buttonwood the kingfisher plummeted down after her but she was no longer there when the sturdy big black bill hit the resting place.

The fry waxed strong on the plankton; in fact she grew so well that now her mouth and stomach were large enough to utilize another tremendous food supply, *diptera*, the little olive gnats that hatch from mud and collect in masses just above the surface. This was the start of a new kind of feeding, surface feeding. Food was snatched from the surface as it was delivered by the current.

In her first August she was introduced to what was to become her favorite food for the next few years: winged ants, countless thousands of them, ants in such abundance that they coated the surface. In the 65° water the growing trout fed as she had never fed before. She sipped ants until she had to rest on the stream bed. For five afternoons they were in tremendous profusion, but throughout the rest of the fall there were usually enough available to furnish a square meal. Cool nights brought forth the old food supply of the spring, *diptera*.

Brood fish moved into the graveled area. One pair was considerably larger than the others. The little trout had no way of knowing it but the biggest trout was her mother, back again, but now over 20 inches in length. This was no place for a 6-inch fish, so discretion being the better part of valor, she moved downstream to deeper water away from the spawning grounds. Some big fish entered her new home pool, but they did not loiter; neither did they feed. On they pushed in their search for clean gravel, the whole intent and purpose being procreation.

The winter may have been safer than spring, summer, and fall, but it was less enjoyable. No trout objects to dangerous living.

Then one spring day she made the first mistake of her life, and the result was near tragedy. A darting and dancing object following a single strand of something flashed before her. Even though it looked like nothing she had ever seen, it was interesting. Forward she shot and took a pass at it. Something hard and unnatural hit her in the face with a sudden jarring sting. The only reason she had a future was because the hook in it did not hold, for there was a new predator at the other end of the line. Never again would a metal lure trailing a strand be of interest to this trout.

A fish is limited to available food, and available food fluctuates with season and stream section. It was a soft golden summer day following a deceptively short spring. A sharp pair of human eyes watched the start of the nuptial dance of the little yellow drake, a water-born insect that is sometimes called sulphur fly. They were milling around the foliage, high above the surface, but by dusk many would be back on the water.

The angler, a real master of his art, was ready with two different imitations and an ultralight leader. One of these he chose. Certainly, he thought, nothing can be more artificial and few things more beautiful than the counterpart of a real fly. He was watching; that meant waiting for a fish, finding it in the right mood for surface feeding, the careful stalk, then the perfect delivery of the right fly.

A trout rose. Most of the spinners were still several feet above the surface, flying upstream. There was another rise in precisely the same place. It was our fish—our friend.

She glanced at a natural insect, then carefully inspected the similar-looking object drifting on the water beside it. She did not know that the second had anything to do with the inherent enemy—man—but she saw it drag on the surface in an unnatural manner. Anything not real was not for her. She might be deceived but never again would she be attracted. The lesson had been learned well from the darting metal lure.

The imitation of the fisherman was acting wrong. It is true that a trout is unable to think like a man, but there are time when it behaves as if it does. Here was a case in point. In spite of the fact that this imitation had worked on many occasions and on many different fish, it was not going to work this time. Three dozen unproductive casts proved that.

The angler smiled to himself, reeled up, then replaced this fly with the other counterfeit. Strange thing, he thought, sometimes one pattern works better, sometimes the other. Both were improved versions of the standard Pale Evening Dun. The first tie would have been the common pattern had it not had a few turns of orange hackle intermingled with the honey, and the second had an orange gantron body substituted for the customary pale yellow. This, it seems, is the way the fish preferred their Pale Evening Duns.

The fresh fly floated in the window of the trout. It looked good. A favorite weapon found a willing taker. This was the second mistake of her young life. This time, however, there was no hardness and no jar, such as the metal lure produced; but she was hooked.

The angler recognized in the trout a real speed merchant, for it seemed to be everywhere at once. In due time, though, strength and speed yielded to the incessant strain. Admiring eyes drank in the rare beauty of this spectacular creature of nature as careful hands removed the barbless hook. The angler murmured to himself, "Too valuable to be used only once," and she was given back to the stream from whence he had taken her.

Time marches on. Dog days had set in; it was mid-August. A man with a rod was sitting on the bank drinking in the reflected greens. The variety of the same locality is amazing and wonderful. This he understood. The sulphur hatch was over for another season but, if the timetable of piscatorial events was on schedule, by late afternoon there should be winged ants on the water. His approach to his art was not haphazard; should they mark their appearance he would be ready. His was a confidence bred of successful experience.

Arthur Woolley, the English angling author, put it this way: "If genius is an infinite capacity for taking pains, successful fishing with fly and rod requires genius . . . careful attention to detail is essential to successful fly fishing."

One minute there was not an ant in sight. A half hour later they seemed to be everywhere, hordes of them speckling the surface of running water. This was a minute ant, so the chosen imitation was accordingly small. The rise started.

What appeared to be a good fish put up across the way, tight against a brush pile. It took up the typical position of a fish feeding on minutiae, about 6 inches under the surface, from whence it would rock up, sip, then settle back, showing only the tip of the dorsal fin and tail. A feeding rhythm developed.

The angler approached unseen, unheard, unheralded to drop his fly a yard above the spot of the rise forms. It was a perfect pitch, the fly coming into the window of the fish in advance of the very fine leader (7X). The trout yielded to the temptation to test a likeness of her favorite food.

The angler's sweet reward that lies at the end of his rainbow is personal satisfaction. The long light-point leader made catching all the greater an achievement. As he carefully returned to the

Eddie Shenk, the noted flytier from Carlisle, Pennsylvania, in operation on Maryland's Beaver Creek. *Photo by Lefty Kreh.*

stream a handsome 14-inch brown trout, he never suspected that this was the beautiful 10-inch fish he had captured earlier in the season, and neither could he know that this fish would become the most valuable brood trout the watershed ever possessed.

It was in the third year of her life that for the fourth and last time she was fooled by her chief antagonist, man. Now a powerful 19-inch trout she was extra heavy because of the formation of roe within her. For the fisherman, situations occur that make possible the existence of opportunity. Here was a superb one. It was hopper time in a grassy meadow.

To a trout an insect diet is preferable to a fish diet because the former has a much higher fat content than the latter. The largest of the aquatic crustaceans are crayfish; the largest of the common terrestrial insects, grasshoppers. Big trout are innately lazy, and because of the size and procurability of crabs and hoppers, these are prime favorites. The hopper is the one insect that can successfully overcome surface tension, for it can kick its way out of a dilemma, and therein lies a story.

The young angler may have been inexperienced but that did not deter enthusiasm and zeal. The feathered hopper he was casting had been highly recommended by a skilled friend, and so had a specialized method of fishing it. The system was to cast across stream to the opposite bank, make the imitation hopper land in tight, drift it by the overhanging grass, then as drag set in jerk it toward midstream, just as the real thing after landing in the water might kick its way across the surface. The section he chose lent itself admirably to this approach. There was something serpentine about the stream as it twisted and doubled back on itself, the chief attraction being deep water and undercut banks—and that is supposed to mean big fish.

In due time near a submerged log there was an explosion at the fly as it kicked its way away from a verdant tunnel. And suddenly there were butterflies in the stomach of the young man. He had gotten by the rise successfully and was attached to what must be a very large fish, a new experience for him.

The trouble was at the big end of the rod. He did not understand that undue ruction might disturb the fish. Suddenly there was a change from a heavy slow thing to a fast and powerful battler. There was a run and a jump. The fisherman walked forward and pulled the fish toward his feet in the belief that the quicker he landed it the less chance there would be of losing it. Just as the angler made a pass with the net the trout experienced a new power from fear. There was an audible snap and the young angler lifted a netful of foam that disappeared like a mocking spirit.

The making of quality trout fishing near centers of population is the combination of release and loss of young fish. Trout learn by experience. Most learn fast and with profit in their game of life. Here was one of that type. Four times this trout had been involved in incidents with man—twice a winner, twice almost a loser. Henceforth she would never touch anything that did not appear to be natural, nor anything that did not act naturally, nor anything that was attached to something. Neither would she show herself, even at spawning time. By day she lived under undercut banks. At night she ranged about. Her meat and potatoes were crayfish. Growth was phenomenal.

That fall she found the perfect spawning place—good clean gravel under a log along the bank in moderately fast water. (It is the hen that chooses the location for the nursery.) Here she spawned year after year for ten consecutive seasons.

She made it into her teens, a giant of the species, in hard-fished water; but not a fisherman knew of or suspected her presence or existence. In the sunset of her life her eyesight was failing so that it was becoming increasingly difficult to pick up a clumsy crab at night. In the old days she would eat only little ones or pink ones, those with soft shells; now she was lucky to latch on to a big hard shell. As the shadows of death lengthened she became lankier and lankier and darker and darker.

With what remaining strength she could muster the once redoubtable trout blindly pushed her gaunt frame into a bed of elodea. In her delirium she turned on her side, even as she so often had in preparation of the redds for the depositing of masses of eggs. With one feeble contortion of the wrist of the 6-inch-wide square tail, she drove her glazed eyes into the soft muck that had collected around the roots of the vegetation. Held there by the stems of the water weed she lay on her side.

Nature's sanitary corps assembled. The crayfish, the shrimp, the sowbugs, once grist for her mill, moved in to play their role. Gaping holes were gnawed in what was once gorgeously tinted and spotted skin. Crawling creatures of the stream entered her gills and nostrils. An eel forced its way into her through the vent to gnaw from within as a snapping turtle chewed and ripped on the outside. She was being devoured alive bit by bit and bite by bite as a stout heart beat its last, nature's hard way of turning her over to the environment.

One week later there lay, deeply imbedded in the elodea, a clean massive skeleton of a fish long since, in terms of trout life, too wise and too strong for man to cope with and too prudent to be observed by him. Here the remains would go unnoticed by human eyes as had been the case with the living creature for a full decade.

In this watershed, however, there fanned the fins of her scions, some from each of her ten different spawning seasons and from each of her ten different mates. Few of them and also few of their unborn generations were destined to die the undignified death of a trout as she did, passage due to the ravages of time. And fortunate indeed are the regular fishermen of this watershed to have for their angling pleasure a native population of her children, trout from such a superior brood fish and of such a superior bloodline.

# 24

# Trout Conservation

It was early spring and two similar incidents, which transpired on consecutive weekends, led me to decide to produce a movie of trout and trout fishing. The picture will be for fishermen and officials alike, an honest effort to demonstrate the advantages of stringent killing regulations. Obviously the policy makers do not recognize the potential of fly fishing for trout as a management tool, and the anglers have failed to link together fly fishing and conservation, a perfect union. Needed is an in-focus, in-depth word picture on screen and sound track.

The picture would show trout in their natural habitat and anglers in operation where there is a minimum of killing. The commentary would connect fly fishing and conservation.

One occasion responsible for the idea of this movie was the combined annual dinner of Trout Unlimited and the Fly Fisher's Club of Harrisburg. The speaker was the top official of the national organization. At the table of so-called old-timers were the Slaymakers, the Allemans, Vince Marinaro, and the Foxes. The speaker was expounding upon the generosity of the state officials in "giving" the fly fishermen some regulated water at the expense of the bait fishermen. He thought of regulated water as a beneficent gift, whereas we regarded it as an essential conservation measure. The wives looked at the husbands for reaction, and they did not like what they saw. Sam was shaking his head; on Harry's face was a frown; Vince's jaw was hard set; I was in a growling mood. Sam poked me and whispered, "He doesn't understand the place of fly fishing in conservation." From the other side Sally Slaymaker asked, "Isn't that discrimination against the fly fishermen?"

The other occasion was the large annual banquet of the southern New Jersey chapter of Trout Unlimited. Even before the introductions of guests were made, the toastmaster pointed out and identified the dignitaries present. It was impressive. The conservation department was well represented.

Knowing that the fishermen in attendance were such great champions of the "limit your kill; don't kill your limit" practice and principle, I was surprised to learn that the entire state trout program was strictly put-and-take—stock, catch, replace—with no regulated areas. A balanced program involves some provisions for tomorrow to go along with something for today. What the hatchery may term "optimum recovery" and "crop harvesting" is in reality fish-truck chasing, a temporary proposition. Of this, Vince Marinaro has written, "Neither victim is worthy of the other." A certain amount of this seems to be important, although not economically feasible, for some people go for it who are not capable of catching holdover or stream-bred fish. There are others who do not want to be caught in the carnival atmosphere that prevails with fish-truck chasers.

So it was that I decided to devote the last part of my thirty-minute talk to trout conservation. After the conclusion, there was, to my amazement, a standing ovation. I realized it was not for my benefit but rather a display of support of regulated fishing for the benefit of officialdom.

The greatness and potential of fly fishing and returning the captured fish, as simple and logical as it is, needed a selling job. The gist of my remarks that night should be the thrust of the commentary for a sound track of the trout picture. What I said went something like this:

The vital organs of a fish are deep in the throat and high in the thorax. Trout frequently swallow a baited hook, with the result that they are doomed. There is not much blood in a trout and any bleeding at all is too much. On the other hand, trout taken on a fly are generally lip-hooked, which is not injurious. This means that many taken on bait cannot be expected to survive if they are returned, while most of those taken on a fly can be expected to recover when they are returned. That is one of the reasons why fly and bait fishing at the same time in the same place are not compatible. Fly fishing, with the return of caught fish, provides a conservation possibility of great significance; unfortunately, bait fishing does not. Lee Wulff puts it this way: "In fly fishing a trout can be used more than once."

Lure fishing with a spinning outfit falls in between these two. The sturdier equipment and heavier, larger hooks have a tendency to rip and tear and drown trout by forcing water down their throats, even though mouth-hooked.

It can be expected that where there are stringent killing restrictions in conjunction with fly fishing, both the number of trout and their average size will increase for several years before leveling off into a very special and unique angling situation. Regulated killing puts to work a population and quality buildup principle. The trout themselves demonstrate something else. Under catch-and-release fishing pressure, they become hyperselective and observant and, as a result, more challenging to the fisherman. Fishing for them becomes more and more a deceiver game, as opposed to the attractor approach. They become less sensitive to people and motion but much more sensitive to fraud, drag, and leader tippet.

The problems are beautifully challenging and the rewards are great. Expertise pays off. It is a must to fish the water well. Success in angling should be measured in terms of personal satisfaction. Here is the ultimate in trout fishing, good fishing that produces great satisfaction.

Do trout remember? That is a good question. Time and again in the regulated water of the LeTort in my backyard I have caught a certain fish feeding in a certain way at a certain location. Sometime later the same fish is seen feeding the same way at the same place. Now it requires various tries on different days to fool him again. This fish is caught and returned a second time, but again the trout feeds in the same old way in the same place, only this time it requires fishing over a period of weeks before the mistake of accepting the fly is made. Envision a whole population of trout, many of which are improving their resistance to the wares of the flycasters. That makes for challenging angling and pretty fishing.

On the one extreme, this is very different from fishing for primitive fish in a remote place; and on the other extreme, it is a different ball game from fishing for newly stocked fish, which are concentrated in a limited area and must experiment in their feeding activity.

It has been interesting to note that many of my angling friends, myself included, are spending either all or most of their fishing time in the restricted-kill fly-fishing stream sections, and we now spend little time and pay little attention to the catch-as-catch-can water.

Teddy Roosevelt, father of the game refuge system even before he became president, looked upon game as a recreational resource and asset, not as food for the market. The game managers of today champion two versions of the refuge system. One type is a wired-off and posted area where hunting and carrying a gun is prohibited. The other is an area where hunting is not permitted without permission of the owners. If the game managers could rejuvenate crumpled game to be used again, they would play that one to the hilt. So would the hunters. Obviously the trout-fisheries manager is the possessor of a special blessing. Ah yes, there can be incursion into and fishing within his refuge and all still remain well.

Suppose a carefully planned trout refuge system were initiated in every watershed. The result would be superb fly fishing in the refuges and improved catch-as-catch-can for the spillover above and below the refuges. In most instances, due to the protection of brood fish, this would also bring about an increase in the native trout population of the stream.

Another use for the refuge system in conjunction with stream-improvement work is in a spawning area. This is generally in the headwaters but it can be at the tail of a pool below a dam. Here the gravel will remain unsilted, as it is washed clean. An annual freshening of the spawning beds is a worthy effort. Unfortunately, common crushed gravel or crushed limestone is not satisfactory. It has to be river gravel; three-quarter-inch has proved to be best for brown and rainbow trout.

Within the bounds of the refuge there is no need for a closed season; therefore there is no opening day. It is common sense, though, not to fish for a hen on her nest, for fear she might be hooked and during her struggle lose her eggs, which would not be fertilized.

From the tourism standpoint, anglers are unique. When they

find what they like they return frequently. A look at their equipment shows they are hobbyists and free-spenders. Often their families go along to indulge in something other than fishing while father—and maybe son—fly-cast. The tourist dollar, they tell us, passes through seven hands before disappearing.

When a rural community with accommodations, attractions, and supplies has a regulated fishing area within easy striking distance, both local people and visitors will use it. A "trout town" can be created. Every borough council and every chamber of commerce at or near a trout stream would do well to investigate the possibility and the potential of a nearby trout refuge open to fly fishing.

Along with the establishment of a trout preserve, it would be great to have a youth program entailing a free fly-tying course and casting clinic and a gift of a fly-fishing outfit to every boy and girl living along the regulated section who wants one.

There is the important matter of nomenclature. One could almost suspect that the person who designated our regulated areas "Fly Fishing Only" and "Fish for Fun," was, for some reason of his own, not in favor of their creation. So he deliberately got them off to a bad start with a poor name. The first reeks of discrimination and the second is irresponsible and silly.

The thought is sometimes expressed by natives, particularly at town sportsmen's club meetings, that the regulated areas discriminate against the bait fishermen. This is the type who fight special archery seasons for the bow hunter. Actually, the shoe is on the other foot. Until such time as the percentage of fly-fishing water equals the percentage of fly fishermen, discrimination is against the fly fishermen. I am sure, however, that the fly fishermen would settle for a trout refuge system used as an effective management tool and a sound conservation practice. Then they would gladly forget about percentages.

Certainly "Trout Refuge" would be a more accurate and more fitting moniker than "Fish for Fun" and it would be more generally accepted and understood. It would be an asset in every respect if the words printed on the top lines above the requirements read:

### TROUT REFUGE
### A CONSERVATION AREA

The sportsman who will benefit from sound conservation practices put into effect today—in this case Chip Fox, in his own back yard along the LeTort.

The Maritime Provinces of Canada are decades ahead of the state conservation departments and fish commissions in the use of fly only as a conservation instrument, as witness the management of their salmon and sea-run trout rivers. Little by little and one by one the conservation department officials will inevitably recognize that you cannot mix successfully the fly fishermen, on the one hand, who preach and practice "don't kill your limit, limit your kill," with the bait fishermen, on the other, who think meat and kill catches.

The refuge system would mean that those who oppose regulated stream stretches would not be battling fly fishermen; they would be fighting conservation.

## TO PUT THEM BACK ALIVE

The fine-leader midge-fly approach is an important, exacting, and fascinating phase of fly fishing for trout. Fish hooked on such tackle must be played carefully lest the leader tippet break and away go the fish with the fly. Careful playing involves time and a wearing-down process.

There are three common turns of event that dictate midge dry-fly fishing. It is called for when we are faced with a hatch of small mayflies such as the little olive *(Baetis vagans)* and little single wing *(Caenis tricorythodes).* It is a requirement for success when the trout are working on a mass of flying ants trapped in the surface film. And the diminutive approach is a must when the dainty surface feeders are sipping jassids.

The length of the season makes this approach truly significant. Little olive has three or four broods a year, a unique situation among the aquatic insects. In the waters I fish, the first duns appear in March, then show up irregularly at various times, October being outstanding. All fishing is then to the duns; the spinner fall takes place after dark. Little single wing is unique, too, in that the emergence of the dun and the fall of the spinner of each individual fly takes place in the morning from about 8:00 to 11:00. The hatch starts in July and continues through mid-October. August is the big month for flying ants; jassids are on the water throughout the hot weather. With such an array of surface-feeding activity, it is obvious that the angler is frequently called upon to trim out his leader to a fine tippet and attach to it a floating midge fly.

The use of terminal tackle in the 7X and 8X category presents two problems. The obvious one is of a sporting nature: the successful hooking, playing, and landing of a fish on ultralight tackle. The more subtle problem and the one I wish to discuss now is of a conservation nature. Often with fine tackle a fish might be played to the point of no recovery, and this is exactly what we do not want to happen, especially in our catch-and-release areas.

In order to guard against loss so that a trout can be used more than once, it behooves us to land them as quickly as possible, to handle them as little as necessary, and to return them in the best possible condition. How best can this be accomplished?

First, all hooks should have the brittle tips of the barbs broken off with pliers. If you tie your own, an ideal time to do this is prior to the construction of a fly. In its barbed form it is a tenacious thing, but with the barb broken away the hook can be removed readily and quickly. Fear not about losing fish on a barbless hook. It rarely happens.

Second, carry a net and use it unless the fish can be led into very shallow water or drawn on top of vegetation. A fish can be landed more quickly and efficiently when one can reach out with a net to meet it. Landing a trout by hand, regardless of how carefully performed, only results in unnecessary handling of the trout. The net will eliminate juggling and dropping and squeezing and rubbing. There is always that tendency to grab too hard or too light.

Third, carry a tweezers or forceps—the instrument that looks like a scissors and is used by surgeons to remove stitches from sutures. With either of these the hook can be rolled out of the embedment. All one has to do is reach down in the net with the hook remover, grasp the body of the fly with the instrument, and, without handling the fish, remove it. Then permit the fish to swim out of the net to freedom without having been touched.

Some of the most intriguing trouting I have experienced is on the restricted killing areas of Pennsylvania streams officially termed "Fish for Fun" sections. In these places the number and average size of the fish are fine, thanks to the population buildup restricted killing fosters; and due to fishing pressure the fish have become sophisticated. They are leader shy and very selective. More often than not the challenge is great and the problems are beautiful.

The hatchery bureaucracy does not think this way. Things are planned to enhance the importance of the bureaucracy and make fishing more dependent on it. The creed is: stock, catch; stock, catch; stock, catch. Only today counts. There is no program for tomorrow. Concern is not to build a viable trout population; it is just to provide trout available for catching at the onset of the trout-fishing season. More and more fishermen are beginning to call this sort of program "put-and-take" or "fish-truck chasing."

Restricted kill areas, which in effect are stream refuges, have their critics. Hopefully, for the conservation-minded fly fisherman, these trout refuges will become the fishing of the future. We do not want the critics to be able to say, "You are playing your fish to death." Neither do we want to have reason to wonder, "Did that one I put back make it?"

# 25

# Anatomy of a Trout Stream

There is something in conjunction with both trout and trout fishing that we'd better recognize because it is true: The finer the native population, the greater the angling potential. Man has managed to produce a substitute for the naturally occurring article with trout stocking. But the "synthetic" is not the same. The more recent the stocking, the lower the quality of angling it provides. This should be expected, because a trout may not have eaten a single *living* thing while being raised in a hatchery. Naturally, this is not conducive to quality and challenging fishing, at least not immediately. In describing the anglers who chase hatchery trucks and the quality of fishing offered by recent stockings, Vince Marinaro coined a classic statement: "Neither victim is worthy of the other." However, it has to be conceded that under certain conditions hatchery trout do learn the how, when, and where of survival and are then worthy of our angling efforts. And also, certain marginal trout streams do benefit from trout stocking, though no stream benefits from fish-truck chasing.

There is also, unfortunately, a very serious side to stocking programs where good native supplies of fish exist—serious in the sense of dangerous. A careful and thorough Montana study reveals that where extensive stocking is done, the native population diminishes. There can be many reasons for this, but I believe that one of the most dangerous stocking practices is the planting of fingerlings. All too frequently baby trout are infected with one or other contagious disease, but have not had time to die before distribution. At the fingerling size in a weakened state, they are soon consumed by the native fish, who then contract and die from the disease.

It appears that the expensive and extensive well-promoted stocking programs, loved so dearly by hatchery-dominated fisheries departments in some of our eastern states, are in reality a management of fishermen rather than a management of trout and trout waters. It is accurate to report that hatchery-oriented fisheries management cares about today only; whereas to the conservation-oriented fisheries management, the *future* is everything.

There are instances where the people who know the least about quality fishing should know the most, and the people who should know the most about native populations know the least. That is the way with a hatchery-oriented bureaucracy, and this is ironic.

With a native population in mind, let us consider the anatomy of a trout stream and possible treatment for imperfection. There are four vital elements: food, homes, productive spawning grounds, and brood fish. The sum of these vital parts determines the degree of well-being of the native population. If all are in abundance as well as in balance, the trouting is of blue-ribbon quality. If something is lacking, man with proper treatment may be able to improve and refine the existing situation, if not completely rectify the imbalance. Often it is only one of these four vital factors that is deficient and deserves attention.

Dr. Ed Cooper, head of the fisheries unit of Pennsylvania State University, each summer conducts an electro-shocking program on different streams in the state for the purpose of fish census and study. Every stream that his team has shocked possesses a native population. The size of the native population reflects the status of the four factors in the trout stream.

An excellent example of how a deficiency can be recognized and rectified is provided by the stream on which I live. The LeTort had homes galore among the beds of elodea and watercress; the food supply was and is superabundant, particularly the sowbugs, scuds, and crayfish; there were sufficient brood fish to maintain population levels; but, due to the interjection and interference of man, spawning conditions had deteriorated, largely due to the influx of silt.

The hatch of trout eggs is controlled by three factors: suitable spawning grounds, a population of brood fish, and relative absence of turbidity—silt rots eggs.

What was needed in the LeTort was more gravel to produce improved spawning conditions for the brood fish. (In addition to spawning, the trout utilize the gravel to clean themselves.) In 1963 I decided to create a spawning area that could be watched and appraised. Over the years it has been enlarged and refined to the point where it is substantial and productive. The greater number of trout and the improved fishing document the effectiveness of this treatment.

The deficiency in the spectacular cascading mountain streams that race down stony mountainsides is most frequently a lack of homes. This can be rectified best by moving large rocks and boulders into the stream to create homes in the backwater of the foreside of the boulder and quiet eddies aft. Conditions permitting, dams and V deflectors can also be constructed to provide homes for trout.

The brooklet, so common to the mountains of the East, has the homes, the brood fish, and favorable spawning conditions; but it is frequently sadly lacking in food. Man can best effect an improvement by opening the overhead canopy of foliage to permit some sunshine to break through, which will increase different plant growths and in turn step up the aquatic and terrestrial food supply.

A weakness of the popular and hard-fished trout streams of the East is most often a deficiency of large brood fish, meaning the big hens. Needed here is less killing.

The standard-type stream-improvement work creates new homes, more food, and frequently, additional spawning grounds. In all instances these improvements will make the water more interesting to fish.

In the consideration of the care of the anatomy of a trout stream, we must have a look at the doctors who prescribe the treatment. In this case they are biologists. Not all of them look upon stringent regulations as a conservation measure and a stream-management tool. With some it is quite the contrary. They say "nothing doing" to fly-fishing-only sections in streams on the grounds that it is discriminatory.

The standard argument of the non-fly-fishing biologist is that fly-fishing, limited-kill stream sections should not exist until such time as it is proven through careful study that they are beneficial.

Some of the biologists who adhere to this line of reasoning are located in states such as New Jersey, Connecticut, and Wisconsin where there have been no fly-fishing-only restricted killing areas; hence a study never could have been conducted.

What would these people say if the fly-fishing clan claimed there should be regulated areas in proportion to their numbers until such time as it is demonstrated through careful study that they are not beneficial?

In considering the qualifications for the employment of a biologist I feel strongly that it should be a requirement that an appointee be an ardent angler who, at least on occasion, fishes with a fly for trout. Otherwise he could hardly have a feeling for quality fishing or even understand what is meant by "Don't kill your limit; limit your kill."

So let's initiate some regulated stream areas on a trial basis on streams where they do not exist, and then conduct a study. I have complete confidence that such areas will prove to be both popular and beneficial to the watershed—in short, a stream-management tool and a conservation measure. Frankly, I am worried about the state of the anatomy of our trout streams.

# 26
# Stream Improvement

One facet of the ever-growing history of trout fishing is stream improvement, the human contribution to increase of carrying capacity, rate of growth, carry-over quality, natural reproduction, and fishability of the water. In many instances streams have been a sort of battleground between nature on the one side and men on the other, men who, in ignorance or indifference, have caused unnatural siltation while bent upon earning a living. In fact, practically every trout stream is in one state or another of man-caused deterioration. But still other men not so engaged who are interested in angling have pitched in to right wrongs—their efforts to offset the damage arising from the others' efforts. Essentially their role has been, and is, a matter of redesigning the stream bed by control of the stream flow.

As is the case of better angling, which is the reason behind stream improvement, there has been refinement by many minds and hands along with the expenditure of considerable time and money. Over the years creative ideas have stemmed from English river keepers, American fly fishermen, and technicians of governmental agencies. Anglers of distinction have recorded some of the practices and part of the progress. There have been starting points; now there are meeting places. The purpose of this writing is to assemble, to correlate, to evaluate data that as of now is scattered about in papers, journals, books, and in heads. The reporting is by an intensely interested advocate who enjoys getting into a stream even to the point of becoming wet and muddy and who has had the good fortune to have known the foremost American trout-stream engineers.

J. W. Hills in his classic, *River Keeper*, wrote: "Angling is an endless quest in which one never attains perfection and we stumble towards it not by conquests but by defeats. . . . You should be impatient, never putting up with defeat. Patience is passive." The very fact that this passage appeared in the biography of William J. Lunn, for forty-five years the keeper for the famous Houghton Trout Club on the river Test in the Hampshire sector of southern England, suggests that these words could have been applied to the biographee. Certainly author Hills would not have taken exception to such application. Lunn worked with spawning beds, weed control, silt removal, streamside plantings, distribution of aquatic insects, and fly boards for the improvement of hatches.

But the great man was not the originator of stream improvement. Frederick M. Halford, the father of dry-fly fishing, wrote a book published in London in 1895 entitled *Making a Fishery*, in which he reported upon trout and stream management of his day, which included work on the stream beds and the banks.

Although the English chalk streams were the cradle of sophisticated fly fishing and also of stream-improvement work, it does not seem accurate to assume that the latter, as was the case with the former, came to America from across the Atlantic. Here it must have had an independent conception, for the problems were totally different in the two environments. There is little similarity between the placid, alkaline English chalk streams and the acid streams of the mountainous sections of America, which flow swiftly and are interspersed in many parts with rocks, riffles, glides, slicks, and pools of considerable depth.

It was in the mid-thirties that the term *stream improvement* became well known. Federal offshoots of the world depression, W.P.A. and C.C.C., made available a tremendous labor pool on the government payroll. States and counties within the states were expected to employ their man quota and spend their dollar quota. It was ruled that, with permission, stream-reclamation projects could be conducted on private property if the materials were furnished. Materials consisted for the most part of stones and logs. Town fish-and-game clubs applied for and cleared the way for work on trout streams. Next to road work, stream improvement became the major public-works activity in some rural sections.

The fishermen of certain states, such as Pennsylvania, with angler Edward N. Jones as director, were fortunate.

Almost overnight the big job became the adoption of a plan or system and the employment of fishing foremen with a scientific twist of mind. Individual bosses and their little groups were going to have to play this by ear, for explicit directions were not available.

Basically there were three recognized and accepted devices: the dam, the slanting wing wall, and the downstream open V. They could be made of stones, logs, or a combination of the two. It was up to the boss. The path he followed was unpredictable, subject to whim or sudden inspiration; his was a fluctuating mental yardstick.

The first work was far from perfect, but it was an improvement in that it did more good than harm. It was not of a temporary nature either, for today, three decades later, some of it is as effective as it was then. This, however, like so many things, is the old story of hindsight being better than foresight. Two errors were common: the main consideration was the fisherman, whereas it should have been the fish; and the improvement was bigger and bolder than was necessary or even good in order that it would stand out to be seen. Walls high above the low waterline are unsightly, veritable snake incubators, and a waste of labor and material.

Refinement, mainly by individuals, has followed those days so that now there are tried-and-tested plans that can be followed, and there are sections of improved water that can be inspected to see how the job is done.

If you wish to become one of that select segment of anglers who attempt to speed up nature's trout-stream potential, it is important that you start with a flexible mind and search out possiblities. The key to observation is knowing what to look for. Facts must be assigned to their rightful causes. It must be realized that aquatic environments are fully as complex as terrestrial habitats and that quality of water is of greater significance to aquatic life than quantity of water. Be prepared to encounter some contradictory evidence. Above all, regard as fascinating the ways of water with obstructions.

In an honest attempt to administer to a damaged environment wrought by the encroachment of civilization, let us see if we can't augment nature's ability to grow fish. One by one we shall examine the stream devices designed by our angling enthusiasts so that the application of each can be considered for a given stretch of water. Before a finger is lifted, though, we want to know as much as possible about this type of work, no matter whether it is to be done by an individual, a trout club, a sportsman's organization, or even a governmental agency.

The best plan is to start the activity upstream and then work down in order that as much silt and sand as possible can be removed from the stretch. More clean gravel and more riffles will increase the hatch of insect eggs and fish eggs. More feeding stations and hiding places will increase the carrying capacity and make the water more interesting to fish. More overhead cover will increase the average size of the evening feeders  More depth will help fish survive the extreme elements of summer and winter.

## DAMS

Bigger water and deeper water is holding water, particularly in summer drought time and winter anchor-ice time. Without the creation of it, trout of some streams are in jeopardy. On the other hand, dammed water is no good for spawning and it is poor for the manufacture of food. A falls from a dam, though, does aerate water, which is beneficial to all life in a trout stream, particularly eggs. The saturation point for oxygen is 15 parts per million; the minimum requirement of trout is almost half that, which is higher than for almost all other freshwater species.

When water is impounded, no matter whether it is a vast concrete structure or a tiny check dam, there is a pileup of water behind it known to engineers as backwater effect. Water pushes against water; water slows up water; and water backs up water. The backup is more than a surveyor's transit would indicate to be the pool of the dam.

A good, productive, inviting piece of trout water should be a combination of deep holding water, riffles over clean gravel, overhead cover, and assorted small homes, which are also casting targets. Our first consideration is the different types of dams because the dam sites should be selected first; then the locations for wing walls, brush piles, and small obstructions as supplementary work should be determined.

Edward R. Hewitt, foremost trout expert of his day, improved his section of the Neversink River of New York. Possibly his booklet of the thirties demonstrating his use of dams and walls was the first written word on the subject published in this country. The Hewitt undercut dam was and is unqiue.

He made the structure from stone, rough lumber, and logs or planks. Two logs or planks, perpendicular to the stream flow, were propped with rocks so that their position was above the surface and almost the length of the boards apart. Rough lumber was then nailed to them, forming a table with stone legs. The next step was to remove the rocks supporting the upstream end of the wooden flat and the sinking of this part with rocks. More rocks were then placed at the sides of the structure so that the entire flow of the stream passed over the boards with no breakout on either side. Thus an incline was formed that created the flat water of a dam on the upstream side, a hollow of quiet water underneath, and a waterfall and gouged pool below the falls.

Hewitt explained that once he had constructed several of these dams on his water, the annual catch of large trout, fish over 18 inches in length, increased tenfold. The cover provided by the boards and the falls of the pool was particularly attractive to the big brood fish on their migrations from the lower reaches after hot weather set in.

John C. Youngman, Esquire, of Williamsport, Pennsylvania, created a dam of ingenious design, a log-jam or brush-pile stream structure. On each bank he anchored a short piece of railroad track with several holes drilled in it by embedding it in a hole filled with concrete. Between these two anchor points he loosely stretched several strands of heavy steel cable, well clamped to prevent slippage. Brush was then woven and hooked into the cables. The result was a brush pile for cover and a flat pool above, which is ideal for evening feeders that come out from under the brush. The current can be forced by judicious trimming to flow over, under, or through the overhead cover as desired.

The Ellis Neuman design, like the Youngman approach, involves a cable, but in this instance holes are drilled through large stones, then the stones are strung on the cable to form a seminatural check dam that will withstand freshet and flood. The ends of the cable are attached to trees or posts.

Fred Everett, the nature artist, did his stream-improvement work on the Kinderhook near his home 10 miles from Albany, New York. Fred was under doctor's orders to take things easy and his helpers were his fourteen-year-old son and two daughters, thus by force of circumstance the line of least resistance had to be followed. To make a dam they stretched hog wire across the stream, stapling the ends to trees on the bank. To support the wire, large stakes were driven into the stream bed so they slanted downstream. In front of the hog wire and the stakes they placed one-inch mesh chicken wire, the kind that is galvanized before weaving. Stones anchored the lower apron of the wire. In due time a profusion of leaves, twigs, and aquatic vegetation lodged against the wire, forcing the water up and over, thus creating a dam with a trout holding pool above it. They called this their "grass skirt body of water."

They then set to work making individual trout homes. Flat rocks were pried up, then the downstream ends were propped up so the water would slip over them and trout could get under them. Other hides were low stone tables. They also gouged out undercuts in the banks back of roots and rocks.

I built in the LeTort what I now call the big-fish dam because I saw in it two trout together, one an estimated 28 inches, the other several inches less. In the middle of the channel an upstream arc made of large and heavy flat stones featuring keystones in the middle was carefully fitted together, then on top of this I placed a second tight-fitting layer. On both sides of this I put pipes perpendicular to the stream flow. Rocks were then piled over the pipes. The ultimate effect was a dam with a chute in the middle. The chute cleaned out a fine pool with a brush pile at the end of it, and, of course, the trout can swim right into the bowels of the dam.

These are the special dams with which one can operate. Circumstances would determine which is most practical.


## WALLS

Sid Gordon was a stream engineer as well as a talented angler, a gifted writer, and an articulate speaker. For a number of years he was head of the stream-improvement team of the Wisconsin Conservation Department. A chapter of his modern classic, *How to Fish from Top to Bottom*, is devoted to the use of wing deflectors and boom cover to prevent erosion. He had some words of advice. "Be sure the deflectors are placed and angled so the intended purpose is accomplished. The height of walls should be such that they protrude above the surface in low water only. Wherever feasible use rocks in preference to logs. Open V dams and open Y dams drive water down the middle of the old channel and away from banks. The wing deflectors, alternating from one bank to the other, speed up the current and clean up the stream bed, thus increase the food supply."

Vincent C. Marinaro, author of the citation-winning book known to the fly-fishing clan as "The Code" designed a special wing wall for a special situation and purpose. Ultimately a group of us, including Vince, constructed a series of them in a meadow along the greatest tiny river I ever fished. Little Cedar Run had a marvelous evening hatch of sulphur drakes from late April into July and it had some great trout, too, which rose to them. This stream section was fished only from the left bank looking upstream, there being an obstruction on the other side. These special wings were to protrude from the far bank so we could cast across to them. The idea was to have the floating insects drift into the best possible hiding places for good fish without damage to the hatch and for the angler to be able to drift his artificial to trout feeding therein.

The stone wing wall Vince designed was shaped much like a fishhook, the open part upstream, the eye tabbed into the bank. Over the bow and above the surface of the water were placed poles and brush. The flies floated down into the hook under the brush and, if not consumed, out they came again to slide around the end of the hook. By casting quartering downstream with a slack leader one could make his dry fly follow the same natural course. Anticipation ran rampant when the artificial floated under the brush pile to the known feeding position of a fine fish. Sometimes the audible rather than the visible generated the answering strike by the angler. This watershed was not subject to violent flooding; but even at that, now and then it was necessary to replace the overhead cover on the hook dam.

An Italian firm manufactures heavy-gauge wire-mesh containers called "gabions," made specifically to hold together loose stones in stream-improvement deflectors. The big American customer is the U.S. Department of the Interior—both Forest Service and Fish and Wildlife Service. Gabions are available in various sizes. This device, when filled with rocks, can be walked upon and it will withstand floodwater without suffering damage.

The so-called Fox Holes are a LeTort innovation in my own backyard, or is it the front yard? These are straight wing walls and open-V dams made of stone but built around pipes or flue liners so they are hollow. Trout love these tunnels, yet the rock walls perform the customary bottom-cleaning functions. Large trout, and there are some very big ones in this stream, spend much time in the tunnels and therefore do not harass the smaller fish in the open channels. There is more visible feeding now in this unstocked water than there was prior to the construction of the stone tunnels. A hollow wall does not require as many rocks as a solid one of the same size, and this can be an important factor. Galvanized corrugated pipe, such as is utilized for drainage under dirt roads, is ideal for this purpose. There is no reason why this principle could not be applied in conjunction with the gabion.

To the best of my knowledge there have been no periodic stockings of legal-size trout where hollow deflectors have been constructed, but it would not be surprising if such were the case that some fish would hide in the pipes and as a result would not be fished over immediately and caught out quickly. It is my humble opinion that fishing over a concentration of newly stocked trout is not an even contest, thus the more spots they can get into where they cannot be promptly hooked the better. If trout are not landed during the initial fishing flurry or if they are put back a time or two, they catch up to the angler.

There is a specialized device in two variations that can be employed to cope with deep silt deposits and/or badly weeded placid water. One is a submerged log crossing the stream and embedded in both banks; the other is a submerged log that extends approximately halfway across the stream in such a position that it is perpendicular to the flow, this too being dug into the bank. In both instances, the greater the diameter of the log, the greater the silt-moving force and action. Care must be taken in either case to place the log deep enough so that after the silt is moved it will still be submerged. Sections of old telephone poles are ideal for this work. Sometimes it is possible to unload them beside the water upstream of their prepared positions and then float them into place.

A favorite feeding station of trout is at the lower end of deep water after it has shallowed. When such a stream-bed bowl is below overhead cover, it is just that much more attractive. The submerged log deflectors create these spots. A word of warning, though: trout that have located in such places are particularly shy and must be approached and cast to with great care.

Some brush piles are made by natural causes and they provide worthy trout cover. Others can be man-made. If copper wire is employed to anchor them, twists of the wire should be used instead of staples, for copper wire corrodes when placed in contact with other metal that rusts.

It is possible to use burlap bags as forms for concrete. A mixture one-third cement and two-thirds gravel will solidify after being submerged. And, too, it might be possible to arrange with a contractor to secure his extra transit-mixed concrete to be poured into wooden forms. Cement is ground limestone. Why can't snails, shrimp, and sowbugs get lime from a concrete wall for the growth of their shells, as they do from limestone ledges.

Very few streams strike a perfect balance between rate of natural reproduction and carrying capacity. Generally speaking, the percentage of hatch of trout eggs is high in the clear mountain brooklets and low in the slow-flowing meadow streams along which there is pasturing and/or cultivation. But the carrying capacity and the rate of growth are low up in the mountains and high down in the valleys. So it is logical to work for a better balance—more food where the hatch of eggs is fine and a better egg hatch where food is abundant. The strange thing is that both need flowing water over clean gravel. Trout eggs rot in silt. If they are to hatch out they must be deposited in clean gravel. Depth is not as important as rate of flow. Slightly broken water is ideal; white water is too fast. Insects are most abundant where spawning conditions are best.

The trampling of stream banks by cattle causes great long-range siltation, which is harmful. Barnyards, however, are beneficial, for they are responsible for more nitrogen in the water, and nitrogen increases the amount of the basic food, zooplankton.

For about ten years I operated my own experimental trout station. Considerable work was done with man-made spawning beds. Three-quarter-inch river gravel proved to be better than pea gravel. Crushed gravel has too many sharp points. It scratches and cuts the hens as they prepare the redds, thus making the fish vulnerable to fungus. The most desirable rate of flow appeared to be about 4 miles per hour or about 5.75 feet per second—walking speed. Large hens are the best brood fish, for they not only lay more eggs, but they work the gravel better to take care of the eggs.

Fine spawning spots and spawning stretches can be made. One cannot go wrong in dumping a deep bed of three-quarter-inch river gravel into the flowing water at the end of a deflector or in the downstream opening of a V dam. The main thing, though, is to put in about twice as much as it appears should be the case. If possible, freshen up these spots with more gravel each fall.

The obvious payoff of stream-improvement work is the catching of trout that would not have been there had the work not been done. A less obvious reward is bigger fish in more interesting water. The hidden happiness is personal satisfaction, just as it is in angling. Then, too, the actual work is more fun than drudgery.

It is not necessary for the trout angler that there be a nostalgic past hidden in a frenzied present. The time is here for the happy epoch of reclamation. For the sake of our children and the unborn generations, angling for trout should be given a future. There is a diversity of knowledge and there can be a perfection of management. Environment is the first consideration.

The starting point for improvement is a survey of the stream section in question. Then comes the sketch with the proposed devices marked thereon. Plans and thinking may be revised, even after work has started; but that is all right too, for we are not bound by something akin to the law of the Medes and the Persians.

# 27
# Man-made Redds

Living creatures come and living creatures go. Always the old must make way for the young. This is a law of nature. To one degree or another man has upset this normal balance in many streams by lowering the carrying capacity or by decreasing the egg hatch so that the continuity is broken of one pair producing and sustaining one pair. Man can bring about a beneficial readjustment in the case of the trout stream with a trout-egg hatch decreased to such a degree that the carrying capacity far exceeds the rate of natural reproduction by the improvement of headwater spawning conditions.

Unfortunately for the trout angler, the typical situation today is a relatively low rate of hatch in the richer streams where the carrying capacity is best, and a high rate of hatch in the poorer streams where the trout are famished and stunted. The rich streams, sometimes alkaline, are in the fertile valleys, and, at least to a degree, are open to sunshine; the lean streams are the shaded mountain brooklets fed by acid water that flows through wood mulch.

It is siltation that decays eggs and silt that coats spawning beds to the extent that they disappear. Man has caused this unnatural condition with his necessary agricultural activity and by grazing his cattle to and into the water in the meadowtype trout stream. Hatch is a matter of degree. Dr. Edwin Cooper of Pennsylvania State University notes that the stream census work that his classes carry on, utilizing electric shocking devices, show that practically all trout waters have natural reproduction. This can be limited or excessive, contingent upon spawning conditions.

"Freshening up" the upper half of the man-made spawning area on the LeTort with an annual planting of gravel. *Photo by Lefty Kreh.*

To rectify the situation where the egg hatch is deficient, a face-lifting, not a head-to-toe overhauling, is in order. The fact of the matter is that this sort of thing is warranted in practically all meadow-type streams but not in the clear tumbling mountain brooklets. The job, although work, is not as extensive as one might think; and it is interesting. The following has to do with a stream section two of us take care of each year.

It was perfectly evident to Ed Weidner and me that this stream could adequately support a much greater head of trout than the existing native population. Old-timers advised that fifty years ago the entire stream bed was sparkling clean gravel edged with watercress, but decade after decade there was deterioration and disappearance of gravel until no gravel could be seen except in the headwater branches. By necessity this was where the existing spawning came to take place.

Siltation was hastened here by the accidental introduction of elodea, a water weed that grows so densely that the root systems collect silt. This weed, however, is not all bad, for it harbors a tremendous amount of food, some of which is always available. In the winter the stems break and the tops float away, many developing roots and catching elsewhere downstream. If the valley is flat, such as this, stream channels form in the weed beds and from year to year these may shift. The result is a widening of the stream, and that in turn slows the flow, a vicious circle. When the banks are broken down by watering cattle, deterioration is hastened.

The stream part that was chosen is a 300-foot badly silted section on a bend one mile downstream from the existing gravel area. New construction work close by provided a bumper supply of chunks of limestone, and a road to the streamside made possible the delivery of gravel to a convenient central place.

The first efforts were with the pieces of limestone. The flow was pinched at the upper end with two wing dams to cause turbulence and aeration. A submerged wall always requires more stone than the original guesstimate suggests. Below this were constructed two fishhook dams, one below the other and one from each side of the stream.

Water action moved the soft silt in a matter of days. Then we gave the bottom a good coating of three-quarter-inch river gravel purchased for the purpose, wherever the rate of flow of the water was medium or fast.

Farther downstream at the end of a bend, we restricted the flow between a rock wall and a mass of willow roots. Altogether two loads, 19 tons of gravel, were moved into the stream by bucket, bag, and wheelbarrow in our two-man operation of 1963. By then it was mid-October and time to sit back and watch for results.

We were not disappointed. During the month of November four major beds or nests were made in the loose gravel by medium-size brown trout. The places they preferred were in medium-fast, well-aerated water, 1 foot to 18 inches in depth in the hook dams and at the ends of the dams. The glaring weakness was limited facilities, no doubt some fish spoiling what others before them had done. In due time there was a hatch of trout eggs. In late March and early April some little parr-marked fish almost 1 inch in length showed up in the shallows, strung out along each bank.

Encouragement was such from our pilot model of man-made redds that it was decided to add more each fall until a model 300-foot stream section would be rehabilitated for the purpose of spawning and also to try to stabilize the sulphur hatch, which is adversely affected by too much weed and which thrives in a rock and gravel bottom.

Prior to the 1964 spawning season, Ed and I laid up some wing walls to confine the stream flow and rolled some large rocks into strategic spots. After the bottom had been given time to scour, 16 tons of three-quarter-inch river gravel were placed where it appeared they would do the most good. Now we believed the new spawning area to be big enough to contribute to the stream population of trout and at the same time improve fly hatches.

The first spawner to work the gravel, a 20-inch hen, appeared October 21 and remained for three days with several males. Each day thereafter for some time new ones moved in, mostly large fish, the ratio being about three males to one female.

Most days there were two or three groups but on November 10 there were seven. Competition between the males was great, which took the form of violent chasing, the largest in the group always dominating.

For the first three weeks it was mainly larger fish, about eight of the hens being 16 to 20 inches. The fourth week smaller fish were present. Peak days were: October 29, 30, 31; November 9 through 12. There were no spawners from December 2 through December 5. The last appeared, or rather disappeared, December 20. One lone brook trout was observed, but there could have been more. Altogether the trout worked twelve different beds.

A pattern had been established. The old nests or spots utilized in 1963 were again the scenes of activity, and the new spots similar to the old ones were well worked. A hen, followed by pugnacious cock fish, moved in. Periodically she turned on her side and by violently contorting her body moved the gravel in a downstream hump. This went on for three or four days, usually the former, then the group broke up or disappeared, all the eggs having been deposited.

An oddity occurred. The major spawning beds of the stream are located in the two branches one mile upstream from our man-made redds. The spawning up there, just one mile away, does not get under way until about two weeks after it commences in the lower area, but it continues there for well over two months after it is all over below. Brook trout spawning in the branches is heavy but almost nonexistent one mile downstream. This starts about the time the last of the browns move out. It should be noted that this is a late-run stream.

Ed and I wanted to know exactly what happens from the day the eggs are deposited until the little ones are capturing their own food. Amazingly, different biologists had made different reportings. For example, there was confused reporting about courtship and actual spawning and there was a difference of opinion as to the duration of time involved in the absorption of the egg sack in the normal conditions of winter.

Observation leads me to believe that brook trout and brown trout make different types of nests and they make their nests in different ways. The female brown trout moves a considerable quantity of light or heavy gravel by turning on her side and violently working the tail, thus with the help of the current loose gravel is rolled downstream into a heap; whereas the female brook trout pushes a small amount of light gravel sideways with her body, first to make a depression for the deposition of the eggs, then to move round pebbles back to crudely cover the eggs. Brown trout do an extensive and elaborate job of it; brook trout put forth a more modest effort. It appears to me that three-quarter-inch river gravel (not crushed gravel) is the best size for placement in man-made redds where brown trout are expected to spawn, whereas a finer size, commercially called "pea gravel," seems best for brook trout; however, we have seen that both will use either.

The female brown trout starts by fanning out a trough in the gravel, the moved pebbles and sand forming a bank or bar below the depression. It certainly appears that the eggs and sperm upon being expelled are to lodge on the upstream side of the bank of gravel. Apparently then more work is done at the head of the trough, which in turn covers the first group of eggs to be deposited. Little by little eggs are deposited, fertilized, and covered. It appears that this process lasts about three or four days. Once the female chooses her bed and starts making it, it is the act of spawning, not courtship.

The very shape of the place where the eggs are laid forces water to flow over and around them, apparently nature's way continuously to wash and aerate the precious contents of the redds. This appears to be vital in the case of brown trout eggs but not in the case of brook trout eggs.

As for the actual egg laying and fertilization Brian Curtis in his work, *The Life Story of the Fish*, writes:

> ...she suddenly drops into the center of this pit, with her vent and anal fin well down in the deepest part. The male immediately moves up into position alongside, with his vent opposite hers, and heeled over so that his abdomen is close to hers. With downwardly arched bodies quivering, with open mouths testifying to the muscular strain of the act, they discharge the eggs and milt at exactly the same instant. This is important for two reasons: first, because otherwise the milt might be carried away by the current without reaching the eggs, and second, because, although the eggs remain fertilizable for several minutes, the sperms lose their potency within forty-five seconds after they have entered the water.

I have observed extra males suddenly rush into a nest when, unlike the usual, there is no attempt by the attending cock fish to drive them out. It very well could be that these fish are so stimulated by the sight or smell of the eggs that they rush in and discharge their sperm, hence they too may fertilize some eggs— nature's way of preventing infertility.

In due course the eggs hatch, the colder the water the longer the incubation period. It would not be nature's plan to permit the eggs to hatch so early in the year that there would not be sufficient food to feed the alevins. The closer to the spring source, the warmer the water in the winter; therefore the shorter the upstream egg-hatching period.

Right at the spring source of this particular stream the water temperature is always about 51°. One mile downstream where we placed the materials for redds, the water chills down in the winter to an average of possibly 40°-45°. Hatchery men have discovered that the hatching time for brown trout eggs in 45° water is sixty to sixty-five days.

Upon hatching, the translucent alevin has a large orange egg sack, which sustains life for about ten days with no feeding. This odd-looking little creature that appears to be more like a grub than a fish rests in its well-aerated dark cavern in the gravel pile while the sack is slowly absorbed. Then comes the time for the trim little fish to wiggle or swim away from the security of the gravel and struggle to the shallows along the shoreline to feed and live dangerously.

Each baby settles in a suitable feeding station from which it will consume microscopic zooplankton. Four hours on end the inch-long alevins will hold their feeding positions, now and then rising to the surface to take a drifting morsel. Always they are strung out, not schooled, each in his own place acting as we like to see big trout perform.

At our setup it is late March and early April when these babies make their appearance and we watch them. Once the grass at the edge of the stream starts to acquire some length, they are most difficult to spot. According to our arithmetic, some should be seen earlier, but for some reason they aren't and we can't fathom it.

The 1965 spawning season in the rehabilitated section was more impressive than the previous ones in regard to length of season, number of fish, size of fish, and quantity of hatch. Ed and I rejoiced in the belief that our continued effort was reaping dividends. "Look at the fruit of the union of our fish at the places we provided," one of us smilingly said to the other.

A badly needed and large water-restricting wall and an effective hook dam below it were built prior to the '65 spawning season, and these used up the last of the available chunks of limestone. To this was added 10 tons of gravel. Our operation could be compared to a stretching spring. The farther we worked our way from the stockpiles of gravel and the scattered chunks of limestone, the harder the pull. Thus our '65 effort did not appear to be as great as that of '63 and '64, but actually it was.

Although there were in use seventeen provided redds, there should be more, for most of them are used by more than one hen. The most groups of spawning trout that were observed at any time were eight but on various days there were four to six. The largest hen seen was approximately 26 inches and the attending cock fish a 2-footer. About half the hens were over 15 inches in length.

Peak days were October 16, November 13 and 14, November 20–26, December 9–11. The first hen we saw working the gravel was on October 6 in '65, as opposed to October 21 in '64. The last of the spawning hens to leave was on Christmas Day, as opposed to December 19 the previous year. Altogether, we believed that over fifty hens had deposited their eggs in the places that had been provided for that purpose. Definitely the '65 spawning season on the man-made redds was a good one.

Spawning time provided a spectacular show. At this time trout are not nearly as wily as is the case the rest of the year, with the result that it is possible to work up with a minimum of motion to within close range. And too, the spawning cloaks are brilliant and beautiful. Several photographers took advantage of this to make colored moving pictures and transparencies. Some of the motion pictures have become a part of a Pennsylvania fishing picture made by Harry Alleman of Channel 8 TV fame.

Going into the '65 season the water was abnormally low and clear, but by mid-November it was cloudier than was the case the same time the two previous years. During the winter the silt caught by the elodea started to move with the breakup of the weed beds. The result was that the bottom could be seen in but 2½ feet of water instead of 5 feet. We were anxious to determine if newly hatched trout would show up. They did on schedule and in good quantity.

Harry Alleman wanted to add to his trout movies the rest of the story, the alevins feeding and a close-up of one. Early in April we easily secured these pictures. It was the best hatch so far, even though the water had not been as clear as was the case the two previous winters.

All the manual activity preparatory to the '66 spawning season was limited to the freshening up of the old nests with more three-quarter-inch-gravel, and we expect to continue this practice each year.

The first baby trout emerge from the gravel in mid-February, at which time they are three quarters of an inch in length. They do not school, but take individual feeding positions in the shallows along the edges.

By the fall of 1975, eleven successful spawning seasons had come and gone for the man-made redds. The uppermost and largest of these areas was located directly below the aerator and was about 25 feet in width. Time demonstrated that only one hen at a time would move in and utilize it. This seemed to be a waste of valuable space and time. So I decided to attempt to divide this large spawning area into several smaller ones. I constructed barely submerged stone walls parallel with the flow and placed fresh loose gravel in each. In effect the area was divided into eight stalls. The stone walls worked perfectly. Now there were eight beds where previously there had been one, and no conflict occurred between fish. In fact, there was one short period when all of the new nests were occupied at the same time. A second section, then a third and a fourth will be subdivided in like manner, hopefully again multiplying the number of nests.

The number of large brood fish is annually increasing. The big hens are the important ones because they lay more eggs than the first-time spawners and they make bigger and better nests. It seems logical that the larger fish could work the so-called one-inch gravel as well as the smaller ones handle the half-inch and three-quarter-inch grade; so experimentation is currently being conducted with the more coarse type, which would catch and cover more eggs and facilitate the escape of the fry.

Spawning takes its toll. What Frank Sawyer adds about this cannot be taken lightly because he was born along the river Avon of southern England and became a river keeper at the age of eighteeen. Now as an elderly citizen he is still a river keeper and one who has gained great renown. In describing the beginning of the end for a trout in his modern classic, *Keeper of the Stream*, he writes as follows:

> Rich summer feeding is needed to make up for loss of feeding during winter and for the strength he expends in spawning, but during the summer following the first three spawnings he is able to mend his condition and add a little to length and girth. But at six years old he finds the balance—the rich feeding of spring and summer does no more than compensate for the loss of condition through spawning. And so it continues. He may live on for several years— losing weight in winter, gaining it again by the following autumn— but slowly, though surely, he finds it more difficult to maintain the

balance. As he ages, so his eyesight fails. Young fish are more active in taking the food supply. Spawning saps his strength, and no longer can he live where maximum food is to be found. A year or two may pass and though he goes to the spawning grounds, he no longer takes an active part. Summer feeding becomes more and more difficult and soon he is forced to feed by sense of smell. Gradually he gets thinner, and now weighs no more than he did at three years old. He seeks the backwaters and quiet places about the river—places where he need no longer use his fins and strength to maintain a position.

As we watch the trout on the redds, certain questions come to mind and some conclusions are drawn.

I think I have observed the same hen at the same redd on successive seasons. Ornithologists have watched the same birds nest in the same localities on successive years. Assuming that such is the case with both, would this be indicative of individual memory or racial instinct?

Some of the eggs in the nests that are worked hard by more than one hen appear to be buried by as much as a foot of gravel. If the gravel is coarse enough the eggs have a chance to live and the alevins a chance to escape, but it does not seem likely that either could be the case with pea gravel.

Why is it that the rainbow trout in the hatcheries are ripe and ready to be stripped in the fall, but once established in a land-locked setup in the East they become spring spawners?

Certainly the most valuable brood hens are the large ones, not only because they deposit more and larger eggs than smaller fish, but because they work the gravel better.

Either there are many more males than females in a native population, or the cocks attend more than one hen at various times.

Nature provides for catastrophe. Such provisions come in the form of an extended spawning season, extended hatching time, extra eggs, extra milt, extra brood fish, scattered spawning, etc.

It is interesting to note that the best environment for spawning is the best environment for most of the aquatic hatches, thus this type of stream rehabilitation serves a dual purpose.

Evidence is strong that there is a slow, upstream, prespawning

Susie Fox displays a burly LeTort brown trout.

migration, a sort of trout shuffle, which coincides with the start of hot weather. This, I believe, is to steer the brood fish into the best feeding environment preparatory to the rigors demanded of them in the process of recreation. Digestion is fastest in water temperature of the low sixties, so under such a condition they eat the most and eat the most frequently; thus nature directs them to the places where they can best prepare themselves for their most important mission in life.

When that powerful urge prompts a brood trout of our stream to seek a bed of suitable gravel in aerated shallows, they now have twenty-four places to examine. That certainly is to the good. The main job now is to have these spawning beds in good shape each fall. However, it would be fine if more were added.

# 28

# *The Commonwealth's Gem*

Beauty is in the eyes of the beholder, association being so important. Among the combined factors are the visual, the emotional, the sought after, and the ultimate. An extensive rise of trout in a scenic setting is to the fly fisherman, beauty in its most enticing and spectacular form.

In describing a scene on a stream, Theodore Gordon wrote in the April 6, 1907, issue of *Forest and Stream*:

> I wish that it was possible to revisit all our old haunts during the best portion of the season. There are many fine streams in Pennsylvania which I have not fished for many years. Some of these are ideal from the dry-fly fisher's point of view, particularly the limestone streams which are formed by great springs which gush from the rocks in large volume. . . . In June I have seen the water covered with the dimples made by rising trout as far as my view extended. This was in the evening after the sun was off the water, in Big Spring, a large spring which flows through Newville, Pennsylvania.

"Water covered with the dimples made by rising trout as far as my view extended"—there is the supreme situation for a trout stream; but here is more by Gordon about the Cumberland Valley and Big Spring, only this appeared in the *Fishing Gazette*, dateline May 26, 1906:

> ...These differ from the mountain streams to the north and south, in flowing through comparatively level country, are slow-flowing, with short riffles and many dams. There is much moss in

these streams; they are full of food for trout and are well stocked [by nature]. It is not easy to take the trout after the first few days of the open season. On one of them usually known as the "Big Spring" . . . the catch used to foot up 3,000 to 4,000 trout in the opening day, over 100 rods being at work.

The native anglers made their own rods of two pieces of hickory, lashed or ferruled together and painted green. Usually they cared not for a reel but wound the surplus line in one place on the rod, carrying it from that point and hitching it at the extreme tip. As a rule they used but one fly, and cast about 35 ft. to 40 ft. When a trout rose and was hooked, the rod was dropped into the hollow of the left arm, and the fish was played and landed by hand. They did not allow much law. As my first experience was gained by the side of one of these old fish-hawks, I very naturally imitated him and fished in the same way until I learned better. The streams just mentioned would be ideal, I should think, for dry-fly. I intend to revisit them, but probably the majority of them are no longer open to the public. If stocked with brown trout they would produce very large fish. I never saw a native [brook] trout in them over 2½ lb. to 2¾ lb., but they are perfect in shape.

What of a greater complimentary nature could be reported of a trout stream, and who could be a more highly respected reporter?

There is no evidence that Theodore Gordon ever revisited Big Spring or the beautiful Cumberland Valley, but had he in his day, or his spirit today, he would find that the stream is still open to public fishing. Furthermore, Big Spring will always be fishable to anyone who cares to give it a try, because the Commonwealth of Pennsylvania has purchased the upper three miles, which for practical purposes is Big Spring.

Like Gordon I can say, "I have seen the water covered with dimples made by rising trout as far as my view extended"; and may I add, "After it is so dark that rises can be seen only on the silvery spots, I have heard the slurps up and down as far as their sound waves carry to eardrums."

Permit me to pick up the Big Spring story where Gordon left off, for I not only cherish the place but have lived my entire life within convenient striking distance of it and have often visited there. Now 11 miles separate home and the spring.

In my judgment the stream deserves fame and notoriety. This is why: the carrying capacity is tremendous, insuring a marvelous rate of growth and some huge fish. The volume and the temperature are constant, insuring a wonderful holdover quality month-by-month and year-round development. The spawning conditions are normally great, creating a heavy native population. All these things for many years were in perfect balance, a normal condition for this stream yesterday, and it can be so again.

Since the conclusion of my college days in 1931, many streams have been visited. Of them all, this one must be placed at the head of the list for productivity. Ecologically it is the top rung of the trout ladder.

Over the years it has featured two types of superb fishing. When there is no breeze to ruffle the surface and the sun is shining, one can spot the fish, then watch the one over which he wants to fish. As the fly drifts into the window of trout vision the receptive or nonreceptive attitude is observed. Either the offering is ignored as though it were not even seen, or the fish moves to take a look, or the fly is accepted. More often than not it is the second.

Such a fish is on the feed; now it is up to the angler. Who said stream-bred brook trout in a rich environment are pushovers? For me they have been more challenging than browns in the same water. The right fly, attached to the right leader, cast right should score; but it doesn't always work out that way. Many fish, for one reason or another, decide your offering is not for them and they cease and desist in their game of coming short. It seems advisable to give an interested fish ample time and opportunity to take a fly. Often pattern appears to be the problem because after some changing, a new fly is finally taken. And, too, certain fish will not come at all for certain patterns.

If a trout ignores your fly, that is, does not move for it after about half a dozen good drifts, it is time to forget this one and look for another. I suspect such fish have eaten well and are asleep.

Under certain conditions it is easier to spot the dark shadows on the bottom made by suspended fish than it is to see the trout itself. Always these Big Spring fish are very light in color and they blend in with the clean gravel bottom.

For this natural fishing for natural trout our best daytime patterns have been little jassids and Cinnamon Ants as basics, plus a

#22 Adams, a #24 Coachman, a tiny Black Spider with gold tinsel body, and a blob of hare's-ear fur dubbed on a #22 hook.

These trout are regularly exposed to fishermen, so they put up with them and live with them. They don't bolt for cover unless almost stepped upon; nonchalantly they ease away to another feeding spot. Bold as they are toward men and boots and moving rods, etc., they are as shy and crafty as they can be to bull-rope tactics, drag, sloppy casts, oversize flies, etc. What appear to be the dumbest of trout turn out to be the most difficult of all to fool with either wet or dry fly. The marvel of it is the ability of the angler not only to watch the trout over which he chooses to cast, but to a degree read its mind by the reaction to the offering.

This highly specialized and intriguing style of angling drifts into another type after sunset. Evening after evening there is a terrific rise of fish of all sizes—rings and dimples as far as the view extends. Every drift or retrieve of the fly covers more than one actively feeding brook trout. It would appear to be a simple matter to catch fish after fish, but try it and see how you make out. They do not seem to be less difficult now than they were earlier in the day. Here is a case of one fascinating challenge melting into an entirely different kind of fascinating challenge, both featuring dry-fly fishing. In writing about the floating fly Lord Grey advised:

> Those who know and practice the art best are the epicures among anglers; they have carried both the skill and pleasure of angling to a height of exquisite refinement.

Basically this is a brook trout stream. It would seem that somewhere between fifty and a hundred of the native species are taken for every one of the exotic brown trout. In a Gordon quotation is the sentence: "If stocked with brown trout they [the limestone streams] would produce very large fish." No browns were planted in it by man, but there are a few there. Where they originally came from, no one can be sure. The first one I heard about showed up in the late thirties, a 4-pounder caught downstream at the town of Newville.

Annually a few brood browns spawn near the head of the stream in early November before the brook trout gather on the redds. One weekend Vince Marinaro and I watched a pair of 6-pounders on a big nest with a 15-inch male hanging around the edges. On our return the following weekend they were gone and there were five other newly made and recently vacated nests, some bigger than the first.

Gordon's prediction brings up the question, what is a large brown trout? The following will answer that question, at least for one of the streams about which he wrote:

### Large Brown Trout from Big Springs

| Length | Weight | Date | How Taken | By Whom |
|--------|--------|------|-----------|---------|
| 31½ in. | 15½ lb. | 6/2/39 | Nymph & Spinner | W. Donald Martin |
| 32 | 16 lb. 7 oz. | 5/28/45 | Pflueger Lure | William McKinley |
| 29 | 8¾ lb. | 6/17/61 | Pearl Wobbler | Wilber Getter |
| 30 | 9¼ lb. | 4/23/66 | Streamer Fly | Jack Escherman |
| 31¼ | 14½ lb. | 7/10/66 | Worm | Bobby Michaels |
| 32½ | 17½ lb. | 7/18/66 | Worm | Kenneth Aspers |
| 28 | 11 lb. | | Worm | Chester G. Bostwick |

The upper half mile produced the state record; then it proceeded to break its own record, then break that. If one can believe what he hears, the biggest of them all is swimming around up there now, a 20-pounder, no less. What an array of battle wagons!

In addition, as would be expected, some huge fish have been lost, and some lesser fish; nevertheless, big trout have been caught by local anglers, including Wilber E. Getter, George D. Ranik, Robert Goldsmith, Lloyd Wagner, Garrett Mortensen, and Dick Swartz.

Why from so few brown trout are there such big ones? It is doubtful if environment alone or strain alone could be responsible, but the combination of the two is something else again.

Maybe someday, or some night, one of these massive fish will come my way. After all, fishing partner of old, Don Martin, set out to get one and he was successful. It would be extra fine if it happened on a dry fly—say a Chauncy Livly Cricket attached to a 2X leader tippet.

The first threat to the stream—probably it was a crisis— occurred at Big Spring in 1937. At the head was a beautiful millpond of about 7 acres and a particularly handsome and large limestone mill nestled in 39 acres of land featuring a primitive appearance. The millers, Messrs. Felix and Lindsey, who owned and operated the grist mill, were ready to retire; so the property was for sale. The streamside scuttlebutt had it that New York City interests were impressed by the local labor market and the manner in which the structure lent itself to conversion into a factory. We fishermen had visions of an eyesore, a running sore, a fluctuating volume of water, and everything else that alarms anglers.

The eight-man board of the fish commissioners was to meet the following Monday. It was the custom of five of them to travel on Sunday and get together in the capital city in the evening. I invited myself to join their gathering in order that the Big Spring tale of woe could be poured forth. What was said was taken seriously because they figured it would be the proper thing to match the out-of-state money in an effort to protect the source for fishing.

Several months later title passed hands and the fish commission and the fishermen owned their second piece of Pennsylvania trout water, the other being the "Paradise" on Spring Creek near Bellefonte. Strangely, though, the new acquisition did not include the cliff side where the great spring outcrops at the head of the pond.

The second crisis came more than two decades later when a newly constructed dam silted the major spawning beds, the purpose being to divert water into the troughs of a private hatchery. The Big Spring fishermen had advocated the construction of a flume instead of a dam in order to prevent siltation of the vital spawning area. Much to their amazement and consternation they were faced with defecting sportsmen. Several faraway officials of a statewide fish-and-game organization with no member club in the area conducted a campaign to destroy the protective efforts of the local fishermen and the State Department of Forests and Waters in this conservation battle to prevent the ruination of an irreplaceable natural resource, in this case a natural reproducing trout stream. Just why they chose to do this poses an interesting question. After considerable wrangling a court order directed a lowering of the dam by 16½ inches, which in turn reclaimed some of the lost gravel beds.

The fish commisison removed the boards of the dam and drew

down the pond, then demolished the massive limestone mill, much to the chagrin of local historians and the lovers of architectural beauty.

During the year 1964 the 150-acre farm at the head, including the actual spring, was purchased by the Commonwealth, thus insuring that in the fullness of time the precious groundwater supply near the outcropping spring would not be subject to injury or ruination from nearby septic fields, spraying, gouging, blasting, or boring.

Shortly thereafter the Pennsylvania fishermen and the Pennsylvania Fish Commission were the recipients of an amazing gift, a gift the like of which was never before heard of, nor is it likely to happen again. It was money from the legislature and the voters—up to five million dollars under so-called Project 70. There are two strings attached: the fund is earmarked for acquisition, and whatever is not allocated by December 31, 1970, will never be. Assuming that it is all spent and spent judiciously, this is a bonanza for the future anglers of Pennsylvania.

But this is not all the story. Between the Commonwealth, through the Department of Forests and Waters and the General State Authority; and the federal government, through the Soil Conservation Service, the Fish and Wildlife Service, and the Corps of Army Engineers, there will be constructed an artificial lake within 25 miles of every citizen of the Commonwealth. These will be warm waters not suitable for trout. Thus it is natural to expect the fish commission to devote a reasonable proportion of its five million dollars to the acquisition of trout stream sections.

In 1966 the fish commission, with Project 70 monies, acquired the upper three miles of Big Spring. Included in the purchase is the private hatchery, which has had a devastating effect on the native trout population, although not all of the fine brood stock of the stream is gone.

Whether it was purchased primarily for the hatchery or for trout-fishing potential remains to be seen. One thing is sure: the two are not compatible here. It may be that the fisherman's officialdom is primarily interested in fishing as opposed to artificial propagation, because there is a tremendous state hatchery 5 miles away at Huntsdale. So the setting in which the gem is located is now a matter of conjecture.

Let us, you and I, dream a dream for our children so that in time they, like Theodore Gordon, will see on Big Spring, "water covered with dimples made by rising trout as far as the view extends"—trout native to the stream, the real thing.

The concrete structures of the hatchery could be leveled with a bulldozer so the area could be developed into a camp-site and parking place with appropriate facilities.

I would restore the millpond at the source by repairing the existing dam: 1) because it is more beautiful that way—presently an eyesore; 2) because it is more fishable in that form; 3) because the water has a chance in the fishing season to climb into the more desirable high fifties before it flows over the blue-ribbon fishing territory; and 4) when it spills over the six-foot falls and splashes on the concrete apron, the saturation point of oxygen is attained (15 parts per million) and undesirable gases are released.

Of the four, the last is by far the most important because the added oxygen increases the rate of natural reproduction.

On the subject of oxygen being a factor in egg hatch Frank Sawyer, the eminent river keeper on the Avon in southern England, wrote in his great work, *Keeper of the Stream*, the following:

> Though eggs may suffer serious mortality through lack of aeration, too much cannot occur, for even though the bubbling water gives a continual movement to the eggs, it has no detrimental effect. I know many people are of the opinion that any disturbance of trout eggs is disastrous during the first three weeks or so of their incubation, but I have repeatedly found that provided the eggs have been properly fertilized and are laid down in suitable surroundings, movement is an advantage rather than the reverse.

With the oxygen-saturated crystal-clear water restoring the high rate of egg hatch, natural fishing for natural fish would be restored. In order to catch the real thing—stream-bred trout of good size—it would not be necessary to travel to some distant and inaccessible place.

Quality fishing would be developed by increasing the size limit and decreasing the creel limit and by the introduction of the conservation practice of returning fish caught when fly fishing with barbless hooks. The basic principle would be to protect the fish until each is old enough and big enough to have enjoyed and indulged in at least one spawning season. A 9-inch limit and a 4-fish creel would do well. There would be none of this robbing of the cradle, and fish-hog kills. Neither would there be ugly competition for easy-to-kill fish, which fosters greed and bad manners. It would be sport fishing only and of the highest order.

Theodore Gordon had his own idea of the minimum size that should be taken:

> I fancy a trout should be big enough to take line from the reel before it is considered large enough to kill. . . . The killing of a large trout is remembered with a thrill of pleasure when heavy baskets of small fish are forgotten. If we reckon our baskets in pounds instead of in numbers it would be better.

It would be well to shave the top off the hatchery dam so the pool of the dam, the flat, would not exceed 100 yards. This would reclaim a valuable and needed spawning area, now defunct, but at the same time maintain a holdover flat for the development of some real trophies.

The graveled area is far too fine and too valuable to be stocked. Here is a stream section where excellent fishing to a fine native population could be maintained at no extra cost, in fact at no cost.

Below the gravel area is a logical division, a bridge that crosses the steram. Below this there could be lure and bait fishing and some stocking so that those who do not choose to fish where the conservation regulations are in force could enjoy the great stream, too. It would be the part these fishermen would like best because this is the bigger and deeper water, where there is room for long spin casting.

A new state hatchery, as proposed, at the head of Big Spring, would be a catastrophe because this would sound the death knell for the wonderful native population about which Theodore Gordon wrote. Anglers know that the area downstream of a hatchery does not harbor stream-bred fish. However, so that it will not be claimed "You are not a scientist; therefore, you are not qualified to pass judgment," I turn to one who received his doctorate in the scientific fisheries field. In effect Dr. Albert Hazzard said the following: "We do not know why stream-bred trout will not use the water below a trout hatchery, but we do know they are not there. The oxygen content, the maximum water temperature and the food supply may be satisfactory, but something else is very wrong."

I offer as a possibility the following reasons: the water does not taste and smell right to wild trout, or the particles of hatchery waste that drift in suspension catch in the gills, or the trout die off rapidly from disease or parasites.

It would be a sacrilege to sacrifice the real thing so that an inferior substitute could be propagated for artificial use and thereby destroy what is a tremendous natural resource and a superb attraction. Then, too, there is the horrible threat of a state activity contaminating an existing municipal water supply.

Nearby to the south is an intake and outlet to Interstate Route 81, the major north-south artery; and nearby to the north is access to and from the Pennsylvania Turnpike, the east-west daddy of all express highways. The Big Spring could become the Pennsylvania showcase for fine stream-bred trout fishing and a popular angling headquarters. Working from this hub in the great limestone spring country, there is Falling Springs 15 miles to the west, the LeTort 12 miles to the east, and the Upper Yellow Breeches 8 miles to the south. As a trout town, attractive little Newville would experience an economic boost.

Sooner or later those who understand the tourist value of colored foliage, blooms, music festivals, antique shows, battlefields, ski resorts, etc., are going to understand, too, the value of quality trout fishing. F$SH$NG it will be.

The biggest business in the United States today is the tourist trade. Experts advise that the tourist dollar funnels down through seven hands before it disappears. Extensive survey reveals that there is a marked swing from spectator sports to participant sports. The pollsters have found that fishing attracts the greatest number of devotees. More miles are driven in quest of it than in search of any other recreation.

When the fly fisherman for trout finds what he likes, he frequently returns. Because of this repetitive feature he is unique among tourists. His season is a long one, too. Furthermore, any hobbyist is a free spender—on his hobby.

Many is the town throughout the extensive trout belt that could capitalize on trout fishing and attract visitors in quantity by a simple means. The bait that catches the avid angler is quality fishing. Quality trout fishing is consistently good fishing. This is developed by the simple means of zoning a stream. The consistent fishing is where flies only are employed in conjunction with a high size limit and low creel limit. The good head of trout is present because a trout is used more than once. Fish taken on flies are lip-hooked, and this is not painful or damaging to a fish. Unfortunately, catching and safely returning does not work so well with other types of fishing.

Any town that develops, maintains, and promotes nearby quality fishing will have many visitors it otherwise would not see, and more likely than not they will appear regularly—substantial free-spending citizens, highly desirable guests.

From the standpoint of management it is most expensive to attempt to hold the borderline trout fishermen in the fishing license fold, for their demands for periodic limits directly following the departure of the fish truck are costly indeed. From the standpoint of economics, this system is not defensible. On the other hand, a stocking can go a long way and last a long time for those who by choice use the trout more than once.

Catering to the trout-angling fraternity really means catering to the habitué, the hobbyist, the regular fisherman, not the periodic local fish-truck chaser.

On the other hand, should the regular angler be ignored and should management be geared to belly fishing for the relatively small band of periodic local limit seekers, the gem will be mounted in a valueless and crude setting. Likewise, the stream can be crippled if the fish commission decides to construct a hatchery at or near the source, for native fish will not use the water below a hatchery. Time will tell what thinking will prevail, which in turn will determine the nature of the setting for the Commonwealth's gem.

It has been more than a decade since the foregoing chapter was written. In the passage of time the landscape has changed in the rural village of Springfield at the head of Big Spring. Pennsylvania authorities elected to construct and maintain a mammoth trout hatchery at the source.

A view of Big Spring, once among the greatest of natural trout streams in America. Hatchery effluent has ruined the stream's spawning grounds, although a population of stocked trout is maintained. *Photo by Vince Marinaro.*

The effluent from the troughs, which in reality is from the trout, stains the once crystalline water and gray slime coats the once sparkling gravel. The great native population of brook trout is no more. There does, however, exist some stocked trout fishing in the water below, which has been "improved," and the average-size fish is 17 inches.

It is not my role to pass judgment on the merits or demerits of the conversion that sacrificed the real thing at one place so that an inferior substitute could be put at another. It is my province, though, to advise readers that this book chapter is no longer a suggestion or recommendation to visit Big Spring in order to enjoy some natural fishing for a unique native trout population; rather it is the documentary of the glory days of a once tremendous stream, the elements of whose anatomy were in near-perfect balance.

As though it were retribution for not preventing the construction of that hatchery, I now, along with twenty thousand others, drink the hatchery sewage in a diluted and treated form.

# 29

# *A Matter of Management*

It is imminent that the trout scene will see a mating of philosopher and scientist, something that has taken place in so many other areas. Being one who relishes fly fishing, I want to be around after such a union has taken place because there will result trouting the like of which never before has been seen or sampled. The scientist may be the better half of the pair, but the philosopher will wear the pants. Ferris Greenslet, man of letters and world traveler, no doubt in his day would have agreed, for he wrote, "Fishing is not a competitive sport but a branch of philosophy." Once goals have been set by the philosopher, the scientist will take over in order to achieve the desired end: quality fishing—supercolossal quality fishing.

A demand for the finest possible stems from the hobbyist, the individual who really cares. He is the one who lavishes time and money on this recreation. As a tourist or as a customer he is a free spender of considerable value to others. When he hears of some quality fishing he samples it, and when he finds what he likes he returns. Thus it is his desires that are important to many non-fishermen involved in interests related directly or indirectly to fishing.

To him the art of fly fishing for trout never was, nor will be, a simple affair. The true greatness of the happy sport is due to two features: the fascination of the problems presented, and the glory of the environment in which the adherent operates. Accumulated knowledge, the powers of observation and analysis, experience and skill combine to meet the challenge of imitation, deception, and approach, all of which are complicated.

Each stream presents an individual problem to be solved and understood, its moods and manners caught. A rising trout of handsome proportions is the ultimate for which the fly fisherman's ear is tuned, his eye is cocked, and his fly is cast. Given this situation, the topside angler is kept in absorbed delight as time gently passes, but it is a hoped-for rather than an expected event.

Thus, the age-old conquest is in progress: man against a creature of nature. Before the dawn of civilization man depended upon wildlife for sustenance. Through the ages necessity forced him to catch food and clothing, to gather food and clothing, to produce food and clothing. He was called upon to provide and protect. That was life; it was fun. Now there exists a latent desire to follow in the footsteps of progenitors. Each generation in turn produces a scion cast from the mold of his fathers. Each generation in turn hears the call that has reverberated through the years. As the regular angler answers this deeply ingrained and powerful pull out of the past, his blood is stirred most when he discovers a big surface feeder up front.

Let us investigate further this discriminating descendant of Cro-Magnon who waves a fairy wand as he wades in a stream. Involved is a strange paradox, in fact the strangest for any sport and something positively confounding to the nonangler. The angler sets forth to catch fish, but he does not want to catch them too easily. He likes to catch large ones, but he does not want all of them to be the same size. He does not like to have the experience of fish getting away, but he does not wish to be successful in landing all he hooks. Just because he is after fish does not mean he must kill each in turn as it is reduced to possession. Obviously, necessary requirements in his success formula are a certain degree of failure and considerable uncertainty. The yardstick of success for the serious angler is the degree of personal satisfaction that is realized. He revels in the challenge of natural problems and glories in the solution of some of them; that is angling.

Quality fishing today, under people pressure, comes in two very different forms, each having its period and its place. The one is reserved for vacation time and involved is a major trip to some primitive place. The fish may not be sophisticated, but there will be solitude and rustic beauty in abundance. Such trout fishing is like gold; it is where you find it. But even as wholesome and enjoyable as major trips may be, they will not suffice for the regular angler. He must fish more frequently than the occurrence of vacation time. The second kind of fishing is within easy reach. It is for weekend junkets, or better yet, week-day-evening angling. Fortunate indeed is the man in waders who can ponder long on the ebbing pulse of many a dying day.

What of the fish, any one of the members of the speckled tribe? They have their way of learning as the law of the survival of the fittest prevails, just as is the case with grouse, deer, wolves, cougar, et al. Harassment and danger, which is what fishing pressure spawns, make trout shy, observant, alert, and resourceful; it produces hypercritical caution. The common phraseology "leader shy" was not coined without reason. For a fish to become sophisticated it must be given a chance to benefit from youthful misjudgment. Now add to this the economic truism that a trout is too valuable to be used only once.

If the philosopher swings into action as the scientist searches out fact, and then the two travel paths that cross, there should be a union resulting in a new dimension in fly fishing for trout, a case of glory even greater than former glory. Today, chief among the frustrations and vexations of the distraught angler is the matter of where to go for some quality fishing. This will stimulate special management. Henceforth the purpose of this article is to explore possibilities that will result in improved trouting in spite of diminishing frontiers, increasing megalopolises, and striptowns.

The important fish to the fly fishermen are the surface feeders, and they become the prime targets because they advertise their position and the fact that they are on the feed. What happens then to fly fishing in a piece of water when the most valuable fish, both catchables and brood fish, are removed?

The philosopher philosophizes: like breeds like, so let the scientist apply Mendel's law and produce a free-rising strain to the natural abundance of small flies. Once the biologist understands the assignment, his task is not difficult, and he likes it, too, because of prime interest to him is the future. He is very different from the put-and-take hatchery man. But the philosopher realizes that more than the trout must be subject to control.

The greatest predator of all, man, presents a problem. By intellect, though, he is a conservationist; but the plan must be explained to him so there can be understanding before support can be expected. Henceforth there should be no killing of small and average-size free risers; they must be returned for future fishing. Take-home reward consists of night feeders, trophy-size surface feeders, and trout caught by means of deep-fishing methods.

The angling philosopher quotes Aldo Leopold, the patron saint of the conservationist. "There must be management which will positively produce rather than negatively protect. . . . Wildlife is a crop which Nature will grow and grow abundantly, provided we furnish the seed and suitable environment . . . Society should know about important fatalities in that new argosy of the intellect which seeks not the conquest, but the preservation of nature."

The blueprint for trout stream improvement has not undergone change in the decades since Edward R. Hewitt first wrote about his experiments. Wing walls, V dams, riprap, undercut dams, and streamside plantings are still what the doctor prescribes. The New York State Conservation Department has done much of this sort of thing. The late Sid Gordon supervised such work for the Wisconsin department; then in his book *How to Fish from Top to Bottom*, he included an illustrated chapter on the subject.

In one of the later years of the amazing angling career of the great Hewitt, he made a trip to Ireland to fish a salmon river. Upon arrival at his destination he found that, due to an extremely wet season, the river was off-color from the water stemming from the peat bogs at the source. There was a good run of fish in the river, but they would not take a fly in the acidic water.

Hewitt had come quite a ways to fish this salmon river and he didn't let this momentary disappointment deter him from his pleasure. He reconnoitered the territory and noticed that not far below a bridge there was a fine pool; he also noticed that in the general vicinity there was a limestone quarry. He immediately ordered several truckloads of crushed limestone to be delivered to the bridge, and when they arrived he asked the drivers to dump the loads into the off-color waters above the pool. The dissolving lime salts from the crushed stone decreased the acidity of the water to the degree that the salmon again felt well or relieved and took his flies.

What is the difference between an acid and an alkaline trout environment? The latter, hard water, produces handsome fish flesh in much the same manner that alkaline soil produces bumper crops of corn, alfalfa, and tobacco. It not only can support more fish and fish food per acre, but thriving therein is certain aquatic life that cannot even exist in water less than neutral—7pH. Occurring in limestone water in fantastic quantity are two forms of insect life, freshwater shrimp and sowbugs, particularly in the watercress, which grows in the protected shallows. As though that is not difference enough between rich and poor water, hard water also harbors a bumper supply of the microscopic organism, zooplankton, which accelerates the entire food chain. Furthermore, some of the consumed food in soft water must be utilized to combat acid, whereas in hard water it is in its entirety converted into growth.

If in an emergency, Hewitt could increase the pH of an Irish river, what might a scientist do for an American trout stream? Needed is research to develop a formula. Suppose that it is feasible to double or triple or even quadruple the carrying capacity of a stream section, and, of course, at the same time increase the rate of growth? The average freestone mountain stream supports around 250 pounds of fish and fish food to the acre; in the average limestone stream the quantity is about 3,000 pounds to the acre, or about twelve times as great. These figures are based on the Sid Gordon formula and water analyses as listed in his *How to Fish from Top to Bottom*. In many places a truckload of crushed limestone to neutralize the acid from leaf mold might be better than periodic truckloads of trout. Hewitt and Gordon may have gathered the nuggets of information to pave the way to golden rewards.

Nature may be a hard master, but nature is also a willing servant; however, opportunities must be recognized before they can be grasped. Trout-fishing frontiers must spill over into biology and chemistry if there is to be valued development and refined management. All our problems can be solved. This one, better trout fishing, is simplicity itself (it goes almost without saying) when compared to splitting the atom or cruising around in outer space.

Cold, clean streams need special protection because new ones cannot be made, as is the case with lakes. Today the character and value of any trout stream in the land is in jeopardy. In the name of progress they could suffer ruination by exploitation from rechanneling, bridging, silting, damming, polluting, spraying, or blasting. There must be recognition of their monetary value for recreational pursuit, particularly for quality troutfishing sections near towns, trout towns. The discriminating angler is a tourist by nature. Hope and care are just the antithesis of resource bankruptcy; from here on it is re-creation for recreation. There should be no fear that the outdoor equipment of our scions will be a rocking chair and a fly swatter.

Needed in the trout world is a meeting of the minds, the philosopher and the scientist; that is all. Then in due time we can add to an improved type of challenging fishing a good companion who doubles streamside joys and halves the griefs and we have it made.

It can be felt by each generation in turn, as Lord Grey put it in the concluding lines of his classic, *Fly Fishing:* "An angler . . . will be grateful and glad that he has been an angler, for he will look back upon days radiant with happiness, peaks and peaks of enjoyment, that are not less bright because they are lit in memory by the light of a setting sun."

# 30

# Pure Water Is Basic

Nature does not operate in separate compartments or with some circuits closed. Everything is interrelated and interdependent. Man calls this "the balance of nature." Furthermore, nature resents and resists interference. This is as true with the distribution and the quality of the water supply of the earth as it is with any other phase of our ecology.

It is not possible to introduce pesticides to water anywhere without threatening the purity of water everywhere. In the entire water-pollution problem nothing is more confounding than the threat of the contamination of groundwater, which would mean the poisoning of streams, lakes, springs and wells.

It is a biological fact of life that minerals in water are passed from one link to another in the food chain. When man introduces poisons into water, they enter the cycles of nature. There prevails an endless cyclic transfer of materials from life to life. It travels from the minute cells of drifting zooplankton, through the microscopic daphnia (water fleas), to the fish that partake of the plankton and the daphnia and are in turn eaten by other fish, animals, or birds. Storage transpires in the tissues and bones of the consumer, where it accumulates.

One day a few Augusts ago, while fishing with Dr. Roebling Knoch, then the president of the Pennsylvania Heart Association he said, "You and I are full of D.D.T." The remark, so surprising to me, was occasioned by our streamside discussion relative to the scarcity of terrestrial insects and how this in turn was a deterrent to the surface-feeding activity of trout for the last half of the

A two-season campaign of man against fish came to a climax when Eddie Shenk, after four failures, finally banked "Gorgeous George," an 8½-pounder from the LeTort.

season. He went on to relate how a friend contemplated conducting research to determine if D.D.T. accumulates in the human body. The expectation was to subjugate some people to a small quantity, then test for possible storage. Upon examination it was discovered that there was already so much D.D.T. in every human tested that the small amount that the doctor contemplated introducing would not be a measurable factor, therefore the work had to be abandoned.

At a Grantham College lecture, Roger Tory Peterson, the famous ornithologist, was discussing the plight of "the big birds." A pair of eagles no longer produces the normal number of fledglings from the annual clutch of eggs. The fish-eating predatory birds are in trouble in all states but Alaska, where the great expanses have not been sprayed with insecticides. By circumstantial evidence and by the process of elimination the reason appears to be that the young are perishing because of D.D.T. in the fish provided for them by the parent birds. The U.S. Fish and Wildlife Service accepts this belief because the fish-hatchery personnel in

New England was ordered to stop killing ospreys, herons, and fish-eating ducks, since pesticide poisoning was causing declines in the fish-eating species.

The late Rachel Carson reported in her great conservation contribution, *Silent Spring:*

> If anyone doubts that our waters have become almost universally contaminated with insecticides, he should study a small report issued by the U.S. Fish and Wildlife Service in 1960. The Service had carried on studies to discover whether fish, like warm-blooded animals, store insecticides in their tissues. The first samples were taken from forest areas in the West where there had been mass spraying of D.D.T. for control of the spruce budworm. As might have been expected, all of these fish contained D.D.T. The really significant findings were made when the investigation turned for comparison to a creek in a remote area about thirty miles from the nearest spraying for budworm control. This creek was upstream from the first and separated from it by a high waterfall. No local spraying was known to have occurred. Yet these fish, too contained D.D.T.
>
> Had the chemical reached this remote creek by hidden underground streams or had it been airborne, drifting down as fallout on the surface of the creek?

In another study D.D.T. was found in the tissues of fish propagated in a hatchery where the water supply came from a deep well. There was no local spraying. The only possible means of contamination was by means of groundwater.

It is plausible for any angler to form a hypothetical case, then visualize disaster in the form of a fish kill. You and I may have our favorite piece of fishing water, which we fish in season at every opportunity and dream about out of season. Herbert Hoover might have described it as "your special place to wash your soul." Suppose it suffered ruination.

Say a field has been sprayed with a pesticide. The partly empty can of the chemical is left outside the barn. Ultimately it is kicked over, the contents spilling into a pile.

A torrential rain descends, transforming the earth from a hard, dry, baked, and cracked surface to one that is soft and muddy.

Trickle joins trickles to form rivulets. The water pours off the land into the stream. The little pile of powder by the barn disappears in its own little stream to be delivered in concentrated form to the main stream. The effect is the same as though the sprayer had been washed by the water's edge. More of the chemical in diluted form is carried off the field and into the stream. This is more than the organic life of a watershed section can be expected to withstand.

Before our eyes fish of various species and varying size struggle on the surface in the agonies of death only to expire and sink from sight. The next people to see your fish live farther down the watershed. In due time the victims will putrefy to the extent that they will bloat and float their way. The death knell has sounded for a cherished piece of water. The only hope left is that someday undisturbed nature will bring it back.

When man upsets a wildlife balance, a law of nature goes to work to rectify the imbalance: predators cease to prey on the species in trouble, seeking a more readily available food supply. This is a part of the overall plan in the fight for continuity. If man will break away and permit nature to take its due course, time will rectify the wrong. But let man heap abuse on top of abuse, then local extermination and even extinction may follow.

Geologically speaking, Cumberland County is one of Pennsylvania's limestone counties. From the standpoint of population growth, since 1950 it is surpassed by only the three counties adjacent to Philadelphia. A survey by the U.S. Soil Conservation Service made of wells divulged the information that 74 percent of those in the limestone belt are polluted. This not only struck close to home, it struck at home—my well. Planning commissions, agencies, and developers understand what can happen to the groundwater channels when septic tanks and cesspools are utilized. Disposal plants have become a necessity of man because they are necessary for the perpetuation of life.

Every big city in the world is built beside water. The second greatest use of water is to remove and dilute man's waste. We as fishermen as well as conscientious citizens must accept this; but we should insist that all wastes, chief among which in most communities is sewage, be properly treated before release. Dilution of pollution brought about by impoundment can work its wonders.

The greatest words ever written and spoken by the late Rachel Carson are:

> The problem of water pollution by pesticides can be understood only in context, as part of the whole to which it belongs—the pollution of the total environment of mankind. The pollution entering our waterways comes from many sources: radioactive wastes from reactors, laboratories, and hospitals; fallout from nuclear explosions; domestic waste from cities and towns; chemical wastes from factories. To these is added a new kind of fallout—the chemical sprays applied to cropland and gardens, forests and fields. Many of the chemical agents in this alarming mélange imitate and augment the harmful effects of radiation, and within the groups of chemicals themselves there are sinister and little-understood interactions, transformations and summations of effect.

Groundwater contamination is a part of what Stuart Udall terms *The Quiet Crisis*, and in his great work under that title he writes: "America today stands poised on a pinnacle of wealth and power, yet we live in a land of vanishing beauty, of increasing ugliness, of shrinking open spaces and of all overall environment that is diminished daily by pollution, noise, and blight. This is the quiet conservation crisis of the 1960's."

In looking far ahead, well beyond the turn of the next century, we might refer to it as "the time when there is standing room only in the concrete jungle." Wars, plagues, physical impotency, and birth control could prevent such a situation; more likely though is a pure-water famine. It could develop that Secretary Udall is far from being a pessimist; in fact he may be overly optimistic, for disaster may be pending. Once the groundwater is contaminated beyond the stage of suitability for human consumption, then all but refined seawater is poisonous to all living things. When the last pure spring finally produces a toxic output, we can still process some nonsalt water from the sea; but when the last freshwater fish dies, all the conservation departments and fish commissions across the land can do naught to replace the loss of organic life.

Today the number one domestic problem is the water problem. Life itself is contingent upon the solution of it. It is natural that we fishermen are among the first to think about water quality and quantity, but the time has arrived when everyone by force of circumstance had better be a conservationist at heart and in practice too. It must be recognized by all that one of the few basic requirements of life is an adequate supply of uncontaminated water.

The following words of Gifford Pinchot apply:

> A nation deprived of its liberty may win it, a nation divided may unite, but a nation whose natural resources are destroyed must inevitably pay the penalty of poverty, degradation, decay.

The warning flag is flying, as witness recent screaming headlines:

HOUSE AND SENATE BILLS
WOULD INCREASE PESTICIDE RESEARCH FUND

NEW HAMPSHIRE GOVERNOR BANS
STATE USE OF D.D.T.

LARGE-SCALE DESTRUCTION OF FISH
BY FARM POISON BEING PROBED IN MISSOURI

As John Milton put it: "Accuse not Nature! she hath done her part; Do thou but thine."

# 31

# The Four Horsemen

How accurate was Emerson when he wrote, "Progress is the activity of today and assurance of tomorrow"? Certainly he appreciated the aesthetic, and no doubt he regarded the best life as one varied in content: activity and inspiration, responsibility and contemplation, toil and pleasure, and security and danger. It is certain that to him, a conservationist, a vital American resource was the outdoors, and a priority was its appreciation and its protection. Since his day, there has developed a different time-space-and-domination pattern. Were he living today there might have been generated within him a suspicious attitude at times toward the planners, the developers, the builders, and the growers, even as this has developed in the minds of many of the present-day anglers and hunters. There are times when we refer to the "dam builders" and we are not sure of the spelling of the first word.

Economic consideration takes precedence over heritage, culture, and the aesthetic, but it will not always be this way. In fact, under the broad spectrum, in the years ahead, abuse and waste will be economically undesirable.

As this is written a state highway department has rearranged the Beaverkill River, the fly-fisherman's temple, to make way for an unlimited-access highway. The engineers at Albany, New York, call it "rechanneling"; the anglers the world over know it as "stream rape." As this is written a federal department would eliminate one of America's finest trout streams, Montana's Big Hole. The plan is to make it disappear in an impoundment. As this is written, a local politician would manufacture a lake in the valley of Maryland's best trout stream. And so it goes.

How about the conversion of Old Faithful into a laundry, Luray Caverns as a storage place for surplus butter, Pikes Peak to be used for road fill, the California redwoods cut into matchsticks? These things are silly to everyone, but unfortunately for the trout fishermen the welfare of the trout streams is not of much concern to any but the fly fishermen, yet these have great value as an attraction to visitors.

The real worth of a place to fish is not measured by license fees paid; it goes far beyond that. One day a successful angler displayed to one not so successful a monster trout he had taken from a stream, whereupon there was an offer from the other to purchase the trophy so that it could be mounted and displayed on the wall of the den. The answer to the buyer's inquiry, "What will it cost?" brought the response, "It would cost you exactly what it cost me"; whereupon the reaction was, "You go to Hell!" Both knew something of their high investments as hobbyists and free-spending tourists.

A stream is an irreplaceable natural resource, the cream of our America, a vital part of the heritage of a free people. Man can make a lake; flowing water is a more precious thing, but the big dam builders seem to get furious at the sight of water flowing freely downhill.

An incident took place that made me think long and hard. It hit close to home; in fact right at home. Affected was only a small stream that involved only a relatively small amount of money, but here was involved the same old conservation principle. It happened to my favorite section of trout stream, one I liked so much I purchased it in 1945. There was wonderful fishing behind it and apparently great fishing ahead. To me it was the prize stretch in a stream of streams and all this in a picturesque and appropriate setting. Actually it was a meadow stream rather than a hill stream, as it wandered through pastoral land and cultivated fields— charming and noble, nature in her finest mood. The part in question was its greatest curve, a serpentine double-back.

The little watershed is less than 30 square miles in extent. A rise of one foot is maximum flooding. The great bridge across the stream is 55 feet in height. The little stream was rechanneled— straightened, widened, and shallowed—so that the flotsam and jetsam it never carries would not damage the massive concrete abut-

A man with his fly rod and thoughts of rising trout. Is he an endangered species? (Irv Swope captured in an intent quiet moment on the LeTort.) *Photo by Lefty Kreh.*

ment high on the banks, which supports four lanes of traffic divided by a medial strip.

As though in mockery the unnecessary channel change and the resultant siltation were approved by a naïve bureaucrat, an employee of the state fish commission and one supposedly dedicated to wildlife. Havelock Ellis, the English scholar and physician, wrote, "The sun the moon and the stars would have disappeared long ago had they been within reach of predatory human hands." The changing years may be saddening, but what we once had and experienced is undimmed in memory.

After the last cast was made on the final day I fished the old bends, August 17, 1960, we scanned the sky at 9:06 P.M. to observe Echo I. As the heaven began to blaze with stars a shining light appeared in the south, crossed the eastern sky, like a moving star, then sank behind the northern horizon. The dramatic event was symbolic of man's achievement and a harbinger of changing times.

It made me think of the Emerson quotation: "Progress is the activity of today and the assurance of tomorrow." Then as an avid angler and hunter I had to challenge Emerson and challenge him in a big way. Suddenly it became time to think about places other than trout streams and people other than anglers. It was time to think of everybody wherever they are. Maybe we'd better make self-preservation our chief impulse, even as the trout do. Ultimately what will happen to the human race? Will man exterminate himself? It is not fair to the unborn generations to shrug off these questions; neither for the sake of ourselves or our children is it judicious to play the part of the ostrich that hides its head in the sand.

As an outdoor man I ponder over the signs I read, as does every outdoor person. Possibly it is later than we think for various creatures of nature.

There is a large dove roost I watch in the fall months. During and prior to 1963 the birds flew in at eventide by the thousands. The concentration and sight was so spectacular that I suggested to my friend Lee Wulff that he bring in his equipment and make one of his great outdoor movies there. Now I hate to think about the roost, let alone boast about it; by 1965 these unmolested birds diminished in numbers to the extent that they appeared by the dozens only.

The songbirds no longer abound in their old-time numbers in the shrubs, trees, and bird feeders around my place. Where I go, the fish-eating birds have disappeared, the kingfisher excepted.

The last several years have brought tremendous change in the terrestrial insect world. Flying ants in August are no longer a factor in the trout streams I fish. Neither is the Japanese beetle. Fireflies, where they used to occur in great mass, have all but disappeared. A friend who likes to photograph butterflies and moths can't find them anymore at his butterfly bushes. The grasshopper supply appears to be down at least 75 percent. One hears very few locusts.

The aquatic insects are in trouble, too. Some of the hatches of the genus *Ephemera* have disappeared; all others have diminished in number.

The briar patches no longer harbor their usual quota of rabbits, and like the big birds (the fish eaters), the ground-nesting birds are in trouble in spots.

I have watched a 100 percent sucker kill in a stream, a violent death amid wild contortion, but trained technicians could not figure out for sure what happened. This is still another one of the changing pictures in the places I frequent, and there are others.

The new era of scientific accomplishment with its arrogant technology appears to be the beginning of the last stand for certain forms of life, possibly man included. What are the signs you read in the places where you study nature in your way?

Could the human race be involved in a race, the kind that is measured in time from start to finish? It might be even worse than that. Could this be the homestretch of the race, the finish being the end of mankind? There may be a parallel between man's fate and that of the dodo.

Earlier in the century we first read about the Four Horsemen of the Apocalypse: War, Conquest, Famine, and Death. Today, I am sure, The Four Horsemen ride again, each racing the others, but their character and names have changed: Strangulation, Thirst, Poisoning, and Radiation. There appears to be no favorite; the race is that close.

When the last gasp has been taken by the last remaining member of *Homo sapiens*, the creature endowed with the large brain and great mental capacity, will the extermination be because of polluted air, contaminated food from poisoned land, poisoned water from polluted ground water, or degeneration of organs caused by radioactive fallout?

How much gas poisoning from people can the thin layer of atmosphere around the earth continue to absorb and still be suitable for human consumption? Fumes from internal combustion motors, industrial processes, and agricultural spraying intensify with an increasing population. And with the increase of the population, the amount of vegetation, which removes impurities from the air, decreases. The smog supply is ever building, ever collecting. For humans there is a limit.

The good earth, the ground that produces our food, is subject to the spraying of pesticides, weed killer, chemical fertilizers, and radioactive fallout, all of which are transferred to the food we eat. They can be conveyed to human bone and tissue directly by the food produced on the land or indirectly from the meat we eat of herds or fowl that feed on the produce of the land.

D.D.T. is stored in the human body, even a young body, from

the milk that is consumed. There it collects and can be measured in parts per million. How would a few more parts per million affect you and me and our children? Then add to that a few more parts per million. There is a limit. D.D.T., unlike Endrin, affects the nervous system. It is not known whether or not either causes cancerous cells, but both might.

Wells, streams, and springs, man's vital thirst quenchers, are clean and clear as normally provided by nature. How much more and how much longer can chemical poisons be used on the land without contaminating the groundwater system? Once this supply in a locality is no longer fit for human consumption, how much time will be required for it to purify itself if the pollution ceases?

Then there is drifting fallout from atomic blasts. A great hope is that the terrific destructiveness of warheads delivered by rocket, rifle, plane, or submarine will be a deterrent against their very use. It is theorized that fallout would cause degeneration affecting procreation—partial impotency of one generation followed by deformity of others.

All creatures, including man, start dying the day they are born. The deterioration is that subtle. Coma and convulsion are obvious and advanced stages, but most troubles are not easily detected at first.

We have always been concerned with life expectancy of the individual. Maybe the time has come to estimate the life expectancy of the human race. Nature is unconquerable. Man cannot win in a struggle against her, but he can live in harmony with her. Webster defines ecology as biology dealing with the mutual relations between organisms and their environment. Instead of ignoring the ecological relationships, it is time to start examining them.

As an angler and a hunter who over the years has tried to train his eyes to be quicker, I say, "Beware of the Four Horsemen of the Ennui: Strangulation, Thirst, Poisoning, and Radiation." A finger is pointing their way, or the signs are wrong. An inspired writer once penned the following, "Where there is no vision, the people perish" (Proverbs 29:18).

# 32

# *In Retrospect*

There are two types of incidents that excite the imagination of the angler: one is dramatic and sudden; the other is subtle and extended. It was the latter that motivated me into becoming a dedicated dry-fly fisherman for trout and salmon, and indirectly it was responsible for my building my home beside blue-ribbon trout water where evening fishing could be a regular part of life. Involved was a wonderful man, and a great outdoorsman. So in looking back I write today in memory of my mentor, Sol Rupp.

I was a youth in a day when few if any tapered leaders and eyed flies were available in the stores in this country. Fly rods were like the buggy whips common to that day and had flopping ring guides tied to the cane. Fly lines were light and level. The collective result of these conditions was that there was no such thing as shooting the line. It was before Ed Hewitt and Ray Bergman advised us how to do it. Thus it happened that I grew up at the same time as did a sport that has no peer—dry-fly fishing in America.

My dad recognized that hunting and fishing were inbred in his firstborn and in effect said, "It is just a matter of the form it takes, not the way it goes with that boy," and he was pleased and cooperative. He turned me over to the best fly fisherman in the area, Sol Rupp, a man who spent much more time hunting and fishing than he did with his law practice. Sol was an innovator and an analyst, keen and skilled. He had been raised along the wonderful little Cedar Run in the limestone stream section of the

This chapter has been reprinted with the kind permission of Winchester Press from the book *Fishing Moments of Truth*.

The author, Vince Marinaro, and Ross Trimmer (left to right) caught in a light moment by fellow angler Lefty Kreh. *Photo by Lefty Kreh.*

Cumberland Valley of Pennsylvania. He knew the brook trout native to the limestone streams—the brown trout had not yet been introduced. His inquisitive mind demanded that he learn about equipment and how to use it. His source for both supplies and information was London, the best possible place at the time.

The first time Mr. Rupp took me fishing with him was to a beautiful mountain brooklet characterized by pools, slicks, and glides and a worthy population of native brook trout. "The dry fly," he had said, "is the most fun; therefore it is best." Fascinated, I watched. A spray of crystal water tumbled into a stony basin causing a swirl. His "dry fly" landed lightly and started on a circular path in the miniature whirlpool. There was a slash and a flash, and the fly disappeared. Possibly I was more thrilled than Mr. Rupp.

The second time out he took me to Big Spring, a limestone spring stream in a pastoral setting. "Here," he explained, "you sneak up to the trout in the clear, smooth water and you watch him as you fish for him. Over on Laurel Run you can't see the fish, you just cast into the good-looking places. It is harder to catch them here at Big Spring."

His fly, which he called a "Light Cahill," landed above one of the better trout and drifted in a course toward him. Ever so slightly the trout rose up, inspected the fraud, and settled back. I expected something else, the sort of thing that had happened on the mountain stream, so I was surprised when Mr. Rupp said with encouraging inflection, "He's interested."

Five minutes and twenty casts later I was a witness to something quite different from the Laurel Run episode. The acceptance of the fly by the trout in this situation was deliberation itself. The fish drifted with the fly, inspecting it at very close range. I saw the trout tip up, the mouth open, and the fly disappear in a dainty dimple. Then I saw more. Suddenly the leader tightened, and as it straightened out above the surface a tiny rainbow of spray accompanied the swish. The trout was jolted in its tracks, the gills flared open with the impact, and then it bolted. Again the whole affair was fascinating, but ever so different from the acceptance of the fly by the mountain-stream trout.

I came to realize later that Big Spring, which flows through Newville, Pennsylvania, thirty miles from my home, was the greatest of all brook trout streams of my state. It featured a perfect balance between a high rate of natural reproduction and a great carrying capacity. Now trout production of this great stream has been adversely affected by siltation and hatchery wastes.

Sol had learned of an English firm, Abbey & Imbrie, where he was able to purchase eyed flies and tapered Spanish silkworm-gut leaders that had to be soaked and tied when wet. Fine strips of this gut, which he called "gut points," were attached to the basic leader as needed with a special "barrel knot." It was just a matter of time before Sol could secure American-made tapered lines and a split bamboo rod possessing backbone. At first these rods were called "dry-fly rods." It was also about this time that eastern anglers were catching their first brown trout.

I entered Lafayette College in the fall of 1927. Because this area was a hotbed of fly fishermen, the fishing-tackle displays in the stores of Easton and Allentown were more impressive than anything I had yet seen. After all, the late Samuel Phillippi, who produced the first split and glued bamboo rod, was a native of Easton, and Big Jim Leisenring, the wet-fly authority, was living in Allentown. Any resident of the Lehigh Valley who fly-fished visited the Brodhead, the Little Lehigh near Allentown, and the Musconetcong and Pequest across the Delaware River in New Jersey.

Present-day fishermen will snicker about this, but with no eyed dry flies to be had locally and no tapered leaders, I did what the others did. I bought 6-foot level leaders with dropper loops and dry flies with 6-inch snells attached. By this time I was the possessor of equipment of sorts, and I also had acquired some degree of expertise from my tutor.

It was springtime, and that meant two things to me: trout and baseball. Glory be, the two did not conflict. I got into uniform promptly, got out on the field to be the first to pitch batting practice, went to the showers early, and then headed across the Delaware River for the Musconetcong River.

The first Musconetcong trip was a very big day in my young life. The site of my adventure was directly below a dam not far from the road to New York. The trout were acting in a manner Mr. Rupp referred to as "jumping." My Royal Coachman came down over a busy fish. There was a slurp, a splash, a flash, and when I came up with the rod tip, the resistance it met was electrifying. That skinny, pale, 7-inch brookie was the first trout I caught on a dry fly and no doubt my first hatchery-reared fish— but still a tremendous one.

At the conclusion of the college year, I returned to the scene of my boyhood worm fishing, little Cedar Run. What had been a twenty-minute bike ride from home was now about a seven-minute ride by car. This is the same Cedar Run along which Mr. Rupp was raised. It was the same stream, too, where I caught my first brookie and, years later, my first brown trout. In due time I learned by comparison how truly wonderful this little limestoner actually was with its superb sulphur-fly hatch and accompanying evening rise of trout. What my small Light Cahills did there was a delight to Mr. Rupp and, of course, to me. But now I was dealing with something different: two kinds of trout, the native brookies and the imported browns that averaged twice the size of the natives.

The story of how the immigrant arrived in local waters is a good one.

Gus Steinmetz, an avid wet-fly fisherman, was both newshawk and political speechwriter. One day in the spring of 1924 he received a call. The voice at the other end of the line said, "I am Herbert Hoover. I want you to take me trout fishing."

"How are you, Herbie?" Gus promptly replied, believing it was a practical joker pulling his leg. "I have been expecting your call."

Well, it was the president, and Gus had been suggested as the one to take him fly fishing in the Harrisburg area. The two arranged an agreeable date, and Gus planned to take the president to Cedar Run.

As the time approached the gillie became apprehensive. Maybe his charge was not slick enough to catch these smart fish? He pushed the panic button. An SOS to the right man in the Department of Interior went something like this. "The big boss is going fishing with me next week. Send in catchable trout." The pump was primed with a truckload of buckets containing eight hundred "Loch Leven brown trout."

As it turned out, pressing business made the trip impossible, and Gus and the president never fished together, but southeastern Pennsylvania and the Yellow Breeches Creek watershed received its introductory stocking of brown trout.

A half-dozen years later we were dealing with the combination of brook and brown trout in Cedar Run. Mr. Rupp decided that the imports were every bit as interesting as the native brookies and twice as big. His crowning achievement was a 4-pounder on his Light Cahill.

Then came the most important thing I ever read about dry-fly fishing technique. Just in time for the 1930 trout season, a book with the title *Taking Trout with the Dry Fly* was published. The author, Samuel G. Camp, sold his readers on the abomination of drag and made *drag* a dirty word. To overcome it he advised, "At the completion of the forward cast hold the rod motionless for a moment until the fly, floating down, has created more or less slack line, in accordance with the character of the water over which the cast has been made." I've always remembered this lesson.

In the decades that followed I fished most of the evenings during the open season and came to appreciate and love the limestone spring streams of the beautiful Cumberland Valley. My plans to live alongside one ultimately materialized.

In 1944 Vince Marinaro and I became fast friends and frequent angling companions. Perhaps the fact that we thought alike was the strongest possible bond. Our game was to try to intercept the hatches and encounter evening rises. We became deeply involved with the dainty daytime feeding activity and with developing imitations of the terrestrial insects on which the trout fed. In effect we were playing two games with the trout, or perhaps it would be more accurate to report that the trout were playing two games with us. Together we also became involved in conservation matters, always, it seemed, losing the battles but in reality winning with the public's increasing awareness of the importance of the conservation of natural resources.

Since the late 1920s, the ranks of fly fishermen and specifically of fly fishermen who fish for trout have swelled into a closely knit army. We have the organizations of Trout Unlimited and the Federation of Fly Fishermen, plus literature the like of which no other sport can boast. The wonderful equipment and techniques now seen on trout streams and salmon rivers is matched only by the increased number of casters.

My trail has led through fifty seasons and it has passed through many waters. Frequently there has been the fly rod for company plus numerous fine companions and great fellowship. I am grateful that I have lived through the time that equipment was refined, when introduced brown trout created their own native populations, and when restricted killing became the vogue in regulated areas. This period has been the foundation for dry-fly fishing in America. It is saddening, however, to see my beloved streams— Cedar Run, Big Spring, and the LeTort—suffer unnecessary deterioration from an instrument they call "progress."

# Epilogue

Stephen Gwynn writes in *The Happy Fisherman:*
"Yet if all this experience has taught me anything it is that a fisherman's best prizes are not accessible by any mechanical estimate. They have their own avoirdupois, which takes into its generous reckoning, amongst other things, the fish we do not catch."

# Index